THE SECRET FILES

BILL DE BLASIO, THE NYPD, AND THE BROKEN PROMISES OF POLICE REFORM

MICHAEL HAYES

THE SECRET FILES

BILL DE BLASIO, THE NYPD, AND THE BROKEN
PROMISES OF POLICE REFORM

MICHAEL HAYES

𝕶ingston 𝕴mperial

— For Ryan, my steadfast champion.

CONTENTS

1

THE ASSASSINATION OF OFFICERS WENJIAN LIU AND RAFAEL RAMOS

On the Saturday afternoon before Christmas in 2014, Ishmael Brinsley walked the streets of Brooklyn's Bedford-Stuyvesant (Bed-Stuy) neighborhood in camo pants marked with blood splattered from the knee down to his shin and ankle. Instead of laces in his green sneakers, there was more blood around the tongue of the 28-year-old's left shoe. In his hand that day, police said he carried a plastic bag with a foam cup inside. Inside the cup was a silver Taurus 9-millimeter pistol.

Brinsley approached two strangers on the street. He first asked about their gang affiliations. Then he asked them to follow him on Instagram. Finally, he said, "Watch what I'm gonna do."

New York Police Department (NYPD) officers Wenjian Liu and Rafael Ramos were parked nearby in a police cruiser on the corner of Myrtle Ave. and Tompkins Ave. The two cops worked at the 84th precinct, which covers a part of Brooklyn closer to downtown, but had been loaned out to the 79th precinct that patrolled Bed-Stuy. Liu and Ramos were assigned to stake out the Tompkins Houses, a sprawling 12-acre housing project. There had been recent reports of violence in the area, but things were calm for now on this weekend afternoon.

Brinsley walked up the block towards the corner of Myrtle and Tompkins. The NYPD later said that he took up a "shooter's stance" as he approached the police cruiser on the passenger side. He pulled out the gun and unloaded multiple rounds into the front seat of the car.

The two ambushed officers sat slumped in the cruiser, bleeding to death from multiple gunshot wounds. Liu, 32, a seven-year veteran of the force, was newly married just two months earlier. Ramos, 40, was a three-year-veteran who joined the NYPD at age 37. He was the father of two young sons. Brinsley meanwhile headed westbound on foot towards the Myrtle Street G train subway stop.

BILL BRATTON, the Commissioner of the NYPD, was home for the holidays in Boston, Massachusetts, when he received the text message from New York City Mayor Bill de Blasio: "We have two cops shot in Brooklyn." Bratton immediately started to make arrangements to get back to New York.

THE DAY BEFORE, Mayor de Blasio talked to a journalist at the *New York Times* about the rising tensions between himself and the police department. The progressive Democrat was still in the first year of a four-year term as New York City's 109th mayor. He had campaigned on a platform of police reform, and in the interview, he called the NYPD a department "in evolution." But in reality, the new mayor had spent his first year in office in an off-and-on feud with his police department.

It's fair to say that he walked in the door of the Mayor's Office at City Hall on day one with a healthy dose of skepticism from the NYPD rank-and-file. De Blasio had staked his campaign on transforming the NYPD into a police agency that was more accountable to the public. Significantly, he promised to end the NYPD's illegal and biased use of "stop and frisk."

Decades earlier, the highest court in the US ruled that it was legal for police around the country to employ stop and frisk. In 1968, in *Terry v. Ohio*, the court held that without probable cause, a police officer may stop and search a suspect if the officer has a reasonable suspicion that the person has committed, is committing, or is about to commit a crime. The court also said that it is not unconstitutional to search someone if they have a reasonable belief that the person may be "armed and presently dangerous."

FOR MORE THAN A DECADE, New York City was engaged in a court battle over the NYPD's use of stop and frisk. The 1999 class-action lawsuit, *Daniels, et al v. the City of New York*, claimed the NYPD's Street Crimes Unit (SCU) racially profiled and conducted stops and frisks without reasonable suspicion. In 2003, the city settled with the *Daniels* plaintiffs and the NYPD disbanded SCU. But the NYPD's use of stop and frisk continued to go up and up.

In 2008, a new lawsuit that built on the *Daniels* suit, *Floyd, et al v. the City of New York*, challenged the NYPD's use of stop and frisk department-wide. After five years of litigation, in 2013, the judge ruled in the *Floyd* plaintiffs' favor and ordered the city to make extensive reforms to its policies. But New York City's mayor at the time, Mike Bloomberg — who once said, "I have my own army in the NYPD, which is the seventh biggest army in the world," — successfully kept the case tied up in court on appeals and stopped the reform process from beginning.

Later that year, de Blasio won the election for New York City mayor in a landslide. And in his first month in office, he made good on this key campaign promise. He dropped the appeal by his predecessor Bloomberg, calling the decision a step "of profound progress" in the city. But a little over five months after de Blasio declared the city would begin a healing process from the stop and frisk era, Eric Garner was killed by a police officer on Staten Island.

Garner's death was one of several police killings of Black men in the second half of 2014 that shook the national consciousness. Just one month after Garner died, 18-year old Michael Brown, Jr. was shot and killed by a police officer in Ferguson, Missouri. The two men's deaths were the spark that ignited a national protest movement in the summer of 2014. Several of the largest protests happened across New York City with tens of thousands of people taking to the streets to call for justice.

Garner's death wasn't the only high-profile police killing by the

NYPD in 2014 either. On November 20, an officer shot his gun in a dark stairwell of a Brooklyn housing project and killed Akai Gurley. While these killings by the NYPD in 2014 were getting attention in New York City, police killings were also getting attention across the rest of the country. On November 22, police gunned down 12-year-old Tamir Rice in a Cleveland, Ohio park. Two days later, the St. Louis County prosecutor announced that a grand jury decided not to indict the Ferguson police officer who killed Brown.

On December 3, 2014, Staten Island District Attorney Daniel Donovan announced that a grand jury declined to indict Daniel Pantaleo, the plainclothes NYPD cop captured on camera putting Eric Garner in a chokehold and refusing to release his grip while Garner pleaded, "I can't breathe."

The DA's announcement that Pantaleo would not face criminal charges in Garner's death set off more protests around the city. Thousands of people flooded the streets. Demonstrators carrying signs reading "Fire Pantaleo," "Justice for Eric Garner," and "Black Lives Matter" shut down city bridges. Some demonstrations turned violent, hundreds of people got arrested, and police cars were set on fire. The NYPD deployed a crowd-control device, commonly known as a "sound cannon," that blared earsplitting high-frequency beeps from a speaker sitting atop a police vehicle.

On December 13, in the largest protest yet, more than 25,000 marched through New York City in a demonstration that stretched over a mile long. The protesters chanted Garner's last words, "I can't breathe." For the most part, the march was peaceful. But as things wound down, some protesters continued to march onto the Brooklyn Bridge, where they would bring traffic to a halt. Police said the splinter group assaulted two police lieutenants. De Blasio called these actions "ugly" and an "unacceptable departure" from other protests but declined to directly criticize the grand jury decision not to indict Pantaleo. Asked about reports that protesters were assaulting police officers, he added that they "allegedly" assaulted the cops.

De Blasio did use the occasion of the Staten Island grand jury decision in the Garner case to talk about his 17-year-old Black son Dante.

The night that the DA announced Pantaleo wouldn't be charged, the White mayor told the press that he and his wife Chirlane, who is Black, often worried that when Dante went out, he wasn't totally safe — not just from the bad guys, but the good guys in blue meant to protect him.

These remarks summoned the ire of Patrick Lynch, the outspoken, brash four-term president of the Police Benevolent Association, the NYPD's union for rank-and-file officers. The top boss at the PBA since 1999, with his slicked-back hair, sharp suits with notched lapels (always adorned with an American flag pin), Lynch was a throwback to the NYPD's tough-on-crime era that he came up in at the police department in the '80s and '90s. In public appearances, Lynch had a propensity for accusatory outbursts directed against his adversaries.

The union boss was outraged by the mayor's defense of the protesters and lack thereof for the police. Regarding the mayor's remarks about Dante, Lynch responded that we should teach our children to respect the police even if we think they are wrong. Regarding Pantaleo, he said he was a good cop caught in a bad situation.

While Pat Lynch certainly remained the most publicly visible police union leader in the city, Ed Mullins, President of Sergeant's Benevolent Association (SBA), was actually the most bombastic.

Mullins joined the NYPD in 1982. Just a few years into his career, he was elected a union delegate for his precinct. In 2002, he became the president of the SBA.

Mullins' personal history of making his issues with city leadership and its treatment of police publicly known predated Mayor de Blasio. For example, in 2006, he demanded that Mayor Bloomberg apologize after he said he was "deeply disturbed" by the shooting of 23-year-old Sean Bell, who was out celebrating on the eve of his wedding when he was killed outside a club in Jamaica, Queens, by plainclothes officers who fired off 50 rounds.

But Mullins and the SBA's rhetoric reached new raging heights during the de Blasio administration. During de Blasio's tenure, Mullins referred to the mayor as a liar and said he was "full of shit." After de Blasio talked about how he and his wife spoke to their Black son after Garner was killed, Mullins called de Blasio "moronic." The SBA also paid for a full page ad in the *New York Post* and *New York Times* after Garner's death that cautioned the Democratic National Committee from holding its next convention at the Barclays Center in Brooklyn as de Blasio had requested. In the ad, the SBA wrote that under de Blasio, New York City is "lurching backwards to the bad old days of high crime, danger-infested public spaces, and families that walk our streets worried for their safety."

A week before the shooting of Ramos and Liu, de Blasio's trouble with the police unions only escalated. The PBA circulated a form asking officers to sign-up if they would prefer that if they get killed in the line of duty that the mayor did not attend their funeral.

While things were tense between de Blasio and the unions publicly, behind the scenes, the mayor and Lynch engaged in a strained dialogue over the PBA's contract. When de Blasio took office every labor union in the city — which amounted to more than 150 different bargaining units — was working under expired contracts. The new mayor managed to negotiate with every union, but the PBA proved to be one of the toughest groups to get a deal done with.

For more than two years, the PBA members had worked without a contract. And the state of those negotiations as the end of 2014 neared could be described as a complete and utter stalemate. In the spring, Lynch and his union had declared an impasse in negotiations with the mayor. By the end of the year, after the PBA had rejected the city's offers, the two sides were no closer to a deal and headed for arbitration.

Despite all the grappling with the police unions since the decision not to charge Pantaleo, de Blasio seemed to believe that cooler heads would prevail. In his interview with the *Times* the day before the officers were shot in Bed-Stuy, de Blasio said, "There's going to be a feeling, sort of a calming dynamic as people settle into a new approach."

About 75 NYPD officers responded to the shooting scene in Bed-Stuy, a witness estimated. Within minutes after the shots rang out, a police cruiser occupied each street corner on the neighborhood grid. Some cops ran towards Ramos and Liu. Others ran towards the subway.

Two Con Edison employees out in the neighborhood doing utility work had spotted Ishmael Brinsley walking towards the Myrtle Street G train and pursued him in their truck. Brinsley noticed them, turned and pointed his gun, and asked them if they "want some." They backed off and called 911. Brinsley disappeared down the subway steps.

Moments later, NYPD officers rushed down the same steps and busted onto the subway platform, yelling, "everybody get down!" A pregnant woman waiting for the train later told the *New York Post* that people started running to try to get out of the subway station. She said she threw herself on the ground. "I was afraid for myself and my baby."

As cops moved in, Brinsley turned and said, "Oh, shit." He raised the gun to his head and pulled the trigger. As officers carried Brinsley's body up the subway steps, the first part of the dead cop-killer that passersby could see emerge from underground were his bloody sneakers and camo pants.

Back on the corner of Myrtle and Tompkins, it was chaos in the street. A crowd had started to gather along with the hoard of cops, all sharing the disbelief that two officers had just been gunned down in broad daylight.

One video shared on social media showed Officer Ramos getting pulled out of the car and carried onto the sidewalk. His fellow officers placed him on the ground and began chest compressions. "Yo, that is crazy," the woman filming on her phone said. Other cops paced around, looking despondent. It appeared nobody was doing much crowd control. Some of the distraught officers, who could be forgiven for feeling overwhelmed, seemed like they didn't know what to do with themselves at the moment. "What's going on?" a person asked the woman filming the scene. "Two cops just got shot in the head," she responded.

Information quickly surfaced about Brinsley — who resided in Maryland at the time — and the hours leading up to the assassination of Liu and Ramos. Early that morning, he arrived at an apartment complex in the Baltimore suburb of Owings Mills. He went to the third floor of the development and knocked on his ex-girlfriend's door. When she opened the door, he pointed his gun at his head. She talked him down from killing himself. But then he shot her in the gut and stole her phone.

Brinsley took off and left the woman for dead. But she was able to struggle her way to the apartment of a neighbor who called the police. Meanwhile, Brinsley boarded a BoltBus destined for New York City. After he left the apartment complex, Brinsley called his ex-girlfriend's mother and said he was sorry for what he had done. She hung up the phone and called the Baltimore police.

On the way to New York, Brinsley posted on his Instagram from his ex-girlfriend's phone. He uploaded a photo of his pants and shoes, covered in her blood. *"Never Had A Hot Gun On Your Waist And Blood On Your Shoe,"* the photo caption said. He also posted his gun with an ominous message that read in part, *"I'm putting wings on pigs today."* He included the hashtags *#RIPErivGardner, #RIPMikeBrown,* and *#ShootThePolice.*

When the Baltimore County police discovered the posts, they alerted the NYPD and told them that Brinsley had his shooting victim's phone. Brinsley arrived in Midtown Manhattan and hopped on the subway for Brooklyn. Police said he dumped the phone near the Barclays Center in downtown Brooklyn at 12:07 pm. From then until two hours later, when he shot the officers, his whereabouts were unknown. At around 2 pm, Baltimore County police sent the NYPD a fax with a wanted poster with Brinsley's picture. But the NYPD didn't receive the fax until 2:46 pm, just one minute before Liu and Ramos were shot and killed.

On the day of the shooting, the *New York Post* ran the headline: *'Gunman executes 2 NYPD cops in Garner 'revenge.'* NYPD Commissioner Bill Bratton was convinced in what he believed had happened to Liu and Ramos. "No warning, no provocation, they were quite simply assassinated, targeted for their uniform," he said.

Rumors and speculation began to swirl about Brinsley and his motive for shooting Liu and Ramos. The New York City tabloids printed a story, citing police sources, that claimed Brinsley was linked to a prison gang that wanted to kill cops to avenge Garner and others. But a federal probe later debunked this theory.

In an in-depth profile on the gunman, the *New York Times* poked holes in this narrative that Brinsley was a part of some conspiracy to wage a revenge war against the police. The *Times* reviewed his history and spoke to those close to him, concluding that Brinsley was an unfocused drifter who was troubled that he could never gain success in life.

He was also not a hardened criminal. Though he had been arrested more than a dozen times and spent a couple of years in jail, most of his arrests were for thefts and other low-level offenses. One detail about Brinsley that stood out — and showed how unstable he was at the time — was that, according to the *Times*, he had told the mother of one of his children he was going to kill himself in the weeks leading up to the shooting.

"Brinsley was like an unmoored, placeless individual," said Matthew Vaz, a historian and professor at City College of New York. "He's like the poor ghetto man of the internet age."

Liu and Ramos were taken to Woodhull Medical Center just around the corner from the Tompkins Houses. Mayor De Blasio and Commissioner Bratton arrived at the hospital that night to meet with their families.

The Woodhull corridors were overflowing with fellow officers from the NYPD. After meeting with the families, de Blasio made his way through the crowd of cops to a press conference with Bratton. As he weaved his way through the officers, several turned their back on the mayor.

PBA President Pat Lynch had also arrived at the hospital. Bratton wrote in his memoir that after hearing rumors that the officers might turn their backs on the mayor, he and his number two at the NYPD, Chief of Department James O'Neill confronted Lynch. They asked him not to do it. Lynch told Bratton he wasn't involved in planning any such demonstration. According to Bratton, this denial caused the typically mild-mannered O'Neill to explode. He told Lynch, "You are full of shit!"

Bratton wrote that O'Neill told Lynch: "These guys will do whatever you tell them to do! Now this is about you fuckers, instead of the two dead cops downstairs."

In the hallway of the hospital, de Blasio was forced to carve a path with bright white block letters laminated on the back of jackets that read NYPD POLICE, glaring back at him. Among the group of officers with his back turned on the mayor was Lynch. Of course, nobody expected de Blasio and Lynch to link arms and console the Liu and Ramos families together at the hospital. But this public display of disrespect seemed designed to increase the tension growing between the union and the mayor.

That night at the hospital, there were two separate press conferences held. De Blasio and Bratton, tears in their eyes, addressed the press together. The mayor called what happened to Liu and Ramos a "despicable act."

"When a police officer is murdered, it tears at the foundation of our society," he said. "It is an attack on all of us. It's an attack on everything we hold dear."

Outside the hospital, Lynch also spoke to the media. Flanked by other union representatives, wearing a blue NYPD windbreaker with a PBA emblem over a shirt and tie, Lynch was as enraged and fiery as he had ever been.

"There's blood on many hands tonight — those that incited violence on the street under the guise of protests that tried to tear down what New York City police officers did every day. That blood on the hands starts on the steps of City Hall, in the office of the mayor."

A week later, the first funeral was held. Two days after Christmas, family, friends, top NYPD brass, and New York City officials gathered to honor Rafael Ramos at Christ Tabernacle Church in Glendale, Queens.

Vice President Joe Biden spoke at the funeral. "Police officers and police families are a different breed –- thank God for them," he said. Ramos's grieving wife wore dark sunglasses, big and round, but not big enough to hide the stream of tears. His two sons, Jaden and Justin, wore matching black-on-black suits. Black shirts, black ties, and black blazers. Over his suit, Justin wore his dad's NYPD jacket.

His dad was "the best father I could ask for," Jaden said at the funeral. On the day Ramos died, Jaden wrote on Facebook: "Everyone says they hate cops but they are the people that they call for help."

Outside the church, 20,000 police officers gathered in the streets to honor Officer Ramos. Cops from New Rochelle to New Orleans and Los Angeles had come to Queens. A video feed of the ceremony happening inside Christ Tabernacle was played for the officers lining the sidewalks on a jumbotron.

When Bratton spoke at the funeral, he acknowledged the animosity and tension between the police force and the protesters in the street after Garner was killed. He started his remarks by talking about the first police funeral he attended 44 years earlier. The slain officer, Boston patrolman Walter Schroeder, was shot in the back by anti-war extremists while responding to a bank hold-up, Bratton said. During the era that Schroeder got killed, Bratton said, "Divisive politics polarized the city and country — maybe that sounds familiar."

Appointing Bratton as his police commissioner was a tactical move by de Blasio. Not only had he served in the role before in the mid-'90s when Rudy Giuliani was mayor, but he was also one of the most well-known and respected figures in law enforcement in the country.

During the campaign, de Blasio's Republican opponent Joe Lhota ran ads claiming that electing the liberal de Blasio would usher in a return to the bad old days when crime ran rampant in NYC. Now that he was mayor, de Blasio hoped that Bratton's stature would provide him cover from these sorts of political attacks while at the same time keep the rank-and-file in step with the mayor's approach to policing in the city.

When it was de Blasio's turn to speak at the funeral, he talked about how Ramos spent ten weeks studying to be a chaplain and said he was "taken from us on the day he was meant to graduate." He said Ramos loved to play basketball with his sons in Highland Park near their home, he loved the New York Mets, and he loved "blasting Spanish gospel music from his car." The mayor told the family: "you epitomize the family of New York." He called Ramos a "peacemaker" in his church, family, and community.

Out in the streets, hundreds of officers turned their backs on the jumbotron as de Blasio spoke.

After the funeral, the mourners filed out of Christ Tabernacle. The Ramos family got in a car to accompany the casket to the Cypress Hills Cemetery in Brooklyn, where the fallen officer was laid to rest. While leaving the church, de Blasio and Lynch nodded to each other. The exchange, however, by no means signified peace between the union and the mayor.

Wenjian Liu's funeral was delayed so that his family could travel from China. On January 4, 2015, the mourners gathered at Aievoli Funeral Home on the corner of 65th St. and 13th Avenue in Bensonhurst, Brooklyn. Yet another crowd of 20,000 police officers filled the surrounding streets.

At the service, Liu's wife of just two months called him her "hero" and "soulmate." His father talked about how his only child would call his parents after every shift to say he was safe. "You are the best son, you are the best husband," he said. "We are very proud of you, we love you forever."

Bratton once again addressed the tension in the city during his funeral remarks. To the police force, Bratton said, "A much larger part of this city, of this country, a much larger part than you think, is proud of you."

In the week between the two officers' funerals, Bratton issued a memo to the department asking officers not to turn their backs again. "A hero's funeral is about grieving, not grievance," it said. Not everyone received his message.

When de Blasio spoke, he called Liu a "young man who came here from China at the age of 12 in search of the American dream."

He also talked about the need for New York City to come together after a horrific year. "Let us rededicate ourselves to those great New York traditions of mutual understanding and living in harmony," he said.

His speech was played on a Jumbotron placed at the corner of 65th Street and 14th Avenue. Once again, hundreds of officers turned their backs on the mayor.

A retired NYPD detective in the crowd that day told the *Associated Press* that the mayor "has no respect for us," adding, "why should we have respect for him?"

Another former NYPD officer who retired after 22 years on the force said to the *New York Times* that de Blasio has been "a cop hater since before he got elected mayor," adding that officers are "not going to forgive him ever."

After the funeral, Lynch once again took it upon himself to speak for the officers against the mayor. "They feel that City Hall has turned their back on them, and they have a right to have their opinion heard, and they did it respectfully in the street, not inside the church," he said.

Wenjian Liu's casket, draped in the green, white, and blue NYPD flag, was carried to the hearse. They drove his body past his house and then up to Cypress Hills cemetery. In the sky above, police helicopters flew at a low altitude in the 'missing man' formation above the crowd.

As for the mayor, even if the tumultuous events of December 2014 with the NYPD dismayed him, it didn't mean that de Blasio could simply just throw his hands up, move onto other political priorities and let the police department be. Progressive New Yorkers, which made up a sizable portion of the mayor's political base, were demanding reform and more accountability for the police. A burgeoning group of activists and organizers, predominantly led by Black and Brown women and LGBTQ New Yorkers, were out in the streets pushing this message. Its ranks included the family and friends of those killed by the NYPD seeking justice for their lost loved ones.

On the other side, de Blasio was under tremendous pressure from the police force. The unions knew how to stir up controversy and would stop at nothing to resist reforms they didn't like and preserve the status quo of the police department. Furthermore, they too were organized, with tremendous legal resources to boot. And they were prepared to do battle in court and in the court of public opinion to challenge any moves by the city that had to do with the police that they didn't approve of.

De Blasio walked out of Liu's funeral alongside his wife Chirlane. If he turned to look down 65th street, he could have seen an ocean of cops as far as the eye could see; waves and waves of men and women in blue. And as for the mayor's relationship with them, it was adrift at sea.

Only a few days after Liu's funeral, the reports of an NYPD work "slowdown" started to emerge. Arrests citywide dropped by over 50%

during the end of 2014 compared to the same time period the year before, according to the *Daily News*. Likewise, the number of people who received criminal summonses for lesser offenses, moving violations, and parking summonses all fell by about 90% during the same time period. In the 84th precinct where Ramos and Liu had worked, police wrote just two tickets for moving violations. Police sources told the tabloids that this drop in police activity was a response to the cops' anger at de Blasio.

On the same day that the slowdown reports started to surface, de Blasio and Bratton commended the NYPD while reporting a 4.6% total drop in crime in 2014. Bratton also said he asked police leadership to do a "comprehensive review" of the past month's police activity. But you didn't need to see the data to know that with more than 35,000 cops spread out across the city if this kept up and police decided not to do their jobs, things could get very bad.

With the NYPD in apparent revolt against city leadership, the only thing that was certain was that nobody was sure what might happen next.

2

POLICE UNIONS AND A HISTORY OF TENSION

The tense relationship between New York City police and the public is as old as the city itself. Before the creation of the professional NYPD in the 1840s, keeping a lid on crime in Gotham was primarily the job of the constables, a bumbling group of partially-employed lawmen that solved few crimes, often failed to arrest perpetrators and were beaten back during the frequent riots that happened in the city. Yet, as crime climbed and climbed during the nineteenth century, New Yorkers were reluctant to establish a more professional police force.

In his book, *Law & Disorder, The Chaotic Birth of the NYPD,* author Bruce Chadwick wrote that this hesitancy had partly to do with lingering animosity towards the British, whose army had occupied several American cities before and during the Revolutionary war. "The people hated the British for doing that," Chadwick wrote. "That sour feeling continued to be felt for generations, and the people saw the proposed police force as another occupying army."

A more modern-day example of the mistrust between the public and the police is the NYPD's persistent resistance to accountability handed down from anyone outside the police ranks.

More than two decades before NYPD officers turned their backs on

Mayor Bill de Blasio, New York City's police staged a very different protest against the city's mayor. On September 16, 1992, the PBA mobilized 10,000 cops to City Hall. The plan was to protest Mayor David Dinkins' plan to establish an all-civilian review board to review misconduct claims against the NYPD.

That morning, starting at around 10 am, thousands of mostly White men and women from the NYPD marched around City Hall, bellowing chants of "No Justice! No Police!" and "The Mayor's on crack!"

The demonstrators — draped in t-shirts that read "Dinkins Must Go!" and holding signs with sayings including "Dinkins, We Know Your True Color — Yellow Bellied" — got riled up as they listened to fiery speeches from PBA President Phil Caruso and Rudy Giuliani, who lost to Dinkins in the mayoral election in 1989 and hoped to unseat him the following year. In the crowd, the officers booed and jeered and cried out racial slurs. Legendary New York City reporter Jimmy Breslin wrote in *Newsday* that he heard an officer call out: "Now you got a nigger inside City Hall. How do you like that? A nigger mayor."

About an hour into the protest, chants of "Take the hall!" broke out amongst the crowd. According to a *New York Times* report, at around 10:50 am, thousands of protesters pushed through the police barriers set up to contain them and marauded up the steps and into the hall. Three hundred fellow police officers assigned to control the event did little to stop them.

At the same time, other cops filled the nearby bars along Murray St. The revelers littered the neighborhood with beer bottles, hopped on top of cars, and blocked the traffic along Broadway. Una Clarke, a Black City Council member, told the media that the protesters blocked her from crossing the street. When she asked an officer to let her through, Clarke told a reporter, the cop turned to a fellow protester and said, "This nigger says she's a member of the City Council."

The event continued to spiral out of control after several thousand protesters left City Hall and marched onto Brooklyn Bridge. With few, if any, police around to quell them, the officers on the bridge brought traffic in both directions to a halt as they jumped on cars, stomped on the hoods, and rocked the vehicles of terrified motorists back and forth.

Another Black member of the City Council, Mary Pinkett, said at the time that she was caught in the standstill while driving with two elderly passengers. Another motorist, Virginia Santana, told the *Village Voice* that she was blocked on the bridge while driving her child to the hospital for chemotherapy treatment.

There would be no mass arrests, tear gas, or rubber bullets deployed against the protesters that day. After the group dissipated, PBA President Phil Caruso admitted that the event got out of hand. "The emotional level did get a little out of control," Caruso said. "But sometimes if emotionalism is not evoked publicly, the responsible elements of the community do not listen."

Dinkins said that the rally bordered on "hooliganism." The following year, the mayor established the city's first all-civilian Civilian Complaint Review Board (CCRB).

The Dinkins years also marked the early beginnings of future mayor Bill de Blasio's career in New York City politics. He started as a volunteer and later became a staffer for Dinkins.

"I see New York as a gorgeous mosaic of race and religious faith, of national origin and sexual orientation — of individuals whose families arrived yesterday and generations ago, coming through Ellis Island, or Kennedy Airport, or on Greyhound buses bound for the Port Authority," Dinkins said during a speech at his inauguration.

"In that spirit, I offer this fundamental pledge: I intend to be the mayor of all the people of New York."

During his 2013 campaign for mayor, de Blasio talked about how he was inside the Dinkins administration when the all-civilian CCRB started. New York City mayors before Dinkins had tried to change the NYPD's disciplinary system by making civilian review of misconduct claims a part of the process. For the most part, those efforts had fallen short thanks to intense pressure from the police unions.

Proposals for versions of a civilian review board in New York City date back to the 1930s, but it wasn't until the mid-1950s that the city formally established one. However, that early iteration of the board consisted of just three deputy police commissioners. It would be another decade — and take another high-profile police killing — before Mayor John Lindsay, who served as mayor from 1966 to 1973, would make a serious attempt to get individuals not connected to the police on the board.

On July 16, 1964, 15-year-old James Powell and other students were sitting on the stoop outside their school, Robert E. Wagner, Sr. Junior High School in the Yorkville section of the Upper East Side. Patrick Lynch, a 36-year-old building superintendent, was outside watering some plants. He asked some of the students to move out of his way. When they didn't, he turned his hose on them. As he sprayed the group of Black teenagers, Lynch, who was White, allegedly said to them, "Dirty niggers, I'll wash you clean." (He later denied saying this.)

Powell became enraged, pulled out a knife, and started to rush towards Lynch. Off-duty NYPD lieutenant Thomas Gilligan was walking by and spotted Powell running towards a building on East 76th Street. Gilligan said that he saw Powell holding a knife and yelling, "Hit him!" at Lynch. Gilligan followed the boy into the building, took out his gun and badge, and said, "I'm a police officer, come out and drop it!" He fired three shots, hitting Powell in the lung and abdomen.

The killing of Powell set off six nights of protests, some looting, and violence in East Harlem. The uprising spread to the primarily Black Bedford-Stuyvesant section of Brooklyn as well. A grand jury declined to indict Gilligan on charges in the killing of Powell. Later, in November 1964, the three-member CCRB also cleared Gilligan of any wrongdoing.

The following year, Lindsay was elected mayor. Early in his first term, he added four civilians to the CCRB. This action granted for the first time individuals outside the police department's ranks the authority to evaluate police misconduct in New York City. The PBA immediately went to work to stop this. In 1966, they waged a successful campaign to have the changes to the review board struck down through a ballot referendum.

It would take another twenty years before the City Council passed legislation that allowed the board to add civilians outside the police department to the board in 1987. However, the board remained under NYPD supervision. But the path was being set for Dinkins to change the CCRB to an all-civilian board in the early '90s.

Dinkins became mayor at a uniquely tumultuous time for New York. When Dinkins took office, crime had been on an unmitigated climb for the last 15 years. During his time as mayor, Dinkins faced challenges that included the AIDS and crack epidemics, an economic recession, and a homicide wave that at its peak saw up to five New Yorkers murdered per day.

Along with reforming the CCRB, Dinkins got some big things done with public safety and policing during his tenure. For example, at the height of the spike in murders, he convinced the New York state legislature to allow the city to hire 6,000 additional police officers. In Dinkins' final two years in office, the decade-plus upward trend in crime started to turn around, too. In 1992 and 1993, according to the FBI's statistics on major crimes, all seven categories — murder, rape, assault, robbery, burglary, grand larceny, and arson — declined in New York City. At the same time, other episodes marred Dinkins' administration — none more than the Crown Heights riots.

On an August evening in 1991, 7-year-old cousins Gavin and Angela Cato were playing with a bike in front of their home on President St. in the Crown Heights section of Brooklyn.

Shortly after 8 o'clock, a three-car motorcade carrying Menachem Schneerson, the grand rebbe of the Lubavitch Hasidic community, was driving the prominent religious figure home through the neighborhood after he visited his wife's grave. The lead vehicle was an NYPD 71st precinct police cruiser; the grand rebbe received a police escort for all his cemetery visits. The second car carried the rebbe himself. A third vehicle was driven by another member of the Lubavitcher community, 22-year-old Yosef Lifsh.

As the motorcade approached an intersection near the Cato house on President St., the light started to change. The first two cars passed through, but the light turned red before the 1984 Mercury Grand Marquis station wagon Lifsh was driving could make it. In an attempt to keep up with the group, Lifsh ran the light (he later told police he believed it was yellow). His car collided with a Chevy Malibu and careened onto the sidewalk, plowing into the Cato children and pinning them against the gate outside their apartment building.

Within minutes of the accident, 71st precinct cops were on the scene. Moments later, a Hatzalah ambulance — a volunteer emergency services organization that operated primarily in areas with high Jewish populations — arrived at the site of the crash. EMS from the city showed up, too. And a crowd of angry people from the neighborhood descended on the scene as well.

For years, relations between the Lubavitcher and Black communities in Crown Heights had been strained. For one thing, the Black people in the community resented the preferential treatment that they felt Hasidics enjoyed from the local police. Lifsh's accident involving the Cato children was about to light a spark that would show the city just how volatile this discontent among the two groups was.

Facing an increasingly angry crowd, the Hatzalah crew took Lifsh from the accident scene and loaded him into their ambulance. Both seriously injured Cato kids were still on the ground when they drove off with Lifsh. The mostly Black group of onlookers became enraged. Angela Cato would survive, but a short time later, at around 9 pm, Gavin was pronounced dead. Crown Heights was about to explode.

Rumors began to circulate about what happened, including that the Jewish ambulance team ignored the children and tended to Lifsh. Groups of Black and Jewish teenagers filled the streets and fought with one another. Windows of homes owned by Jews got smashed out. The new commander in the 71st precinct didn't realize that things were spiraling out of control until he had a rock hurled at his head while leaving a B.B. King concert in the neighborhood. He deployed an additional 30 cops to the area, but worried it was too late.

At around midnight, Yankel Rosenbaum, a Hasidic scholar visiting Brooklyn from Australia, was walking near the intersection of President St. and Brooklyn Ave. when a group of about 15 Black teenagers surrounded him. A 16-year-old in the group pulled out a knife and stabbed him four times. Rosenbaum died three hours later at Kings County Hospital.

For two more nights, the violence continued in the neighborhood. Thirty-eight people and 150 police officers were hurt, according to a report by the governor's office. Mayor Dinkins and NYPD Commissioner Lee Brown got roundly criticized for not doing more to quell the uprising. Another future mayor, Bill de Blasio, who served as an aide to first deputy mayor Bill Lynch, was stationed at City Hall fielding calls from Jews in the neighborhood about the violence. On Thursday, following three nights of violence, Dinkins ordered 1,800 additional NYPD cops to the area. After that, things in the neighborhood finally calmed down.

His political opponents claimed that Dinkins ordered the police to hold back and allow the Black community to vent their frustrations. Some, like former mayor Ed Koch and Rudy Giuliani, took their criticism a step further and called the riots a "pogrom" against the Jews in neighborhoods. Over the years, Dinkins vehemently denied all of this to be true. Years later, when he was asked about these scandalous accusations, Dinkins told *Gothamist*, "There is nothing worse than being falsely accused."

A report commissioned by New York Governor Mario Cuomo called the riots "the most extensive racial unrest in New York City in over 20 years." The investigation overseen by Richard Girgenti, the state's Director of Criminal Justice, determined there was no evidence to support the claim that Dinkins and Brown held back police. The Girgenti report came down hard on Commissioner Brown's leadership of the police and his communication with his boss, Mayor Dinkins. The authors wrote that Brown assured the mayor that the situation was "under control." They noted that Brown "failed to fulfill his ultimate responsibility for managing the Department's activities to suppress rioting and preserve the public peace."

Girgenti's report also criticized Dinkins' top aides, including his first deputy Bill Lynch. They wrote that evidence is "persuasive" that top City Hall officials who were in frequent communication with the mayor "were given crucial information." They wrote that reports of violence in the community were provided to the officials "in a dramatic and sustained manner, and was conveyed well before" Dinkins said he was made aware.

"If the Mayor was told, fundamental questions would arise as to why he did not act on this information," the report said. "However, if the information was not provided to the Mayor, systemic problems in City Hall's flow of information and decision-making would be revealed."

Dinkins was contrite but put some of the blame for what happened on the NYPD leadership. At a press conference, he reiterated that he received incomplete information about the rioting. At the same time, he acknowledged he should have questioned Commissioner Brown's tactics sooner than he did.

"The report concludes that I should have rejected the Police Department's assurances about their response to the violence on the second rather than the third night of unrest," Dinkins said. "I accept that criticism."

Politically, Dinkins never recovered. In November 1993, his reelection bid fell short as he could not put together the same coalition of voters that put him in Gracie Mansion four years earlier. He lost out to Rudy Giuliani by just two points.

Dinkins paid the ultimate political price after Crown Heights. But his staffer, de Blasio's political career was just ramping up. After working for Dinkins, de Blasio joined Bill Clinton's White House administration as a regional housing administrator. He later managed Hillary Clinton's successful US Senate campaign in New York. Then, in 2001, he won his first of two terms as a New York City councilman representing the 39th district, which included the Park Slope, Brooklyn neighborhood where he resided with his family.

De Blasio wasn't known on the City Council for being very active or having many opinions on policing. However, in 2009, he and another councilman drafted and introduced legislation to expand the power of the Civilian Complaint Review Board. The bill aimed to bolster the agency's clout by granting the CCRB the power to prosecute cases against NYPD officers if the board found evidence that they had committed misconduct. At the time, the most the CCRB could do was recommend that the police department hand down discipline against officers that it investigated.

De Blasio's proposal included data that showed in the previous year that the NYPD had pursued no disciplinary actions in 33% of cases where the CCRB determined there was reasonable evidence of police misconduct. That number had increased from just 1% of cases that the police department turned down in 2003. De Blasio said granting the CCRB the authority to prosecute cases "will help restore public confidence" in the agency.

At an event on the City Hall steps to announce the bill — along with another bill that expanded the CCRB's funding — de Blasio talked about how he was inside City Hall when Dinkins enacted the all-civilian board. He said that they did not go far enough in reforming the oversight agency and that the changes he was proposing would enable New York City to "rededicate ourselves to getting it right."

That same year, in 2009, de Blasio was elected Public Advocate for New York City. The citywide position had little power. The public advocate was technically a member of the City Council but didn't have a vote. That said, the job was seen as a good stepping stone for politicians with eyes on more prominent, influential offices.

This lack of real power certainly didn't stop Public Advocate de Blasio from criticizing more powerful city officials about how the NYPD behaved on their watch.

In May 2011, he wrote NYPD Commissioner Ray Kelly a strongly worded letter asking for him to investigate after a massive "ticket-fixing" scandal hit the police department. A probe by the Bronx District Attorney's office revealed that hundreds of cops on the force had made traffic tickets vanish for friends and family. A wiretap ensnared several high-ranking officers in the scandal, and more than a dozen cops got criminally charged. Bronx DA Robert Johnson said the actions had cost the city in the ballpark of $1 to $2 million in revenue. De Blasio pressed Kelly, writing that New Yorkers "need the facts and we need them sooner rather than later."

"I think it's time that they come out and say, 'Here's an investigation. This is how long it's going to take. This is what we're looking at,'" de Blasio said.

Later that year, de Blasio criticized Mayor Mike Bloomberg for ordering a police raid to tear down the Occupy Wall Street encampment at Zuccotti Park in Lower Manhattan. On November 15, 2011, police entered the park at 1 am and started handing out eviction notices. A half-hour later, officers in riot gear began taking down tents and kicking the protesters out of the park. Bloomberg defended the action citing health and safety conditions. De Blasio said that these "provocations under cover of darkness" by the NYPD and the Bloomberg administration would "only escalate tensions in a situation that calls for mediation and dialogue."

During his tenure as public advocate, de Blasio continued to criticize the NYPD. In February 2012, he demanded a quick investigation into the police killing of 18-year-old Ramarley Graham, who was shot to death by an officer who chased him into his own home in the Bronx. "Time is of the essence. The Bronx District Attorney must expedite his investigation into the incident," he said in the statement.

As many expected, in January 2013, de Blasio announced his candidacy for mayor. Notably, in this election cycle, voters wanted to hear from candidates on police accountability. The city was reeling from controversies with the police department's treatment of Occupy Wall Street protesters, and the police killings of young black men like Ramarley Graham and Mohamed Bah, a 28-year-old who was fatally shot 8 times inside his Harlem apartment while suffering a mental health episode. However, one policing issue stood above the rest in terms of widespread public interest — the NYPD's enforcement of its stop and frisk policy.

3

BILL DE BLASIO AND A NEW ERA OF BROKEN WINDOWS POLICING

On a February afternoon in 2008, 28-year-old David Floyd, a Black college student at City College, left his apartment on the way to class. He ran into his neighbor who lived in the basement of the building where they both rented apartments from Floyd's godmother. The other man had been locked out. Floyd had a spare set of keys. He ran back inside and retrieved a key ring.

Floyd set down his backpack and started trying different keys on his neighbor's door. About a minute later, three plainclothes NYPD officers ran up to Floyd and his neighbor and told them to put their hands against the wall. The officers told the men they suspected they were burglarizing the home. They claimed that there had been a pattern of burglaries in the neighborhood. The officers then frisked both men for weapons.

The cops found no weapons on either man. They asked them for their IDs. When Floyd produced an out-of-state ID, they had him retrieve his Con Edison utility bill to prove that he lived at the address.

That year, David Floyd became the lead plaintiff in the landmark class-action lawsuit, *Floyd vs. City of New York*, which challenged the NYPD's long-standing policy of "stop, question, and frisk."

The *Floyd* lawsuit claimed the NYPD's practice of stop and frisk violated New Yorkers' Fourth Amendment rights to be free of unreasonable searches and seizures. It also claimed the NYPD was being racially discriminatory in violation of the Equal Protection Clause of the Fourteenth Amendment.

After five years of litigation, the case went to trial. Asked during his testimony how he felt about the incident where police suspected him of breaking into his godmother's home, Floyd said that he felt humiliated. The officers who stopped him that day would testify at the trial, too. They claimed they became suspicious after observing him and his neighbor looking up and down the block as they tried to open the door. The officers said that they saw a bag on the ground that they believed could have been "burglary tools." It would also be revealed at trial that there had only been one burglary in Floyd's immediate neighborhood in the two months prior to this stop, though the NYPD disputed that analysis of the data, claiming that it didn't reflect the number of burglaries in the precinct, which was considerably higher.

"I felt like I was being told I should never leave my home," Floyd testified.

David Floyd represented just one of the thousands of mostly Black and Latinx New Yorkers the lawsuit claimed police had stopped for no good reason. During his opening statement, Darius Charney, lead attorney for the plaintiffs, said, "really this trial is 14 years in the making."

Charney's organization, the Center for Constitutional Rights (CCR), a progressive non-profit legal organization focused on civil rights, first challenged the NYPD stop and frisk policy after the killing of 23-year-old African immigrant Amadou Diallo. In February 1999, four officers from the NYPD's notorious Street Crimes Unit — a squad of about 300 cops whose chief mandate was getting guns off the street — shot the unarmed Diallo a shocking 41 times after stopping him in front of his apartment. Later that year, the New York State Attorney General issued a report that found that the Street Crimes Unit made more stops than any other "non-precinct command" in the NYPD. They also found that the majority of those stopped — 60% — were Black.

CCR's initial lawsuit, *Daniels vs. City of New York*, specifically challenged the stop and frisk practices of the Street Crimes Unit. After it settled, the NYPD promised to make changes to the policy to make sure its officers weren't racial profiling. However, during the *Daniels* settlement period from 2003 to 2007, the number of stops by NYPD officers skyrocketed — from about 160,000 per year in 2003 to over 470,000 in 2007. The racial disparities of who was being stopped persisted, too. While the number of guns recovered during stops — the NYPD's own stated reason for the policy to exist — remained at less than 1%.

Charney said *Daniels* simply "did not fix the problem." So after the settlement expired in 2007, his organization filed the *Floyd* lawsuit. This time they would challenge the use of stop and frisk department-wide.

The filing of a new lawsuit did not deter the NYPD from using stop and frisk. At the trial, the plaintiffs came armed with stats that showed that the number of stops just kept going up. According to findings from the New York Civil Liberties Union, at the peak in 2011, the NYPD stopped a total of 685,724 people. That total is more than 80,000 greater than the record set the previous year in 2010. 87% percent of the people stopped were either Black or Latinx, and 51% were between the ages of 14 and 24.

Professor Jeffrey Fagan, a Columbia University criminologist who analyzed more than 4 million stops by the NYPD over an eight year period from 2004 to 2012, testified that he found that in 88% of those stops the person was neither arrested nor given a summons. As for guns, Fagan found that they were recovered in just .15% of all stops.

Along with the ballooning numbers, the plaintiffs presented testimony from NYPD officers themselves who believed that they were being asked to racially profile while they patrolled the streets and juice the statistics in order to meet quotas. To back up their explosive claims, these officers brought secret recordings to court.

Adhyl Polanco, a patrol officer in the Bronx, testified that he was instructed to write 20 summonses and make one arrest per month to meet the department's expectations. At trial, a recording Polanco made of his union delegate, Officer Angel Herran, was played in which Herran mentions the "20 and 1" requirement. On the tape, Herran tells

Polanco and the other officers listening inside the 41st precinct station house to "crush the fucking city" and make their numbers. Anyone who can't, Herran said, is a "zero." During his testimony, Herran confirmed that the "20 and 1" comment referred to the 20 summonses and 1 arrests that the department expected from officers each month.

Other recordings played at trial just showed an utter disrespect for the local community by the officers' superiors. Adrian Schoolcraft, an officer in the majority Black Bedford-Stuyvesant section of Brooklyn, recorded a lieutenant telling officers at a November 2008 roll call that they are "not working in Midtown Manhattan where people are walking around smiling and happy. You're working in Bed-Stuy where everyone's probably got a warrant."

The most contentious episode caught on tape presented at the *Floyd* trial came out during the testimony of Officer Pedro Serrano.

Serrano, a Puerto Rico native whose family moved to the Bronx when he was young, worked as a patrol officer in the NYPD's 40th precinct not far from where he grew up. The "4-0" as it is known is a very busy precinct, Serrano testified. He would sometimes go out on 20 or more radio calls per night, responding to all kinds of activity. "Some people have called me because their cat was stuck in a pool table," Serrano said during his testimony. "That actually happened."

In the winter of 2013, Serrano received what he thought was a bad performance review. On a scale of 1-5, Serrano received a 3. He was concerned because he had gotten 4s and 5s in the past; plus, he knew that if that number went any lower he could be put on performance monitoring.

Serrano thought that the rating was unfair so he disputed it. On Valentine's Day, he found himself in a meeting about his evaluation with Deputy Inspector Chris McCormack. Before he walked into the meeting, Serrano reached into his pocket and activated the recording app on his phone.

McCormack was seen as a rising star at the police department. Two years earlier in 2011, at age 38 he was promoted to command the 40th precinct. Born and raised in the borough, McCormack testified at the

Floyd trial that he was "excited" to get the job in the Bronx. As Deputy Inspector of the 4-0, he oversaw more than 200 officers policing one of the most violent and crime-laden parts of the city. Lately, they had particular trouble in the Mott Haven section, which housed a dozen housing projects and had seen a rash of shootings and burglaries.

"I was very excited about going back to the Bronx and assisting them in getting back to where it should be with no violence," he said.

In March 2013, as Serrano sat on the stand at the *Floyd* trial, his tape of the meeting with McCorrmack rolled.

During the meeting, the Deputy Inspector came down on Serrano for not having enough stop reports in his file. He said that Serrano's file showed he had stopped only two people during the prior year, though Serrano was sure he had stopped more than that. McCormack told Serrano that the numbers made it look "almost like you're purposely not doing your job at all."

As the conversation continued, both men got more heated. McCormack had earned the nickname at the NYPD "Red Rage" because of his red hair and the way his face would turn red when he lost his temper. McCormack told Serrano he was looking for him to be stopping "the right people, the right time, the right location."

"And who are the right people?" Serrano asked him, repeatedly.

"Depends where you are," McCormack said. He brought up Mott Haven.

Serrano shot back: "Mott Haven. Full of Black and Hispanics... What am I supposed to do? Stop every Black and Hispanic?"

McCormack repeated that "this is about stopping the right people, the right place, the right location."

"Again take Mott Haven where we've had the most problems, and the most problems we had, these was robberies and grand larcenies," he said.

"And who are those people robbing?" Serrano said.

McCormack responded, "The problem was, what, male Blacks. And I told you at roll call, and I have no problem telling you this, male Blacks 14 to 20, 21. I said this at roll call."

When it was McCormack's turn to testify he was asked what he meant by "the right people." He said he was referring to the victims' descriptions of who were committing these crimes in the precinct. When he was asked if he ever instructed officers in the 40th precinct to stop all Blacks and Hispanics, he responded, "Absolutely never."

Following the two-month non-jury trial, Manhattan federal court Judge Shira Scheindlin ruled in August 2013 that the NYPD's policy and practice of stop and frisk were unconstitutional and discriminatory. In a nearly 200-page long decision, the judge determined that the stops revealed a widespread violation of New Yorkers' Fourth Amendment and Fourteenth Amendment rights. Calling it a "policy of indirect racial profiling," Scheindlin wrote that officers routinely stopped "blacks and Hispanics who would not have been stopped if they were white."

In her report, Scheindlin noted that over an eight-year period, from 2004 to 2012, about 83% of the stops by police were of Black and Hispanic people. These two demographic groups made up only about 50% of the city's population at the time. In her report, Scheindlin wrote that "nearly 90 percent" of those stopped "are released without the officer finding any basis for a summons or arrest."

While she made it clear she was "not ordering an end to the practice of stop-and-frisk," Scheindlin appointed a federal monitor to oversee reforms to the police department.

On the day Scheindlin released her decision, Mayor Mike Bloomberg called a press conference and angrily accused her of denying the city "a fair trial" and claimed she did "not understand how policing works."

Bloomberg was determined to fight Scheindlin's decision. He said the city would appeal the case. But unfortunately for him, his time as mayor was up in a few months. And as for the four leading candidates most likely to succeed him — Christine Quinn, John Liu, Bill de Blasio and William Thompson — they all said that if elected they planned to drop the appeal.

Two weeks before Scheindlin's ruling came down, de Blasio, who was trailing in the polls to the frontrunner, City Council Speaker Christine Quinn, was asked about stop and frisk during an appearance on *MSNBC's Morning Joe*. "I think, particularly for young men of color, it's sending a horrible message to them that they are not part of this society in the same way," he said. However, de Blasio never said that he would completely end the practice of stop and frisk during the campaign. Instead, he said he planned to reform it and end the racial profiling.

As the summer of 2013 wore on, de Blasio still trailed Quinn. But just a few days before Scheindlin delivered her ruling in the Floyd case, de Blasio's campaign debuted a TV commercial that would put their candidate over the top.

The ad was titled "Dante." It debuted about a month before the primary election. As it begins, Dante, a 15-year-old Black boy with an impressive afro from Brooklyn, appears on the screen. "I want to tell you a little bit about Bill de Blasio," he says.

In the ad, Dante said that de Blasio was the only Democrat "with the guts to really break from the Bloomberg years." The teen said de Blasio will raise taxes on the rich to fund early childhood programs, has a plan for affordable housing, and "he is the only one who will end a stop and frisk era that unfairly targets people of color."

Dante continued: "Bill de Blasio will be a mayor for every New Yorker, no matter where they live or what they look like..." And then, the payoff: "...and I'd say that even if he weren't my Dad," Dante closed, as the viewer watched him walking down a tree-lined Brooklyn street with his dad, Bill de Blasio.

Before the ad featuring his son aired, de Blasio had started to gain on Quinn. But, as her campaign told *The Daily Beast*, "the ad" — referring to the Dante spot — "killed us." The following month, de Blasio won the primary and became the Democratic nominee — and overwhelming favorite — to become New York's next mayor.

In the general election, de Blasio faced off against Republican Joe Lhota. Even though Lhota had formidable credentials, having served as budget director, finance commissioner and deputy mayor for operations under Rudy Giuliani, he trailed heavily in the polls from the start. So Lhota sought to work some of his own magic with an attention-grabbing campaign ad. He went right after de Blasio on the issue of public safety.

On a Wednesday morning in early October, the day after the candidates faced off in a televised debate, Lhota's ad "Can't go back" began to air. The ad opened with recent images of a biker gang attacking motorists on the West Side Highway. It went on to show a series of shock images purported to be from the New York City of the 1970s, '80s, and early '90s — the eras before crime went down.

The commercial showed a lifeless body laying on the ground in a duffel bag next to a shopping cart, an overturned police car, and a Black man with a gun drawn in a stairwell. As the still images played, a sinister voice said: "Bill de Blasio's recklessly dangerous agenda on crime will take us back to this." The de Blasio campaign responded by accusing Lhota of using "fear tactics" to divide New Yorkers.

Fact-checkers had a field day with Lhota's ad. One headline in *The Nation* read: *Lhota's Mistake-Filled Attack Ad Depicts de Blasio ad as Soft on Crime*. The body lying next to the shopping cart was an image from 2012 when Mike Bloomberg was mayor and crime was on the decline. The Black gunman turned out to be a picture of an undercover police officer.

One image included in the ad that was indeed from the earlier high-crime era was the photo of an overturned police car. This photo showed an NYPD cruiser flipped on its roof on Eastern Parkway in Brooklyn during the Crown Heights violence in 1991.

A week after the ad aired, Lhota took shots at de Blasio over his role in the Dinkins administration during the Crown Heights riot. With less than a month to go in the race, the *Daily News* broke a story that said de Blasio had a "front-row seat" to the crisis in Crown Heights in his role as special assistant to Dinkins's top deputy Bill Lynch. The story mentioned the Girgenti report's findings that Lynch and other Dinkins aides mismanaged communications to the mayor during the riots. The story quoted a former Dinkins aide describing de Blasio as Lynch's "right hand."

The Girgenti report never mentioned de Blasio, however. In an interview responding to Lhota's allegations that he gave to the *Daily*

News, de Blasio said, "I remember vividly being on the receiving end of a deep, deep concern, particularly from members of the Jewish community" during the Crown Heights riots.

He confirmed he was fielding calls from Jewish people in the neighborhood complaining about the unrest. "I came away with very strong views, but I did not participate directly," he said. De Blasio added that he believed there should have been "a very, very strong show of force from the very beginning." He said that he would have sent more cops to Crown Heights "from day one. No question."

After the story broke, Lhota called the city's response to Crown Heights an "unmitigated failure" and said de Blasio deserved some of the blame. "Bill de Blasio was given information by people in the community," Lhota said. Unfortunately, Lhota claimed, that information "stayed with Bill de Blasio."

These criticisms by Lhota, the attack ad, and the reports on Crown Heights did not, however, substantially move the polls or change Bill de Blasio's message on public safety and policing, especially stop and frisk.

Just days before the election, the Second Circuit Court of Appeals, which handled the city's appeal of Scheindlin's ruling in the Floyd case, handed the outgoing Bloomberg administration a win. In a stunning move, the court ruled that Scheindlin "ran afoul" of the judicial code of conduct and froze the reforms she ordered from taking effect. They also removed her from the case. Two weeks later, the judges put out an explanation clarifying that they had made "no findings of misconduct, actual bias or actual partiality" by Scheindlin. Following the court's ruling, de Blasio reiterated that he would still drop the appeal and allow Scheindlin's decision to stand if elected. A few days later, de Blasio defeated Lhota in a landslide — winning more than 70% of the vote.

Before he even took the oath of office, Mayor-elect de Blasio began to frustrate and anger Progressives who supported him because they hoped he'd be different.

In early December 2013, de Blasio announced that he would appoint Bill Bratton as his police commissioner to lead the NYPD. Bratton was arguably the most famous cop in the country. He had appeared on the cover of *Time* magazine with the headline *Finally, We're Winning the War Against Crime. Here's Why.* The title of Bratton's 2008 memoir also referred to him as *"America's Top Cop."*

De Blasio tapping Bratton marked his second stint as NYPD commissioner. From 1994-96, he held the position under Giuliani. Bratton became well known for deploying the "broken windows" policing strategy during the Giuliani era. Broken windows calls for addressing small, sometimes called "quality of life" offenses like graffiti and drinking in public before those petty crimes in the community lead to larger crimes like rape and murder.

The term broken windows was introduced by two social scientists, James Q. Wilson and George L. Kelling, who published an article under the same name in *The Atlantic Monthly* in 1982. Kelling later worked with Bratton as a consultant at the NYPD. Both Bratton and Kelling vehemently defended the broken windows strategy throughout the years.

In the academic world, the jury is still out on whether broken windows works or not. A few studies over the years have attributed the steep drop in crime in cities across the country since the mid-90s at least partly to broken windows. In contrast, other academic studies and papers claim that broken windows had little to do with the crime drop and instead caused tremendous harm and resentment in communities with the number of criminal records it helped create, especially for young minorities.

Kelling and Wilson themselves had concerns about broken windows becoming racist in practice. In their original article in *The Atlantic*, they wrote:

"The concern about equity is more serious. We might agree that certain behavior makes one person more undesirable than another but how do we ensure that age or skin color or national origin or harmless mannerisms will not also become the basis for distinguishing the undesirable from the desirable? How do we ensure, in short, that the police do not become the agents of neighborhood bigotry?"

On this question, Kelling and Wilson wrote, "We can offer no wholly satisfactory answer to this important question."

George Mason University's Center for Evidence-Based Crime Policy looked at seven studies that evaluated policing approaches that incorporated some principles of broken windows. Three studies concluded the approach led to a meaningful reduction in violent and more serious crime, while three of the studies did not, and a fourth had "mixed results." In conclusion, George Mason said the effectiveness of broken windows was "difficult to evaluate."

One of the people who apparently agreed it was difficult to conclude whether brokens windows worked or not was James Q. Wilson, one of the men who coined the term in *The Atlantic*. In a 2004 interview, Wilson told the *New York Times*, "I still to this day do not know if improving order will or will not reduce crime."

"People have not understood that this was a speculation," Wilson said.

One of Bratton and Kelling's defenses of the broken windows strategy is what happened with the murder rate in New York. In a paper they co-authored that was published in 2015 by the Manhattan Institute, a think tank that supports the broken windows approach, they note that in 1993, the year before Bratton took control of the NYPD, the city's murder rate was 26.5 per 100,000 people, and New York City accounted for about 8% of all US homicides. In 2014, they said the city's murder rate had drastically been reduced to 4 per 100,000 people — which was lower than the national rate of 4.5. In addition, New York's share of the country's total homicides dipped to 2.4%.

"These conditions didn't just happen," they wrote. "They resulted from thousands of police interventions on the street, which restored order and civility across the five boroughs."

One issue that some take with Bratton's characterization of his success is the fact that from the mid-'90s on, cities all over the country saw dramatic drops in the level of violent crime whether their police used broken windows or not. In 2002, criminologist Richard Rosenfeld wrote, "homicide rates also have decreased sharply in cities that did not noticeably alter their policing policies, such as Los Angeles, or that instituted very different changes from those in New York, such as San Diego."

While stop and frisk has been associated with broken windows by some, Bratton and Kelling disagree. In the Manhattan Institute article, they argue that stop and frisk is "entirely distinct" from broken windows. They write that a stop and frisk "is based on reasonable suspicion that a crime has occurred, is occurring, or is about to occur." On the other hand, broken windows, they write, "is not a tactical response based on reasonable suspicion of possible criminality."

Bratton and Kelling continue, writing that unlike stop and frisk, broken windows "is a more broadly based policy mandating that police will address disorderly illegal behavior."

However, whether he separates these concepts doesn't change the fact that stops of New Yorkers climbed in the mid-'90s as Bratton applied the broken windows strategy in his execution of Giuliani's "zero tolerance" policing policy and cracked down on low-level offenses.

During the early months of the de Blasio administration, it became apparent that broken windows was still a big part of Bratton's strategy. The rates of arrests and charges for minor offenses soared. For example, arrests of people begging and peddling on the subways tripled during the first few months of 2014. In New York public housing projects, data showed that arrests for minor offenses like drinking in public and riding a bike on the sidewalk increased by over 20%, while at the same time, felony arrests declined 5%.

With low-level arrests surging in early 2014, Bratton gave a speech at the swanky Waldorf-Astoria hotel in midtown Manhattan to the New York City Police Foundation, a non-profit that raises money for the NYPD. At the event, Bratton said, "Broken windows works, and it will remain the cornerstone of the New York City Police Department."

"We will be focusing on ensuring that aggressive begging and squeegee pests, all those activities that create fear and destroy neighborhoods, graffiti, all those seemingly minor things that were so much in evidence in the '80s and early '90s here, don't have the chance to come back," he continued.

On broken windows, de Blasio also backed Bratton. When Bratton stepped down from the department two years later, the mayor called

Bratton's strategy "still the right approach." In fact, during his entire tenure as mayor, de Blasio never denounced broken windows.

Little did the mayor and the police commissioner know that four months after Bratton heralded it as the "cornerstone" of NYPD strategy, the most infamous act of broken windows policing in history would tragically play out on a random sidewalk on Bay Street in the Tompkinsville section of Staten Island.

4

"NOT A BIG DEAL. WE WERE EFFECTING A LAWFUL ARREST": THE POLICE KILLING OF ERIC GARNER

NYPD sergeant Kizzy Adonis told investigators that "the perpetrator's condition did not seem serious," and he did not appear to get worse. She also said she "believed she heard the perpetrator state that he was having difficulty breathing."

Another NYPD sergeant on the scene, Dhanan Saminath, told the investigators that the officers were "maintaining control" of the man and that he "did not appear to be in great distress."

That is how two senior officers who were there that day initially described the arrest of Eric Garner, an asthmatic 43-year-old father of six, on July 17, 2014, according to an internal NYPD report obtained by the *New York Daily News*. The officers did not state that Officer Daniel Pantaleo put Garner in a chokehold before tackling him to the ground. Pantaleo and his partner, Justin D'Amico, were not interviewed by the NYPD investigators for the report at the time due to a possible criminal investigation.

In contrast to these officers, Mayor Bill de Blasio and NYPD Commissioner Bill Bratton agreed that it looked like Pantaleo used a department-prohibited chokehold on Garner when they watched the video that night. At a press conference the next day, Bratton said, "As defined in the department's Patrol Guide" — which is like the NYPD's bible — "this would appear to have been a chokehold."

The NYPD banned the use of chokeholds by officers two decades earlier in 1993. That, of course, hasn't stopped New York City cops from using them. After Garner's death, the city's outside oversight agency for the NYPD, the Civilian Complaint Review Board, released a report stating that between July 2013 and June 2014, the agency received more than 200 complaints from civilians that officers used chokeholds against them.

The NYPD's use of chokeholds became the subject of more oversight review following the death of Garner. The year before he was killed, the City Council created a first-of-its-kind Office of Inspector General (OIG) to investigate the policies and practices of the NYPD. For its first report, OIG looked at ten illegal chokehold cases investigated by the CCRB between 2008 and 2012.

In each instance, the CCRB determined the claims were credible and recommended the accused officers face serious discipline, the OIG review found. And in each case, Commissioner Ray Kelly departed from the CCRB's recommendation and handed out penalties that ranged from no punishment to instructions to a loss of five vacation days.

At the July 18 press conference, Bratton said that the department had issued an order as recently as a year earlier "that chokeholds are in fact prohibited by the NYPD." On what this all meant for Pantaleo, he added that the "final determination" of what, if any, violation he committed would be made by the Staten Island District Attorney's office and the NYPD Internal Affairs Bureau (IAB).

De Blasio agreed with the commissioner, saying it was "too early to jump to conclusions" about what had happened. But as the accounts from those officers on Bay St. that day showed, not everybody in New York City law enforcement saw the incident the same way the commissioner and mayor did.

There is a remarkable amount about the Garner case that you can see with your own eyes. The details were captured by bystanders in nearly 15 minutes worth of cell phone video.

"I'm tired of this! It stops today!" Eric Garner yelled at Officer Justin D'Amico while his friend, Ramsey Orta, filmed the two men locked in an argument. D'Amico claimed that he observed Garner illegally selling loose cigarettes on the Staten Island block where he and Officer Daniel Pantaleo stopped him.

Earlier that day, Lieutenant Chris Bannon was driving by Staten Island's Tompkinsville Park. Bannon spotted a group of people hanging out on the sidewalk on Bay St. He wasn't close enough to see what the group was up to. But he had been directed by the bosses to crack down on the sale of illegal cigarettes at this location. Bannon directed Sgt. Daminath to send some officers to check it out.

"To who? To who?" Garner asked D'Amico in protest about the officer's claim he saw him selling cigarettes, adding, "I did nothing."

Eric Garner did indeed sell illegal cigarettes at this spot near the park. There was a sizable market for this sort of enterprise thanks to the very sizable tax that the previous mayor, Mike Bloomberg, had imposed on cigarettes.

In an effort to promote public health while raising tax revenue for the city, Bloomberg slapped a tax on each pack of cigarettes sold in stores that brought the combined city and state tax to a whopping $5.85. This pushed the total price of a pack in New York City at the time north of ten bucks. This also opened the door for Garner and others to purchase cartons from southern states where the cigarettes were significantly cheaper and sell them on the street for a profit.

Garner had been arrested, ticketed, or just given a hard time by the NYPD over the sale of loose cigarettes many times before. But, according to Garner and Orta, an illegal cigarette transaction wasn't what he was up to when Pantaleo and D'Amico stopped him on July 17. "I was just standing here minding my own business," Garner told the officers.

Orta and Garner tried to convince the officers that Garner just finished breaking up a fight moments earlier. And while they were busy hassling him about a street sale that didn't happen, the two people who were fighting ran off. Two witnesses would later tell the *New York Times* that Garner was telling the truth about breaking up a fight moments before police stopped him. While Garner continued to plead his case to D'Amico, Pantaleo called for back-up on his handheld radio.

As Pantaleo approached him from behind, Garner told him, "don't touch me." Pantaleo wrapped his right arm around Garner's upper right arm near his shoulder. He swung his left arm around Garner's neck. He pulled him back, and the two men stumbled into the glass storefront window of a Bay St. beauty shop before toppling in a heap onto the sidewalk.

On his hands and knees, Eric Garner tried to crawl forward. Pantaleo was on his back, now with both arms around Garner's neck. In Orta's video, you hear Garner plead, "I can't breathe," as Pantaleo wrestles with him on the pavement. With his hands locked, Pantaleo appeared to squeeze Garner's neck tighter. D'Amico, cuffs in hand, tried to reach out to grab Garner's left hand, but he missed as Pantaleo and Garner jerked around on the sidewalk. Throughout the struggle, Garner continued to plead, "I can't breathe" — he said it 11 times total.

Three other NYPD officers moved in to assist Pantaleo, who finally released his grip from around Garner's neck and began pressing his face into the pavement with both hands.

A manager inside the beauty shop would later tell the *Times* that Sgt. Kizzy Adonis approached the officers, telling Pantaleo and the others, "Let up, you got him already."

The officers got off Garner, cuffed and now lying on the ground unresponsive. They attempted to get him up, but he slumped back down onto the pavement. For the next 7 minutes or so, the officers left Garner on the pavement while waiting for the ambulance to arrive.

From inside the beauty shop, Taisha Allen recorded on her phone as the officers stood over Garner waiting for the ambulance. She captured D'Amico going into Garner's pockets and pulling out a couple of packs of cigarettes. When the ambulance arrived, an EMT appeared to try to get Garner, who hadn't moved in minutes, to get up himself. "Sir? We're EMS. We're here to help you...Get in the stretcher," she said to Garner. She checked for a pulse then nodded to the police.

In Allen's video, you can hear a person ask why they aren't giving Garner oxygen. A cop turns and says "he's breathing."

Just before the officers and EMTs lifted Garner onto the stretcher, Allen turned her phone's camera on Daniel Pantaleo, who was still standing nearby. He gave her a wave.

On the way to Richmond University Medical Center, Eric Garner went into cardiac arrest.

He was pronounced dead at the hospital.

Afterward, Sgt. Saminath texted Lieutenant Bannon. "Danny and Justin went to collar Eric Garner and he resisted," he wrote. "He went into cardiac arrest and is unconscious. Might be DOA."

"For the smokes?" Bannon wrote back.

"Yeah they observed him selling," Saminath responded. "Danny tried to grab him and they both fell down. He's most likely DOA."

"Not a big deal. We were effecting a lawful arrest," Bannon texted back.

In a memoir published after his death, Eric Garner's mother, Gwen Carr, recounted the last conversation she had with her son. On the morning of July 17, she called Eric. They hadn't spoken in a few days, which was odd. He didn't answer at first, but he eventually called back. They chatted for a few minutes and then Carr reminded Eric about their family reunion that Saturday in Brooklyn.

"Don't forget on Saturday it's our family reunion in Prospect Park," Carr said.

"I didn't forget. What do you need me to bring?"

"Just bring soda and water. We got the rest."

"OK, bye, Ma. I love you."

"Love you too."

Carr wrote that she could picture Eric working the grill at Prospect Park, joking and carrying on with everyone while he flipped burgers. It was a role he typically played at family gatherings. And she was sure that's how it would be on Saturday. But in the end, the family reunion never happened.

Carr had suffered loss in her life before. She wrote in her memoir that when Eric was six, her husband and father of her children, Bernard, had a stroke and died at the age of 33, leaving her a single mother. Twenty years later, her son Emery was shot and killed in his early twenties in 1996.

What was different this time was Carr's grieving for her son Eric was going to be done in public. A short time after his death, she was going to become famous as "the mother of Eric Garner." The time for peaceful and quiet grieving over the years to come would be interrupted by the numerous legal fights with the NYPD, the police unions, the city of New York, and the federal government in pursuit of justice for her son.

For Mayor de Blasio and the city's top officials, there would be plenty of time to deal with the legal side later. In the immediate aftermath of Eric Garner's death, the people in power in New York City needed to run damage control and try to parry away the anger being directed their way from multiple fronts. Protesters were calling for Pantaleo to be arrested or, at the very least, fired from the NYPD. Furthermore, activists were calling for Bill Bratton to resign — taking to the streets with signs that read "Fire Bratton, End Broken Windows."

The day after Eric Garner's death, Bratton highlighted that the location where he died was a hotbed for broken windows enforcement on Staten Island. He noted that the "immediate area had been the subject of numerous community complaints by local residents and merchants." Then he ticked off the stats. "Year to date at that location there have been 98 arrests for various offenses, 100 C summonses issued mostly for quality of life offenses, as well as 646 nine-eleven calls for service within the immediate area of that very small park."

A week after Garner died, *The New York Times* editorial board echoed the people in the streets' condemnation of Bratton's policing strategy. In an editorial titled "Broken Windows, Broken Lives," they wrote that the mayor and the commissioner should "begin a serious discussion of the future" of broken windows.

The *Times* called for Bratton and de Blasio to "acknowledge the heavy price paid for heavy enforcement."

"Broken windows and its variants — "zero-tolerance," "quality-of-life," "stop-and-frisk" practices — have pointlessly burdened thousands of young people, most of them black and Hispanic, with criminal records," the board wrote.

As for the mayor, he caught flack for taking an 8-day vacation to Italy just after Garner's death. De Blasio was supposed to leave for the trip on Friday, July 18. But he decided to delay departure by one day to deal with the aftermath. Still, not canceling the vacation meant that he would miss Garner's funeral the following week. In her memoir, Gwen Carr wrote that she thought "that wasn't right."

"As a mayor, when something horrible happens in your city, you change your plans and show up," Carr wrote.

De Blasio defended his trip at the time, telling *The Wall St. Journal* a couple of days later that he needed to recharge from what he described as the "incessant and draining and intense" job of being mayor.

When he returned from Italy, de Blasio called a press conference to show that he had everything under control. He also used the occasion to let people know that broken windows policing wouldn't be going anywhere.

At the press conference held 11 days after Garner's death, a reporter posed a question to de Blasio and Bratton about comments that the commissioner made earlier in the year during his swearing-in. After the ceremony, Bratton had extolled the city's "steady drop in crime" of late. He said because of this, "There should be an expectation that the intrusion of police into citizens' lives should also diminish."

The reporter asked if at the time Bratton was just referring to a decline in the use of stop and frisk — de Blasio's cornerstone police issue from the campaign — or was he also talking about other low-level offenses?

The mayor jumped in first and gave an emphatic defense of broken windows. He said that they wanted officers to use discretion and resolve situations, if they can, through dialogue rather than arrest, but "breaking a law is breaking a law, and it has to be addressed in one form or another."

The tension of those initial public appearances by the mayor was paltry compared to what was to come. Two weeks after Garner's death, on July 31, de Blasio hosted a public discussion dubbed "a roundtable on police-community relations" at City Hall. For the quasi-public affair — the press were only allowed in for part of the discussion — de Blasio invited high-ranking NYPD officials, City Council members, clergy, and members of his staff to attend. But the headliners for the event were Bill Bratton and the outspoken civil rights leader Reverend Al Sharpton.

Two days after Garner's death, Sharpton led a march along with Garner's family in Staten Island. He said there was "no justification" for what Panteleo did to Garner. He also derided the release of Garner's arrest record following his death, calling it a tactic to "scandalize the deceased" and "distract" from the real issue, which was "how an unarmed man was subjected to a chokehold and the result is he is no longer with us."

At Garner's funeral, Sharpton rallied the mourners, telling them, "Fight back, community. Don't back down. We got to win. We don't choke people. We're redeemers of this city."

Sharpton had clashed with Bratton in the past, particularly during his first stint as NYPD commissioner in the 1990s. But after his appointment by de Blasio, Sharpton published an editorial in the *New York Daily News* where he sounded optimistic that they could work together under this new regime.

"When Bratton was under Giuliani, we had a very distant and adversarial relationship, and we knew him as 'enemy,'" Sharpton wrote. "But when he served as police commissioner in L.A., we worked together closely on gang violence and other issues, and knew him as 'friend.'"

He continued by writing that despite their differences in the past, Bratton and him "have had shared interests in keeping our streets safe."

"It's important to remember, that though we may be strange bedfellows, we cannot forget that at the end of the day we are all in the same bed," Sharpton said.

Bratton's recent dealings with Sharpton suggested he saw room for the two to work together as well. After his appointment the previous December, Bratton called Sharpton. He arranged to make his first appearance as Commissioner-appointee that month at the Harlem headquarters of Sharpton's organization, the National Action Network.

During the appearance, Bratton invoked the words of former South African president Nelson Mandela, who died just two days before. He said the NYPD would "practice what Mandela preached: freedom for all, respect for all, compassion for all."

At the roundtable two weeks after Garner's death, Councilwoman Debi Rose, the New York City Councilmember representing the Staten Island district where Garner was killed, spoke first. "It ends today," Rose began her remarks, "Those were the prophetic words that were uttered by Eric Garner on July 17 just before he was put into a chokehold."

Rose was seated next to the principal combatants for this discussion. Immediately to her right was Sharpton. Bratton sat two seats over from Sharpton. Sandwiched in between the two was Mayor de Blasio.

Next up to speak was Sharpton. "Let me be very direct," he began.

He said that when de Blasio ran for mayor, he "captured the hope of the city" because he "seemed sensitive" to the fact that the city was "caught in between two serious problems." One was violence in some communities and crime, and the other was the police that had "gone over the line."

"But now...we have to go from that hope to actuality," Sharpton said. He told de Blasio that it was time to prove that he could be "transformational" and "not just another politician."

Sharpton called out Bratton's broken windows strategy and its disproportionate adverse effect on Black and Latino communities. Then he got even more direct with de Blasio.

"If Dante wasn't your son, he'd be a candidate for a chokehold," Sharpton said, referencing the mayor's half-Black teenage son.

Shifting his focus back to the police, Sharpton balked at the suggestion that training would solve the problems associated with the policing that they all witnessed two weeks earlier on Bay St.

"You don't need training if a man saying 11 times I can't breathe, and you still hold him in a grip," Sharpton said.

Next, it was time for Sharpton to address Bratton directly. "I heard the commissioner say race wasn't involved. We don't know that...So we're gonna prejudge what we want and tell the community to wait on the results?"

A few days after Garner's death, Bratton had told *The Observer,* "I personally don't think that race was a factor in the incident involved in this tragic death." He said that based on the "circumstances" that he saw in the video, "I don't think the issue of race entered into this at all."

As he neared the end of his speech, Sharpton made a blunt suggestion to the police commissioner: arrest Pantaleo. "The best way to make police stop using illegal chokeholds is to perp walk one of them that did."

Bratton spoke next. He didn't seem phased, only telling Sharpton that he "disagreed in some respects" with what he had said. Bratton retorted that training would be an "essential catalyst" and said they would retrain the whole department on proper Use of Force protocol. He said he'd institute annual retraining if he had to.

Bratton spoke calmly, mentioned a couple more times how great his plan to fix the NYPD's "deficient" training would be, and assured people in the room that part of the memory of this tragedy will be "the good that came out of it, not just the negative."

The final member of the trio to speak was de Blasio. The emcee for the event, one of de Blasio's aides, introduced him as "the man who put an end to stop and frisk."

The emphasis on the "end" of stop and frisk was curious here. For one, the remedial process in the *Floyd* case had not even started yet — and wouldn't get started for several months.

After de Blasio took office, he announced in late January 2014 that he intended to drop Mayor Bloomberg's appeal of the case. "The unions don't take this lying down," said Darius Charney, lead attorney for the *Floyd* plaintiffs. "They say 'we want to continue the appeal.'"

So the stay in the case remained until the end of October 2014. Then, on Halloween, the Second Circuit Court of Appeals dismissed the appeal once and for all.

De Blasio said during the roundtable discussion he remained "deeply troubled" by what he saw in the video of Eric Garner. "It pains us to this hour," he said.

"It would be a great disservice and injustice to not find change and reform out of this moment," he said.

De Blasio went on to commend the police department for the low crime numbers in the city of late. Indeed, at the time, the steady downward trend in crime had continued. But, he said, part of the job was also to "create a mutual respect" in the communities while keeping crime low.

"We have to do both…one without the other is a disservice to the communities we all serve," he said.

PBA President Patrick Lynch panned the mayor for putting Sharpton on equal footing with other city officials. The union boss said in a TV interview after the roundtable that the NYPD "protect Al Sharpton's right to have his opinion, but his opinion should not be elevated."

A few months later, Bratton was asked about the talking-to that Sharpton gave him at de Blasio's roundtable while appearing at the $1000-a-plate Crain's Business Breakfast Forum. "I'll shake hands with the devil if necessary to keep this city calm, safe, and secure," Bratton responded. He later insisted he wasn't referring specifically to Sharpton as the devil.

One day after the roundtable, the New York City Medical Examiner announced that Eric Garner's death had been ruled a homicide. The medical examiner said that the cause of death was "compression of neck (choke hold), compression of chest, and prone positioning during physical restraint by police." In the excerpt of the report that they released, the medical examiner said Garner's asthma, obesity, and hypersensitive cardiovascular disease were "contributing conditions." The complete medical examiner's report was never released.

Now, in addition to the 15-plus minutes of video evidence, the case had a medical examiner's report that said Garner's death was a homicide. Yet over the remaining months of 2014, it seemed like justice kept getting further out of reach for the Garner family and their supporters.

The Staten Island District Attorney's criminal investigation moved at a glacial pace. DA Daniel Donovan conducted 38 interviews, including 22 civilians who said they saw at least part of what happened between Garner and the NYPD. To decide whether or not to indict Pantaleo, Donovan impaneled not just a regular grand jury but a special grand jury that would hear just evidence in the one case. The group of 23 spent over two months hearing evidence. Fourteen members of the grand jury were White, and the rest were Black and Hispanic. They listened to the testimony of 50 witnesses that included civilians, police officers, emergency personnel, and doctors. On December 3, 2014, Donovan announced that the grand jury found "no reasonable cause" to indict Pantaleo on criminal charges.

Most of what happened behind closed doors during Donovan's special grand jury remains a mystery. A coalition that included the Legal Aid Society, NYCLU, and the NAACP sued to have the grand jury minutes released to the public. That effort failed when a Staten Island judge ruled in March 2015 against them.

The shroud of secrecy over the grand jury didn't stop at least one of the 22 civilian witnesses from speaking out about their testimony. Taisha Allen, the Garner friend who filmed video from inside a Bay St. beauty shop, told the *New York Times* a prosecutor told her not to say Garner was put into a chokehold while she testified. "I said they put him in a chokehold," Allen told the *Times*. She said the prosecutor responded, "Well, you can't say they put him in a chokehold."

Pat Lynch came out in defense of Pantaleo after the DA's announcement that he wouldn't be criminally charged, calling him "a mature, mature police officer who's motivated by serving the community."

"He literally, literally, is an Eagle Scout," Lynch said.

He called Pantaleo's takedown of Garner "textbook."

"We feel badly that there was a loss of life," Lynch said "But unfortunately Mr. Garner made a choice that day to resist arrest."

The end of the Staten Island DA's investigation meant that the family's remaining paths to see Pantaleo and the NYPD held accountable for Garner's death were the department's own administrative investigation and the federal civil rights investigation. Both seemed poised to drag on for quite some time. Meanwhile, Pantaleo would remain on the force collecting a paycheck.

Any reconciliation between Bill de Blasio, the police unions and rank-and-file officers he had angered was also not happening. After the DA's announcement, de Blasio's speech about telling his Black son in the past to "take special care" around police triggered the unions to accuse the mayor of throwing the NYPD "under the bus." A few weeks later, they turned their back on him after officers Liu and Ramos were killed.

Still, the fact remained that this was year one of the de Blasio administration. He was going to be in office for at least another three. And surely the mayor and police had to find a way to fix their relationship, as well as the relationship between police and the public. But how?

Politically, the July roundtable with Sharpton and Bratton turned out to be a huge miss by the mayor. But during the discussion de Blasio managed to lay out an outline of the areas where he would be judged in terms of enacting police reform.

At the end of his remarks — or at least the end of the part before they kicked the media out — de Blasio, in classic politician speak, moved to assuage the concerns of the listeners by ticking off a list of his accomplishments you might've missed. "We have a team here that's focused and ready to get things done," de Blasio said.

De Blasio then proceeded to give props to the team he had appointed to handle critical roles related to his policing agenda. He talked about Bratton, who he said "understands the important role of oversight," adding that he doesn't see it as a "burden." And he touted his new head of the Civilian Complaint Review Board, Richard Emery, a highly regarded civil rights attorney around town who was given the CCRB job just a few weeks earlier on the morning of the day that Garner died. De Blasio called Emery "a well-known reformer and change agent." He said that Emery is the person "to help us make" the CCRB "what it should have been long ago" — a police oversight agency that is "fair to both community members and police officers."

De Blasio also mentioned Zachary Carter, who he had made Corporation Counsel at the New York City law department. As New York City's chief legal officer, de Blasio tasked Carter with representing the city, the police department, and its officers in civil lawsuits brought by alleged victims of police misconduct.

Carter's resume included being the first Black man to serve as US Attorney in the Eastern District of New York. He had notably handled the federal prosecution of the police officers who tortured and sodomized Abner Louima in the bathroom of Brooklyn's 70th precinct station house in 1997.

When de Blasio announced he was appointing Carter that past December — just a few days after he announced Bratton's appointment — it was praised by many, including Al Sharpton, who told the *New York Times* that Carter's appointment was an "unprecedented and huge step for progress." At the roundtable discussion, de Blasio said that since he had brought Carter in, he already "aggressively settled outstanding lawsuits" related to stop and frisk.

"The change has been happening. The change will continue to deepen. And it will be felt in every neighborhood of this city," de Blasio said.

By listing off these specific players and their agencies — and suggesting that they would exist in harmony — de Blasio seemed to suggest he had a tight handle on police accountability and transparency. He sounded confident that he could deliver the sort of accountability that the public was asking for after watching Eric Garner die for unnecessary reasons.

Of course, a big overarching question was how would the NYPD, an agency of immense power, respond to de Blasio's plans. To put it quite bluntly, Karen Hinton, a former de Blasio press secretary, said of the NYPD, "They've always been allowed to do what they want to do."

"The police department is an independent agency. You don't manage them, you manage your relationship with them," another former de Blasio staffer said.

"The NYPD is what I call a super agency," another former de Blasio press secretary, Eric Phillips, said.

"They have more clout, more public perception, and more resources than the vast majority of agencies. That gives them, naturally, a unique leverage in public power that, for example, the Department of Transportation or Parks might not enjoy."

"And they know that, most importantly," Phillips added. "This clout is not lost on the police commissioner or the cops on the street."

The mayor's relationship with — and his authority over — the NYPD was also being questioned by the media. After the July 2014 roundtable, the *New York Post* ran a photo from the event with de Blasio, Bratton and Sharpton with the not-so-subtle headline, "Who's The Boss!" However, several of de Blasio's former colleagues said that the idea that he was openly feuding with the department and its leadership during the early days of his administration after Garner was killed and officers Liu and Ramos were assassinated was not true.

"I never saw the mayor get into any kind of disagreement or fight with the police commissioner," Hinton said. "You would think they were the best, closest friends in the world."

"He got surprised by the reaction of the department to him saying he had 'the talk' with his son. And It was unfortunate that some time after that the two officers were assassinated," said Rev. Fred Davie, a former chairman of the CCRB who has known de Blasio for decades dating back to when they worked together in the Dinkins administration.

"He really worried about not having the police force alienated," Davie said.

Whether Sharpton's lecture of Bratton and de Blasio during the roundtable discussion was helpful or not, he did hit on one point that pretty accurately summed up de Blasio's situation with the police at that time. If de Blasio could pull it off and get the NYPD and City Hall to play nice, the mayor would have a damn good argument that to quote Sharpton, he was "transformational."

But if it went another way, as Sharpton said, the question would have to be asked: with his ideas to transform the New York City police department, was de Blasio just playing "spin games?"

5

"THEY KILLED MARLEY!": THE POLICE KILLING OF BRONX TEENAGER RAMARLEY GRAHAM

On a Thursday morning in February 2012, Constance Malcolm was on her way out the door to her job as a nurse's aide. A Jamaican immigrant who had come to New York City when she was 13, Malcolm was about to leave her apartment that she shared with her children and mother in the Wakefield section of the Bronx, when she spotted her oldest son sprawled on the living room couch.

18-year-old Ramarley Graham was lying there wrapped in one of the burgundy blankets that Malcolm's aunt had given to them from the hospital she worked at. She didn't dare disturb him. Ramarley looked so peaceful, Malcolm thought. She headed out the door to work.

When Ramarley woke up, he helped his little brother, Chinnor, get ready for school. Chinnor was having a tough time in school. He didn't want to go that day. But his older brother told him he had to. Ramarley said he'd be right here waiting for him when he got back.

The brothers were close. Even though they were twelve years apart, Ramarley made sure to make time for his little brother. He played video games and watched *Animal Planet* with 6-year-old Chinnor. He was also showing his younger brother how to defend himself. They would play-box each other. Ramarley told Chinnor he had to stand up for himself and not let anybody mess with him.

Malcolm said she was glad that Chinnor got to spend some time with his older brother before it happened.

Ramarley Graham spent the afternoon of February 2, 2012 hanging out at a friend's house. They smoked some weed. Then they walked to a bodega on East 228th Street. After the store, Graham started for home. He wanted to change his clothes. He had plans to meet up with some girls that night.

Plainclothes NYPD officers from the 47th precinct's Street Narcotics Enforcement Unit were parked in a Lexus on the corner of White Plains Road and East 228th Street staking out the bodega, known as the "ice box." Officers Tyrone Horne and Andrew Jarvis watched the three teens enter the store then exit quickly. The officers saw Graham adjust his pants as he was walking. Under Graham's shirt, Horne said he believed he saw the butt of a gun.

Horne relayed the details over the team's tactical radio channel. NYPD Sergeant Scott Morris replied and asked the officers to confirm the information. Jarvis backed up his partner and told the sergeant that he saw a gun, too.

The Street Narcotics Enforcement Unit, or SNEU, was known at the NYPD as narcotics-lite. Its officers were restricted to arresting people for drug deals they spotted with their own eyes. The SNEU teams weren't authorized to conduct the more elaborate undercover buy-and-bust operations. They didn't try to go up the chain and take down higher-level distributors either. The units mostly stuck to staking out spots that they believed were known drug buy locations, like the bodega Graham walked out of on that Thursday afternoon.

The three friends kept walking up White Plains Road. The police stayed on them. As he neared his block, Graham peeled off from the others and continued on his way to his home on East 229th Street.

Two other members of the SNEU team, officers John McLoughlin and Richard Haste, were nearby in a 12-passenger Ford Econoline van used for prisoner transport. They followed Graham in the van. When he got about half a block from his house, McLoughlin and Haste got out and started running.

Graham got to his building's door. He unlocked it, looked over his shoulder, walked in, and locked the door behind him. Then he made his way upstairs to his family's second-floor apartment.

Moments later, Haste ran up to the building door. The 30-year-old ex-Marine had joined the NYPD about four years earlier. In that time, he racked up 175 arrests. But he'd only been a member of the SNEU team for about two months.

Haste pulled the door, but it wouldn't open. He tried to kick it in. It wouldn't budge. A couple of minutes later, another tenant on the first floor of the building opened their door and let McLoughlin and Haste inside. The officers raced up to the second floor.

They banged on Graham's door and shouted commands. *Police! Open up!* Nobody opened the door. McLoughlin asked Haste "you ready?" then kicked in the door. Haste rushed into the apartment.

Haste spotted Graham in the hallway. "Show me your hands!" the officer yelled. Graham's grandmother, who lived with them, Patricia Hartley, said she was standing with Ramarley in the hallway when the officers busted in. His brother Chinnor was off to the side in another room.

"Fuck you. Suck my dick." Graham responded, according to Haste.

Graham darted into the bathroom. Haste followed him with his gun drawn.

As they came together in the bathroom, Haste claimed he saw Graham reaching into his pants. He said he believed he was going for a gun. Haste fired one shot into Graham's chest.

Hartley screamed at Haste, "Why did you shoot him? Why you killed him?" He told her, "Get the fuck away before I have to shoot you too." She said he pushed her out of the way and into a vase. In an interview with *New York Magazine*, Haste admitted that he yelled at the grandmother. He didn't deny using profanity, but he said he didn't threaten to shoot her.

Standing off to the side in just his t-shirt and underwear, Chinnor could see his brother laid out on the bathroom floor, his tan boots with the toes up twitching in the hallway.

It was three o'clock in the afternoon. Ramarley Graham was officially pronounced dead at 3:53 pm at Montefiore Hospital. Investigators never found a gun in the house.

Constance Malcolm was already on her way home from work when she got the first call from her downstairs neighbor, Eric. He told her there were a bunch of police in the backyard, and she needed to get home. They hung up, but a few minutes later, Eric called her back. He asked her how close she was. Malcolm thought, Eric never calls me. *Why is he calling me twice?*

By the time she got to the block, police had cordoned off the street. She showed the police her ID and told them where she lived. An officer in a white shirt asked her if she would come with them to the precinct. Malcolm agreed to go.

A cop took Malcolm upstairs at the station house. The police still hadn't told her what was going on. When they got to the next floor, Malcolm said, the officer said to another cop they were coming from "the homicide." That was the first time that she said she heard that somebody was killed back on her block.

Moments later, her mother, Patricia Hartley, spotted Malcolm as police were taking her back for questioning. Hartley, crying and hysterical, screamed out to her daughter, "They killed Marley!" Malcolm remembers at that moment feeling confused, thinking *what is this crazy lady talking about?*

The officers at the precinct brought Malcolm into the hallway to sit on a bench and wait. While she was sitting there, she got a call from Ramarley's father, Frank. He told her not to let the police talk to her mother. She needed a lawyer with her.

Malcolm got up and began frantically going door to door, looking for her mother. When she found her, she tried to pull Hartley out of the interview room. She said an officer pulled her mom away and pushed her to the ground. Even though nobody at the precinct had confirmed Hartley's earlier outburst about Ramarley, Malcolm blurted out, "You gonna kill me like you killed my son?"

A little later on, Malcolm left the precinct. She had no idea where Chinnor was. Surveillance video that surfaced later showed an officer leading Chinnor out of the apartment on that cold February day in just his t-shirt and underwear.

Some members of the community would stay with Hartley at the precinct, she figured. She had to find her younger son.

Chinnor, it turned out, was taken in by Eric, the downstairs neighbor. After Malcolm located her younger son, she needed to take Ramarley's dad Frank to the hospital. His blood pressure was spiking from stress.

Hartley claimed the police kept her at the precinct for seven hours that day. The NYPD later said it was about five and a half hours. She also said she was denied her heart medication and forced to give a statement against her will.

In the whirlwind of activity that day, the family wasn't able to locate the body. It would take them three days because the city registered Graham under the wrong name at the morgue.

One of the city officials that called for a speedy investigation after Graham's killing was Public Advocate Bill de Blasio. A few days after his death, de Blasio put out a statement: "Part of the healing process for the Graham family, and for the city as a whole, derives from a fair, speedy and transparent investigation."

"That work should begin immediately," the statement added.

The NYPD had been in the news a lot that week due to confrontations with suspects that turned deadly. Graham was the third person killed by police in the city in the past five days. On January 26, an off-duty NYPD officer shot and killed a man suspected in a carjacking who police said fired upon them during the pursuit. Four days later, another off-duty cop shot and killed a man that police said tried to mug the officer in the Bushwick section of Brooklyn.

The same week, NYPD cops were also caught on video beating 19-year-old Jateik Reed with a baton while they had him pinned on the sidewalk in the University Heights section of the Bronx. In the cell phone video that surfaced, an officer appeared to threaten to pepper-spray the person filming the beating. Nearly five years later, Reed settled a lawsuit with the city for more than $600,000. The cop that struck him with the baton was ordered to contribute $5,000 to the settlement.

Two weeks after Graham was killed, de Blasio put out another statement calling on the Bronx DA to "expedite his investigation" into Graham's death. "Time is of the essence," de Blasio said.

De Blasio couldn't have predicted it then, but the controversy over this particular police killing — which happened more than 22 months before his inauguration — would drag well into his time as mayor.

According to Constance Malcolm, she would get "farther than most" people who have a loved one killed by the police during the years she spent seeking justice for her son. "But there's no justice," she said.

From its onset, the investigation did not go smoothly. That night, the NYPD told the media that Graham struggled with the officer who shot him in the bathroom. The police department's top spokesman Paul Browne told the press that it was unclear whether the officer's 9-millimeter semiautomatic pistol was fired during the struggle.

The next day, Police Commissioner Ray Kelly walked back the department's comments. He said that the report that Graham struggled with an officer was not accurate. On the investigation as a whole, the commissioner said, "We're still evaluating the actions here."

"We see an unarmed person being shot. That always concerns us," he said.

As the investigation continued, so did the negative media campaign against Graham and his family. After Graham died, his arrest record was leaked to the press. It showed that he was arrested eight times. Most of the incidents ended up without charges. Several had occurred when he was a juvenile, meaning the records should have been sealed, and whoever shared them with the media should not have had access to the reports in the first place.

The Bronx DA's investigation took months to reach the grand jury. Then on June 13, 2012, Richard Haste's 31st birthday, he was indicted on first and second-degree manslaughter charges. He became the first cop indicted in a police killing since three officers were charged after the death of Sean Bell in 2006. In the case over the killing of Bell, all three cops were acquitted of the charges.

A year after the Bronx DA brought charges against Haste, the case fell apart. After he was indicted, Haste's defense team argued that the instructions from the prosecutor led the grand jury to ignore Haste's "state of mind" at the time of the shooting, including the fact that he heard another officer in his unit communicate to the team that he saw a gun on Graham. The judge agreed with the defense and tossed the indictment. The DA's office presented the case to a second grand jury. But this time, they chose not to indict. The state's criminal investigation against Haste was done.

As for Officer Haste, the NYPD placed him on "modified assignment," which means he was stripped of his firearm and sent to a "non-enforcement" team. In Haste's case, the NYPD assigned him to the motor fleet division, which maintains the department's cars. Whether he kept his job long term with the NYPD would now be determined by the department's internal investigation.

One level of closure came for the family in early 2015. On the one year anniversary of Graham's death, in 2013, Malcolm filed a federal civil rights lawsuit against the city and the police. She hired attorney Royce Russell to represent her. He said that compared to some lawsuits he has brought against the city, this one moved quickly.

On January 30, 2015 — just under two years after Malcolm sued them — the city announced they had reached a settlement with the family for $3.9 million. "This was a tragic case," a spokesperson for the city Law Department said. They said that settling the case was "in the best interest of the city."

The settlement in the Graham case came just six months after the announcement of the historic $41 million settlement for the Central Park 5. The five Black teenagers wrongly accused of the rape of a White female jogger decades earlier had fought with Mayor Bloomberg over the lawsuit throughout his administration. When de Blasio took over, the city moved to resolve the matter.

Weeks before the Graham settlement, City Comptroller Scott

Stringer publicly said he was also trying to resolve the $75 million dollar lawsuit brought by Eric Garner's family against the city.

For years, Constance Malcolm didn't touch the settlement money. She publicly decried it "blood money." But after a couple of years passed, she used it to buy a house and move out of the apartment where her son got shot. Still, she said the city could have kept the money — what she wanted was accountability. "Me having the money didn't make me any happier," she said. "I'd rather be broke."

Her lawyer Royce Russell knew that for Malcolm, the settlement money would never represent justice for Ramarley's death. "By the time we got to the end, that was a different person than I met," Russell said about Malcolm. "Articulate, knew certain laws. She knew this is what I want, what we need."

What she wanted more than anything was for the officers who killed her son to be taken off the force. But she said she was kept in the dark about the department's investigation into Haste and the other members of the NYPD involved in the shooting. Russell had warned her about setbacks. He told her that as she continued to fight, there would be "potholes" along the road in her journey — and also "that potholes can be very deep."

Malcolm tried to meet with Mayor de Blasio to express her frustration with the department's investigation, even writing his office multiple letters. "I did everything in my power to get de Blasio to listen," she said. "This man would not listen."

Malcolm doesn't know why de Blasio, the man who had called for a "speedy investigation" into Graham's killing, wouldn't meet with her. She suspects it's because it didn't serve his political purposes. She mentioned how around the same time, he met with the professional tennis player James Blake after the police manhandled him during a botched investigation.

In September 2015, Blake was tackled by NYPD detective James Frascatore outside the Grand Hyatt Hotel on East 42nd St. in Manhattan. He was waiting for a car to take him to the U.S. Open in Queens. Frascatore had mistaken Blake for a suspect in an identity theft ring investigation. His takedown of the tennis pro was captured on video.

The footage of the arrest went viral and made headlines around the globe. Within two weeks, Blake had a meeting with de Blasio and Commissioner Bratton.

De Blasio publicly apologized to Blake and pledged reform. Years later, Blake expressed his outrage that the officer had only lost vacation time over the incident and wasn't fired. He said Frascatore "should not be allowed to sully the badge that so many other good cops wear with honor."

Still, to Constance Malcolm, de Blasio and Bratton meeting with a celebrity like Blake and not her revealed a double standard. "They looked at me and probably said, 'Poor little Jamaican girl, she's nobody,'" Malcolm said.

Even after being denied her meeting with the mayor, Malcolm wasn't deterred. She worked with others in the community to organize rallies for Ramarley after his death — 18 in total because he was 18 when he was killed. They always held them on Thursday because the police killed him on a Thursday. Her activism in her son's memory brought her in contact with organizations in the city working for police reform. One of the people she met was Loyda Colon, the director of Justice Committee.

Justice Committee was founded by prominent Puerto Rican activist Richie Perez in 1988. Over decades, Perez and his team built the organizations into a force for activism and organizing against police brutality in New York City. They regularly organized rallies and protests against police violence. They also maintained a healthy presence in the media in an effort to sculpt the narrative around the injustice they saw being perpetrated by cops largely against the city's minority population. After Amadou Diallo was killed, Perez worked to bring the *Daniels* stop and frisk case to the Center For Constitutional Rights who filed the lawsuit.

A major part of the Justice Committee and Perez's focus was on the work of advocating for the families of victims of police violence. Joo-Hyun Kang, the former director of Communities United for Police Reform, was trained by Perez. She said that he taught the young organizers to "meet the immediate needs" of survivors and help them figure out their options, define what justice looks like for them, and try to secure some accountability.

Unlike some of the people who came to the rallies for Graham — and predicted that Haste was definitely going to jail and all her problems would be solved — Colon and Justice Committee were "honest and brutal" with Malcolm, she said. Colon told her, "I'm going to be real with you. This is going to be very hard. Many families do not win." However, Malcolm said Colon promised that their organization would be with her until the end.

If it took years of her life, Malcolm was determined to fight so long as the cops that killed her son remained on the force. And that's what it would take: years. Not just to see some accountability, but for Malcolm to learn the details of what went down that day inside her apartment.

6

WHO WAS OFFICER DANIEL PANTALEO?: THE FIGHT OVER CIVIL RIGHTS LAW 50-A

A fter seven years in private practice, attorney Cynthia Conti-Cook took a job at the Legal Aid Society in early 2014.

Founded in 1876, the Legal Aid Society is the oldest and largest provider of free legal assistance to those who can't afford representation in the country. Conti-Cook worked out of the Manhattan office for Legal Aid but that July she made a trip to the Staten Island office. It was the day after Eric Garner died.

"I remember vividly, one of the attorneys, he and I walked over to where he was killed," she said. She remembers people were just "milling around," still in shock about what had happened on the Bay St. sidewalk the day before.

A few months later, in December 2014, she sent a Freedom of Information Law request on behalf of Legal Aid to the Civilian Complaint Review Board seeking any records of misconduct that the agency had for the officer who put Garner in a chokehold, Daniel Pantaleo.

Conti-Cook filed her records request the same month that a Staten Island grand jury declined to indict Pantaleo. Because the grand jury's decision to end the criminal case against Pantaleo happened behind closed doors, how the Staten Island DA presented the evidence was a mystery. Now it was up to either the federal government or the NYPD to punish Pantaleo. While Garner's family and the public waited to learn what would happen to the officer in the future, Conti-Cook and Legal Aid hoped to pry loose anything they could learn about his past. However, a 40-year-old New York state law that kept police officers' records secret stood in their way.

Even before the recent spate of highly publicized police killings of Garner and other Black men across the country, in New York, civil rights and criminal justice reformers, organizers and advocates, including Conti-Cook, had been focused on the issues of police accountability and transparency for some time.

During her time in private practice, she handled around 100 civil rights lawsuits, many against the police. She noticed something about her cases against the NYPD: she was suing the same cops, over and over again.

Daniel Sbarra ran an NYPD narcotics team out of Brooklyn North. The cops from this patrol borough were so notorious in the community for their aggressive tactics they earned the nickname the "Body Snatchers."

Over the years, Sbarra and his crew racked up more than their share of complaints. By 2013, Sbarra himself had been the subject of 30 civilian complaints in 15 years with the police department, among the highest number on the whole force. Hand in hand with the heavy amount of complaints came the lawsuits — a whole lot of lawsuits — from people claiming that this unit violated their civil rights.

The year before Garner died, the *Daily News* revealed that Sbarra and his team had been sued a staggering 58 times. The cases that settled cost New York taxpayers at least $1.5 million. Sbarra was personally named in at least 15 lawsuits. Together, those suits cost the city almost $500,000 to settle.

In one case, a Black man claimed that Sbarra and his team repeatedly called him a "nigger" and illegally searched him during a traffic stop while hiding their badge numbers with tape. Sbarra was personally ordered to contribute $1,000 to the $19,500 settlement of the man's lawsuit.

In one of Conti-Cook's cases, her client accused Sbarra and his team of smashing his face into a glass window at the station house and ripping out a handful of his dreadlocks. The man's lawsuit was settled for $50,000.

Despite costing the city so much, Sbarra had faced very little discipline over his career. After one complaint, the police department docked him 20 vacation days but then promoted him the following month to lieutenant.

Her experience going after the Brooklyn North narcotics crew left Conti-Cook dismayed by the lack of officer accountability at the NYPD.

"There were no repercussions," she said. "It sparked my quest to collect police misconduct data."

Legal Aid attorneys handle heavy caseload. On average, the New York office handles around 230,000 cases per year. To keep up with the sometimes overwhelming amount of work, the attorneys need to be creative when it comes to defending their clients. Conti-Cook had an idea to help them do a better, more efficient job: a "bad cop" database.

Her goal was pretty straightforward: create a centralized hub where attorneys could learn if the cops arresting their clients had a history of running afoul of the police department rules. She had been ruminating on the concept before joining Legal Aid. But after she joined the organization, she kicked into high gear.

Cynthia and her team worked tirelessly to pull information from multiple sources such as news reports about alleged police misconduct, civil lawsuits, and criminal trials where a police witness was found not credible by a judge. In less than a year, they built a database with details on 3,000 New York City cops.

Another substantive source of information that Legal Aid tapped into to learn about the cops involved in their clients' cases was the CCRB. When she first arrived at Legal Aid, Conti-Cook said they had some luck getting summaries of the disciplinary information that the CCRB had on officers the agency investigated. These letters contained limited information such as the number of complaints about a particular officer and what, if any, penalties they received. The Legal Aid defense attorneys would then take those letters into court and ask the prosecutors to turn over more information on the officers.

On Christmas Eve, the CCRB responded to Conti-Cook's request for Pantaleo's files. It was short and blunt: her request was denied. The city agency claimed the documents related to Mr. Pantaleo's records were confidential. They cited an obscure state law: Civil Rights Law Section 50-a.

———

50-A, as it is commonly referred to, was passed by the state legislature more than four decades earlier. The law stated that all "personnel records used to evaluate performance towards continued employment or promotion" for police officers, firefighters, and corrections officers are deemed "confidential and not subject to inspection or review" except by a judge's court order. The law's stated intention was to prevent defense attorneys from engaging in "fishing expeditions" for information to attack officers' credibility in court.

The author of the bill was State Senator Frank Padavan, who wrote the original draft of the bill in 1974. The Queens Republican made it clear he was introducing the legislation on the police union's recommendation. In a memo describing the bill, Padovan wrote: "The Patrolmen's Benevolent Association of the New York City Transit Police has pointed up a very serious problem which exists whereby some attorneys engaging in 'fishing expeditions' subpoena personnel records as a possible basis for attacking the credibility of police officers on cross-examination and have abused and misused these files."

Padavan noting how the PBA brought this "very serious problem" to his attention, spurring him to act, illustrated how the political power of the police unions was growing during this era.

During the civil rights movement in the 1960s and '70s, persistent police brutality repeatedly drove minority groups into the street in protest. Some of those protests turned violent. In 1964, Black residents in Harlem, Chicago, Philadelphia, and Jersey City, New Jersey rioted following instances of police violence in their cities. Three years later, demonstrations in response to more police brutality in Detroit and

Newark again turned violent. During the Summer of 1967, violence and riots broke out in 150 cities across the country.

In response, President Lyndon Johnson formed The National Advisory Commission on Civil Disorders — known as the Kerner Commission after its chairman, Illinois Gov. Otto Kerner — to study the unrest. The Kerner Commission blamed the riots on several factors, including the lack of economic opportunity for minorities, failed social programs, police brutality, and racism. The commission put it bluntly in the report: "Our nation is moving toward two societies, one black, one white — separate and unequal."

At the same time, the highest court in the land handed down change mandates for police in America. In a series of rulings in the 1960s, the Supreme Court started to reshape and limit police power. In 1961, the court held that any evidence obtained by unconstitutional search and seizure is inadmissible in court. A couple of years later in 1964, the court ruled that statements made by a suspect after they requested and had been denied an attorney were also not admissible at trial. In 1966 — in one of the most well-known Supreme Court rulings on criminal justice — the court said that a police officer must inform a suspect that they have the right to remain silent and consult an attorney before answering questions. These rights are commonly known as the *Miranda* rights, after the name of the case.

In the face of these recent legal developments expanding civilian rights when dealing with the police, and in response to the sharp critiques of police during the civil rights movement, the police unions adopted an *"us vs. them"* mentality. The unions subsequently began pushing a political agenda that opposed transparency and accountability for law enforcement. One example of how this political strategy was put into practice in the 1960s was when the PBA blocked New York City Mayor John Lindsay's attempt to usher in civilian oversight of the New York police department.

Going back more than ten years earlier, in 1950, a coalition of 18 organizations in New York City called the "Permanent Coordination Committee on Police and Minority Groups" aggressively lobbied the city to address police misconduct in general, and "police misconduct in their relations with Puerto Ricans and Negros specifically." In response, the city established its first Civilian Complaint Review Board in 1953. However, having the words "Civilian" in the group's name did not mean in this early iteration that people outside the police department were involved. In fact, when the CCRB was established in the 1950s it operated solely within the police department. The board was composed of three deputy police commissioners, who were tasked with investigating civilian complaints and deciding whether or not to recommend discipline against any police officers.

In 1965, John Lindsay promised during his campaign for mayor he would create a "mixed" review board of police and citizens. After he was elected, the following year in 1966, Mayor Lindsay attempted to reform the CCRB and appoint non-police civilians to the board. In May 1966, Lindsay's police commissioner Howard Leary issued General Order No. 14, creating a seven-person CCRB composed of four civilians and three police officers. The PBA was not the least bit happy about this change.

By 1966, the PBA had grown its ranks to 20,000 members. Although still technically not an official union, it became one of the strongest and politically-effective groups in the city.

The PBA staged a rally to protest the mayor's restructuring of the CCRB. PBA president John Cassese angrily told the 5,000 officers who gathered outside City Hall, "I am sick and tired of giving in to minority groups, with their whims and their gripes and shouting. Any review board with civilians on it is detrimental to the operations of the police department," he said.

The PBA set out to get a referendum to repeal Lindsay's CCRB placed on the New York City ballot. That summer, they needed to collect 30,000 signatures to get the item on the ballot in the November election. Within about two months, they collected more than 51,000.

In the lead-up to the vote, the PBA waged a fear-mongering media campaign urging New Yorkers to vote against Lindsay's CCRB. A pro-repeal television spot delivered the message: "The addict, the criminal, the hoodlum — only the policeman stands between you and him." A newspaper ad pictured a Philadelphia street with smashed storefront windows and a cash register lying in an empty street during the 1964 riots. "This is the aftermath of a riot in a city that had a civilian review board," the ad said. (Philadelphia established the first civilian review board of police misconduct in 1958.) This ad was a direct swipe at Commissioner Leary — who was the police commissioner in Philly during the riots.

In New York City, posters and billboards went up around town urging New Yorkers to vote to repeal the CCRB. One infamous poster depicted a young White woman in the rain standing outside a subway entrance on a dark street that read: "The Civilian Review Board must be stopped...Her life...your life...may depend on it." The NAACP's executive director Roy Wilkins called the ad the "slimiest kind of racism." Lindsay said, "The only thing it didn't show was a gang of Negroes about to attack her. It was a vulgar, obscene advertisement if I've ever seen one."

Later that year, New Yorkers voted overwhelmingly to stop Lindsay's attempt to put civilians on the CCRB. The referendum passed by almost a two to one margin, 63 to 37 percent.

Over the years, the police unions in New York grew this reactionary political machine. They hired lobbyists, mobilized their members to rally against police reforms, and pushed police-friendly legislation at the state and local levels of government. Anthony V. Bouza, a former New York City police officer and chief of the Minneapolis Police Department, wrote in a 1985 article tracing the history of police unions, "Police Unions: Paper Tigers or Roaring Lions?" that the New York state legislature in particular, which "wielded crucial authority over legislation substantially affecting the police ranks" became a "focus" for the PBA.

"Accustomed to lobbyers, the representatives and senators welcomed the PBA as a source of campaign funds, support, and good times," Bouza wrote.

During the de Blasio years, the PBA's spending in Albany was significant. During a five year period, from 2015 to 2020, the union shelled out more than $1.4 million on campaign contributions and lobbying fees, according to an analysis by local NYC media outlet *The City*. This big spending came as the PBA fought to lobby against reforms on the legislative docket, including legislation aiming to repeal the state law that kept police disciplinary secret, 50-a.

From January 2015 through May 2020, *The City* found, the PBA's political action committee cut $650,000 in campaign checks to New York politicians. The biggest beneficiary during this time was the state Senate Republican Campaign Committee, receiving $78,500 between 2015 and 2018. The PBA also spent big bucks on lobbying during these years. From 2017 to 2019, they forked over $768,000 in union dues to outside lobbyists, according to filings with the state Joint Commission on Public Ethics.

In 1974, the same year Padavan introduced the 50-a bill, a very interesting thing happened in New York's legislature related to government transparency: the state enacted its first Freedom of Information Law (FOIL). This came about eight years after Congress passed the Freedom of Information Act (FOIA) at the federal level, which required federal agencies to disclose information requested under FOIA unless it fell under a list of exemptions meant to protect interests such as personal privacy or national security. Now, the law passed in New York created a new mechanism for individuals to request information and documents from government officials in the state, which presumably included police departments.

In 1974, Padavan's 50-a legislation came up for a vote in Albany. This first iteration of the bill would have prevented grand juries, district attorneys, and even the state's Attorney General from accessing police records. Prosecutors across the state opposed it. The bill passed, but Governor Malcolm Wilson vetoed it. Padavan tried the following year again, and this time when it passed, the new governor, Hugh Carey, vetoed it again.

In 1976, Padavan tried yet again. The legislature amended the bill to allow DAs and other key individuals more access to police personnel files. Nevertheless, there was still opposition to 50-a. For example, the state's budget office said the bill created unnecessary court procedures. The budget examiner argued that judges already weighed the disclosure of police records against their public interest. Also, they pointed out that 50-a would make personal records confidential for law enforcement officers but not other civil servants.

The amendments allowing more access for specific groups helped it gain support from most prosecutors in the state, but not all. In a two-page letter, Deputy Attorney General Joseph Hoey wrote: "All the participants in the criminal justice system should constantly be reminded that their employment in this system is a privilege...and the greatest part of this privilege is being charged with the trust of maintaining the public's right to justice."

Hoey, who had served as the US attorney in Brooklyn, acknowledged the concern over defense attorney "fishing expeditions" but said he believed that judges could handle this issue on a case-by-case basis. He argued that Padavan's bill went too far, saying it was "analogous to a village placing a glass dome over Town Hall to keep the mosquitos out in the summertime, because the Mayor fears the custodian will forget to put up the screens in May."

The police unions lobbied heavily for 50-a to pass. In 1976, John Maye, president of the New York City Transit Patrolmen's Benevolent Association, wrote a letter to Gov. Carey that read: "In today's milieu police officers are bearing the brunt of fishing expeditions by some attorneys who are subpoenaing personnel records in an attempt to attack officers' credibility, a tactic that has led to abuse and in some cases disclosure of unverified and unsubstantiated information that the records contained. It also has resulted in the disclosure of confidential information and privileged medical records."

"These abuses can be stopped and the civil rights of police officers upheld by enactment of this bill," Maye's letter continued.

This time, when the bill passed, Gov. Carey signed it into law.

In the years to come, the police secrecy law would be used to protect against more than just the discovery requests of overly aggressive defense attorneys. One way that police departments and municipalities expanded their use of 50-a was to invoke the law to deny FOIL requests from the media and the public. When they did so, the highest courts in the state sided with them.

In 1999, a group of off-duty cops from Schenectady, New York, on a bachelor party riding in a chartered bus pelted two people in a car with eggs. The police department confirmed the incident to *The Daily Gazette*, telling the upstate New York paper that the cops were disciplined. But the department denied a public records request by the paper for which officers were involved and their penalties.

The Daily Gazette sued and the case made it to the New York Court of Appeals. The state's highest court ruled in the police department's favor citing 50-a. The court said that the law shielding the records applied not just to disclosure in the courts but also to the public and the press.

Frank Padavan died in 2018. But in a 2016 interview, he told the *Albany Times Union* that the only intention of 50-a "was to stop private attorneys from using subpoenas to gain unfettered access to personnel records of police officers." He said that "if the law is being misused, then obviously an amendment might be in order."

————

In 2014, those fighting to find out what was in Daniel Pantaleo's CCRB file saw the Christmas Eve denial of the public records request as yet another expansion of 50-a. So Legal Aid decided to take the matter further and sue the CCRB and the city for Pantaleo's records in early 2015.

Legal Aid said in the suit that it was only after the number of substantiated complaints against Pantaleo and the CCRB's recommendation to the police department on discipline. The public defenders insisted that they were not asking for full details of the disciplinary reports or background information on the alleged incidents.

The city's lawyers and an attorney for Pantaleo argued that these files were confidential because they were part of his personnel file and therefore covered by 50-a. They also argued that giving the files to Legal Aid would subject the officer to further harassment. In a sworn statement, Pantaleo said he'd already received a death threat from a person in Michigan on Facebook, leading to 24-7 police protection.

Manhattan Supreme Court Justice Alice Schlesinger ruled that the

CCRB files were not part of Panteleo's personnel records because a third party holds them. Therefore, the judge said, they're not shielded by 50-a.

Regarding the threats, Schlesinger said that "any adverse reactions expressed toward Mr. Pantaleo have their roots in the video of the incident, which speaks for itself," and "in the Staten Island Grand Jury's subsequent decision not to indict him."

On July 17, 2015, the first anniversary of Eric Garner's death, Schlesinger ruled in Legal Aid's favor. It was a big deal. If Schlesinger's decision stood, it would set a new legal precedent for the public's ability to learn NYPD disciplinary history. But seeing the court ruling's effect would have to wait because the next month, the city filed an appeal over the release of Pantaleo's records.

Richard Emery, chairman of the CCRB during this time, said he didn't believe that the city expanded its use of 50-a to deny requests for police records during de Blasio's tenure.

"As much as I didn't agree with it, 50-a is simple, it's clear — the statute was clear," he said.

Emery had been announced as chairman of the CCRB the same day that Eric Garner died. At the press conference that day, de Blasio acknowledged the shortcomings of the CCRB during its history as a police oversight body. "For decades, there was the fight to have a CCRB," de Blasio said. "And now, over the last 20 years, the fight to have an effective CCRB — we've never seen that work in a consistent manner."

He tapped Emery at the suggestion of Bratton and one of the commissioner's most trusted advisors and one of Emery's close friends, John Miller, the NYPD's Deputy Commissioner of Intelligence and Counterterrorism at the time.

Before he was appointed CCRB chairman, Emery had earned a bit of a rock star reputation in the New York legal world by handling some headline-grabbing cases. For instance, a few years earlier, Emery won millions in a settlement paid out to about 100,000 people who claimed they had been illegally strip-searched as prisoners at Rikers Island jail.

He was also the attorney behind the exoneration of Bobby

McLaughlin, a 19-year-old Brooklyn man who spent six years in prison after he was falsely identified as part of a mob that killed three during a violent hold-up of a dozen people in a park. After years of work, Emery and the Innocence Project, a leading nonprofit legal organization that fights to exonerate the wrongfully convicted, got McLaughlin's conviction thrown out, and the city agreed to pay him $1.9 million. The case inspired a made-for-TV movie, *Guilty Until Proven Innocent*, starring Martin Sheen and Brendan Fraser, which aired on the USA network in 1991.

In what was perhaps his most impactful case, in the late-1980s, Emery challenged the validity of New York City's Board of Estimates, an opaque, 200-year-old government body made up of representatives from each city borough that had tremendous decision making power. Starting in the late-1800s, the city had given the Board of Estimates free reign to cut deals for a number of things including land use and approving budgets. The board hashed out these often lucrative deals in smoke-filled rooms while the public remained in the dark about what was going on.

The clandestine nature of the system made it ripe for corruption. But beyond that, the representative math didn't add up. Each borough received the same number of seats on the Board of Estimates. So Staten Island, for example, had just as many members on the board as Brooklyn, despite having nearly 2 million fewer people. Emery argued that this violated the constitutional principle of "one person, one vote." He lost the case in federal district court but won the appeal. And when the city kept up the fight and petitioned the US Supreme Court, Emery went to Washington to argue his case before SCOTUS, his only appearance at the nation's highest court. The justices ruled in his favor 9-0. After that, the city eliminated the Board of Estimates.

When Emery took the reins of the CCRB its critics saw the agency charged with investigating police misconduct complaints as ineffectual and toothless. Emery shared this opinion about the CCRB. He said it was a place of little consequence when dealing with police accountability.

Statistics about the agency at this time revealed its ineffectiveness.

For example, from 2008 to 2012, NYPD Commissioner Ray Kelly chose to not punish officers in 23% of the cases where the CCRB substantiated the complaint, meaning it found that there was a better than 50% chance that the misconduct took place based on the evidence. In another 41% of those substantiated cases, Kelly gave officers "instructions" as a penalty, the lowest possible level of discipline.

Emery set out to reorganize the operation. He created a unit that would visit the scene of every complaint within 24 hours. He set and held people to deadlines for cop interviews. He reassigned supervisors as investigators to increase the agency's evidence-gathering muscle. Doing this also lowered each investigator's caseload from 40 to 50 open cases at a time to about 10 or 12.

To raise morale, Emery held regular meetings with the whole staff and encouraged even low-level personnel to come to him directly if they had concerns about the agency.

Emery also had to contend with some ugly internal politics that permeated the CCRB. The agency's executive director at the time he arrived, Tracy Catapano-Fox, was a holdover from the previous administration who had been in the job since 2013. Within four months, Emery fired her after she refused to step down.

Emery and Catapano-Fox disagreed about several issues of agency function, one of which dealt with the sharing of disciplinary information about officers with attorneys making Freedom of Information Law requests. At Catapano-Fox's direction, the agency had fulfilled these requests and shared summaries of disciplinary records with the attorneys filing FOIL requests.

Emery's position was that this violated 50-a. In the CCRB's 2014 year-end report, Emery addressed the agency's behavior regarding these records disclosures.

"During the CCRB's internal review of past practices, it came to light that for approximately one year, from October 2013 until October 2014, an employee of the CCRB had been improperly responding to Freedom of Information Law (FOIL) requests from attorneys for CCRB records pertaining to the complaint histories of specific police officers," the report said.

The report said that in response to 70 FOIL requests involving 95 officers, the CCRB turned over disciplinary records "even though this information is confidential and protected from public disclosure."

"The person responsible for these breaches is no longer an employee of the CCRB," the report said, referring to Catapano-Fox.

The Pantaleo situation quickly became a complicated affair for the CCRB in 2015. On the one hand, they were tied up in the Legal Aid lawsuit over their files on the officer. At the same time, Emery and the CCRB were also trying to prepare to prosecute Pantaleo in an NYPD disciplinary case over the death of Garner. And in that effort, *the city was blocking them* from learning more about what happened on Staten Island on July 17, 2014.

After Garner's death, a complaint was filed with the CCRB, so the agency began investigating Pantaleo's conduct. Emery said that Bratton asked him to prosecute the case personally. "I told him I would do it — actually go in and do the prosecution myself," Emery said.

If he was going to prosecute the case, he felt it was appropriate for the CCRB as part of its investigation to get the grand jury minutes from the Staten Island DA's criminal investigation. He petitioned the district court, thinking that the CCRB had a pretty good argument for accessing the secret files. However, he was pretty sure he'd lose with the Staten Island district judge — the court had made it clear that it was *case closed* when the grand jury voted not to indict. Indeed, the Staten Island judge denied Emery's request for the files.

He planned to appeal and thought the CCRB had a decent shot at convincing a panel of appellate court judges that the agency had a particular interest that merited turning over the grand jury minutes. "We were going to keep them a secret. It was just for us," Emery said. "We would have had a sealing order, and we would have abided."

But to file the appeal, Emery needed the approval of New York City's Corporation Counsel, Zachary Carter. The Corporation Counsel is the chief legal officer of New York City. The person in the job is responsible for handling claims against the city, including negotiating settlements and defending the city when it is sued. According to the City Charter, any agency litigation had to be approved by Corp. Counsel. Carter, it turned out, disagreed with Emery about the Pantaleo grand jury files.

"I had to go to Carter to appeal. He would not grant the appeal," Emery said.

Emery addressed this at a September 2015 board meeting after Carter shot him down. He said Carter had told him "he felt that the judge's opinion was right, that we did not have what is called particularized need, especially since we had the police file, to proceed with our appeal."

"And I strongly disagree with him," Emery added in his remarks to the board that night. The grand jury testimony of the Staten Island DA's criminal investigation into the killing of Eric Garner remained hidden from public view.

However, it was correct that Emery and the CCRB had gained access to some investigatory files in the Garner case through the NYPD's Internal Affairs Bureau. Emery said he went through that whole file, which included a taped interview of Daniel Pantaleo where the officer "completely undercut himself."

In the interview, Pantaleo denied that he had used a prohibited chokehold during the Garner altercation. An NYPD Internal Affairs Bureau investigator asked Pantaleo to define what constitutes a chokehold. He said that it required that the person lock their two hands for a grip to be categorized as a chokehold. The investigator showed him the video, which showed Pantaleo with his hands locked and his arms wrapped around Garner's throat. Still, Pantaleo denied using a chokehold.

Pantaleo also claimed in the interview that he didn't apply pressure to Garner's neck. However, according to Emery, the autopsy photos in Garner's files he reviewed showed "horrible ligature marks" — discolored grooves that can appear on a person's neck when pressure is applied to the area. Emery said it looked like the blood vessels in Garner's neck "had exploded."

"I thought the case was airtight," Emery said.

But he would never get the chance to prosecute it for the CCRB.

The same day Emery fired Catapano-Fox, she sued the city and him over her termination. In the complaint, she made several accusations against Emery directly, including that he "colluded" with the NYPD over police disciplinary matters. Emery, at the time, dismissed the suit as "frivolous."

After Catapano-Fox was out, Emery hired Mina Malik, a former prosecutor who worked in both the Queens and Brooklyn DA's office, as the new executive director. It wasn't long before they began to butt heads as well.

In September 2015, Emery was sitting on a three-person CCRB panel reviewing cases. One of the cases included a video of officers wheeling an Emotionally Disturbed Person (EDP) strapped to a gurney into a hospital. At one point in the video, the EDP spit on one of the officers. Emery said that the video showed the officer punch the person multiple times. He said that he made a remark to the panel calling the officer a "pussy" for unloading on the defenseless victim.

A couple of days later, he got a call from Malik. She wasn't present at the panel's meeting but had heard about Emery's comment. She asked him if he had used the term "pussy" during the session. He said yes, but told her that he was referring to the cop in the video who punched an individual strapped down on a stretcher. Malik said to him that she thought that she had to report it. Emery said that if that's what she felt she had to do, she should do it.

Later on, Emery recalls that he received a call from the Corporation Counsel's office about a complaint that he made the "pussy" comment. Emery admitted he had said it. That was the last he heard from anyone from the city about the episode. But the comment would come back to haunt him later on.

While dealing with this internal strife, Emery was also in a public fight with the police unions. In early 2016, two of the city's unions — the Police Benevolent Association and Sergeants Benevolent Association — called for Emery's removal after claiming he had a conflict because his law firm was representing a person who also made a complaint to the CCRB.

Before becoming agency chair, the city's Conflict of Interest Board cleared Emery on the question of whether it was appropriate for his firm to continue to sue the police while he held the position of CCRB chair. The board just said that he had to recuse himself in any cases involving the CCRB. And as for Emery's response after the unions called for his head, he said he wasn't going anywhere.

"I'm not going to deprive the public and people who are abused by police officers of having access to excellent lawyers because some union is squealing like a stuck pig," he told the *Daily News*, who broke the story about his firm's case and their client's CCRB complaint. He later apologized for the "squealing like a stuck pig" comment.

Two months later, in April 2016, Mina Malik sued Emery and the city, alleging sexual harassment at the agency. In her complaint, she said Emery "takes every opportunity to trample on the rights of and retaliate against those who complain about his misogynistic views." The suit mentioned the episode where he used the term "pussy." His comments about the police unions "squealing like a stuck pig" also made it into the court papers.

One day after Malik filed the lawsuit, Emery stepped down from the agency. Malik dropped her suit a month later. Around the same time, the city settled with Tracy Catapano-Fox for $275,000.

Emery said that he was disappointed that de Blasio didn't back him. He said that the mayor told him he'd been too controversial even though he made the CCRB into more than de Blasio conceived it could be.

Emery felt that he was falsely accused. He thought that de Blasio felt the same and should simply remove Malik as executive director. He was wrong.

"In typical de Blasio fashion, he was happy to have me resign, even though he said I did wonders with the place," Emery said. "My political issues with the unions, and even with him...it was plain to me that politics were driving him and not the merits."

With the de Blasio administration fighting to protect Pantaleo's records, leaning on the shield of 50-a, it looked like it would take a lot more fighting in court to learn if Pantaleo had a history of misconduct, with no guarantee of success.

But then, in the Spring of 2016, about ten months after the state court judge initially ordered his files to be turned over to Conti-Cook and Legal Aid, something unexpected happened. The local press started to reveal that Pantaleo indeed had a history of bad police conduct.

In early April, the *New York Daily News* reported that Pantaleo was accused of an illegal stop and frisk in June 2012 — more than two years before Garner's death.

According to NYPD and CCRB records obtained by the *Daily News*, Pantaleo and his partner recognized someone they might have stopped in the past in the Park Hill section of Staten Island. They stopped the man and searched his pockets, allegedly spotting a "bulge."

After the officers initially found nothing in the man's pockets, Pantaleo ran his hands around his waistband. They let the man go, but later, he filed a complaint about the stop with the CCRB.

The CCRB recommended department charges against Pantaleo. The department found him guilty of an "unauthorized frisk without legal authority." But the NYPD docked Pantaleo just two vacation days instead of the eight that the CCRB recommended.

As for how the *Daily News* learned about the incident, it turned out the reporters had seen the information posted on a clipboard hanging inside NYPD headquarters that the department updated daily with officer personnel information like promotions, transfers, and yes, disciplinary actions.

Cynthia Conti-Cook was somewhat taken aback by this report in the press. Here was information about Pantaleo that she had been fighting with the city over in court for more than a year. And yet, some reporters just learned about it by walking into an NYPD office and reading a printout tacked to the wall?

Conti-Cook called one of the *Daily News* reporters who wrote about Pantaleo's record of misconduct. He laid out for her how it worked: Each day, the police department would update these clipboards with personnel information about its officers. The daily rundowns were hanging in precincts around the city and inside the NYPD's press office.

The month after the press revealed at least some of Daniel Pantaleo's history of misconduct, Conti-Cook and Legal Aid upped the ante in their pursuit of NYPD disciplinary history. They filed another Freedom of Information Law request, this time requesting that the department turn over its disciplinary files on all officers dating back to 2011. Armed with the new information from the *Daily News* on the department's clipboard updates, Conti-Cook explained in the FOIL request that the information she was after was publicly posted regularly in police shops around the city each day.

In August, the NYPD denied the FOIL request. In their response, they thanked Legal Aid for bringing it to their attention that these records were being shared on their clipboards. The department said that this practice had been a mistake. Commissioner Bratton called it "a lapse in oversight on our part," adding that when it was "brought to our attention, we corrected it."

The NYPD said that putting out this information violated police officers' rights covered under 50-a. They intended to correct that mistake by simply stopping to update the clipboards. On the criticisms of the 50-a law, Bratton said these complaints should be directed not at the NYPD but the lawmakers in Albany.

"So all the focus, all the ire, all the concern, basically go a couple hundred miles north and bang on those doors, rather than continuing to harangue the New York City Police Department," he said.

Mayor de Blasio also defended the decision to stop updating the clipboards. "In terms of the specific disciplinary pieces that state law precludes that disclosure, so we obviously have to honor state law," he said.

But one former de Blasio staffer said that since the NYPD and the law department had already made up their mind to stop releasing disciplinary information, the mayor was essentially forced into this position of defending 50-a. Eric Phillips, former de Blasio press secretary, said the city and the police took a "legal posture" on 50-a and "by the time it percolated to [the mayor], we were already in a position of defending it."

"The mayor was screwed because the city effectively adopted a position before he got to adopt a position of his own," Phillips said.

By the end of 2016, the fight over the secret files was front and center in the story of Garner, Pantaleo, and the accountability of the police. A few months after its latest request for NYPD disciplinary history dating back to 2011 was denied, the Legal Aid Society once again sued the city.

As the year closed, the de Blasio administration was locked in a handful of litigation fights over NYPD misconduct records. On top of this latest lawsuit from Legal Aid, they were still appealing the judge's decision to release Pantaleo's CCRB file to the public defenders. At the same time, Legal Aid was in court seeking other individual officers' records. Along with the litigation brought by the Legal Aid Society, a 2011 lawsuit from the New York Civil Liberties Union seeking ten years of police disciplinary records from the NYPD was also on the docket.

The reports that emerged that revealed that Pantaleo did have a history of misconduct didn't help the public perception of the de Blasio administration and the NYPD while they fought to keep police disciplinary files confidential. But that information only came out because of some industrious newspaper reporters who had the good fortune to find out about one misconduct case against the embattled officer. Advocates and the public were left wondering what else might be in Pantaleo's file that the city was keeping secret?

Indeed, legal precedent surrounding 50-a meant that the chips were stacked in the city and the NYPD's favor in these various legal fights over the misconduct files of the New York City police. But there was one more twist here that nobody saw coming.

It turned out that inside a building downtown, there were binders — many binders — with details on thousands of police misconduct cases. Beatings. Thefts. Officers lying in court. Ticket-fixing. Domestic violence. Even killings. The only thing was, nobody knew about it. Well, almost nobody.

7

HE'S STABBING ME! SHOOT HIM!": THE POLICE KILLING OF MOHAMED BAH

"He's stabbing me! Shoot him!"

That is what NYPD Detective Edwin Mateo yelled out to the other members of the Emergency Services Unit (ESU) inside the Morningside Heights apartment of Mohamed Bah on September 25, 2012.

Seconds before, the ESU team entered the fifth-floor Manhattan apartment of the 28-year-old African immigrant from Guinea. Bah was in the throes of a mental health crisis. For 45 minutes, police officers stood outside his door and tried to get Bah to come out. He did not respond. According to the NYPD, after Bah's door was eventually opened, he charged them with a 13-inch knife. Bah began stabbing at the officers, piercing two of their vests with the blade, police said.

The four-officer team attempted to subdue Bah with tasers and a bean bag gun. But they said he wouldn't back down.

An hour before this, Bah's mother Hawa called 911 to request an ambulance for her son. She told the dispatcher that her son wasn't acting like himself and wouldn't come out of his apartment. Police from the NYPD's 26th precinct responded. Officers went up to Bah's apartment and knocked on the door. One of the officers looked in and saw Bah standing half-naked with a large kitchen knife. He opened it part of the way. He wasn't saying anything, just grunting in response to the officers. They called for a Hostage Negotiation Team and the Emergency Services Unit, which were trained to deal with barricaded suspects.

The confrontation between the ESU team and Bah lasted about 15 seconds. When they tried to subdue Bah, Det. Mateo felt a hot sensation radiating through his body. His muscles spasmed and he froze. Mateo fell backward, landing on his left side. Thinking he'd been stabbed, Mateo called out for the other officers to shoot. Two other cops shot Bah. His body twisted, and he fell to the ground, landing face-up, an ESU team member later recalled. Leaning on his elbow, Mateo extended his hand and fired five bullets at Bah during the confrontation.

The officers shot a total of ten bullets, hitting Bah in the chest, arm, abdomen, and left side of the head. The final shot to his head killed him.

This was essentially the story that the NYPD put out on that night: Mohamed Bah was shot and killed while stabbing the officers. He plunged his knife into their protective vests, injuring two cops — one of the injured officers, Det. Mateo screamed out for the others to shoot.

But then, three years after Bah's death, Mateo changed that story. He said that Bah was not stabbing him when he called out to his fellow officers to shoot him.

Mohamed Bah immigrated to the United States twelve years earlier at the age of 16. He initially stayed with family before later settling into a tiny 400-square foot apartment in the Morningside Heights neighborhood of Manhattan. He supported himself by working as a cab driver. At the time of his death, he was also taking classes at Borough of Manhattan Community College. His mother, who ran a successful company back in Guinea, wanted him to quit his job and focus on school. She said that she'd support him so he could finish school faster. Bah insisted on working and continuing to earn his keep.

"Mohamed told me, 'I see all my friends working. Let me do the work. I want to be independent,'" his mother said.

After Bah left Guinea, his mom visited him every year. She would take two months off from work to travel. When she came to America to see him, she would cook and clean for him and they'd go see the Statue of Liberty together, which he loved. A few years before he died, they spent her birthday together in New York. When he dropped her off at the airport, Bah told his mother, "Mommy, you'll be proud of me. I will buy a house." She responded, "Don't worry about it, my child."

During the last week of September 2012, Bah's brother called Hawa and said Mohamed was not acting like himself. He was lashing out, calling his brother "jealous," and saying strange things like "I am not Mohamed" and "we are not the same people." She learned that her son hadn't been showing up for work or school either. Hawa decided to make an emergency trip to see her son.

When she got to New York, the situation just kept getting worse. Bah refused to leave his home. She found him inside his apartment, acting lethargic and limping around. On September 25, his mother tried to get him to leave the house, but he just retreated, half-dressed into his bedroom. So Hawa and another family member decided to call 911 and try to get her son medical help.

When the police showed up, Hawa said she told them, "I don't call the police, go away."

"My son, he didn't do nothing wrong. He's sick. I just want to take him to the hospital," she told the officers. They told her not to worry and that they would take care of her son.

"The police said, 'This is the system, we come first, we all work together,'" she recalled.

Det. Mateo was about to eat with another ESU officer when they got the call to respond to 113th street and Morningside Avenue. The ESU team showed up with bullet-proof vests, ballistic shields, a bean bag gun, tasers, a water cannon, a sledgehammer, and a Y-bar halligan that can either breach a door or hold back a suspect.

The ranking officer on the ESU team, Lieutenant Michael Licitra, spoke with Hawa Bah. She told him that her son was not acting normally. Licitra also talked to a lieutenant from the 26th precinct who advised him that "a male black opened the door, that he had a knife in his hands, and then the door was closed." Licitra ordered his team to enter the brick apartment building and head up to apartment 5D, where Bah holed up inside.

Bah's mother also spoke to the NYPD hostage negotiator, who responded to the call. The negotiator tried to reach Bah three times by phone but was unsuccessful. He planned to go up to the apartment shortly. He was just waiting for his helmet to arrive. The negotiator never got the chance to go inside.

Before they went in, the ESU unit popped out the door's peephole and inserted a special camera with an LED light. They saw Bah standing motionless, holding the knife, police said. He was quietly whispering something that sounded like, "Allah, Allah, Allah." On the other side of the door, the officers commanded him to drop the knife. Bah didn't respond.

After the officers removed the camera, the door opened. Lieutenant Licitra gave the order to his team to "go." He recalled later that the shooting lasted only "two seconds" with "all the pops going off at the same time."

Hawa Bah was outside when the shooting happened. While she waited, she felt a sharp pain in the left side of her chest. She thought, "those people have done something to my son." Then she saw more police running towards the building.

As the minutes passed, she pleaded with the police to let her see her son. "They told me, 'No, we're taking him to the hospital. You'll see him.'"

A woman came out of the building. She was hysterical. She started to yell towards Hawa, who was trying to get some, any information from the police. The woman told Hawa, "Don't trust them! Those men, they kill your son!" Hawa said the police told her not to listen to her, that the woman was crazy, and they were taking her son to the hospital.

At the hospital, Hawa was brought into a room to wait. Finally, a doctor came to talk to her. He told her, "Mommy, sorry for your loss, they shoot your son and kill him."

A familiar refrain of many police killings emerged after Bah's death. An internal investigation by the NYPD found the shooting justified. A little over a year later, in November 2013, a grand jury declined to indict the officers on criminal charges. As for officer discipline, only Lieutenant Licitra was reprimanded over his supervision of the ESU team that day. His penalty was a letter asking him to review department policy.

Just before the first anniversary of his death, Hawa Bah sued the NYPD and city for $70 million.

———

NEW YORK CITY pays out hundreds of millions of dollars each year to people who sue the NYPD claiming to be victims of police misconduct. Most of the money comes after cases settle. According to data from the city, in 2020, they spent $205 million to settle claims against the NYPD. This figure was a slight decrease from 2019, when the city paid $225 million. Over five years, from 2015 to 2020, the data shows that the city spent over a billion dollars settling suits against the police.

The taxpayers almost always foot the bill. In the vast majority of cases, the city indemnifies the officers accused of wrongdoing. The cops always pay little or nothing out of their pocket.

This is how it works in cities across the country. According to a study by UCLA law professor Joanna Schwartz, from 2006 to 2011, municipalities around the United States paid 99.98% of the money that plaintiffs recovered in civil rights lawsuits against the police.

Schwartz examined more than 9,000 lawsuits against 70 police departments, including the NYPD. In her research, she found that NYPD officers weren't required to pay anything in more than 99% of all cases. In fact, during the study's six-year period, only 35 of the NYPD's 36,000 officers contributed funds to a settlement or judgment. When NYPD officers were ordered to pay, even then, half of the payouts were under $2,125, Schwartz found.

If a lawsuit against the NYPD has merit, the city almost always settles. Very few cases make it to a trial. The prospect of an expensive settlement is not necessarily a reason for the city to take its chances with a jury. For instance, in 2015, NYPD officers tackled NBA player Thabo Sefolosha outside a Manhattan club. One of the cops whacked him with a police baton and broke his leg. Sefolosha sued the city and the NYPD. A year later, the city agreed without putting up much of a fight in the case to pay him $4.5 million — the largest settlement for a police brutality case in New York's recent history at the time.

As Bill de Blasio entered his second year as mayor, he was reeling in his relationship with the NYPD rank-and-file. In the waning weeks of 2014, at the behest of the police unions, officers turned their back on the mayor not once but three times. Those public displays of discontent and disrespect were followed by a full-on work slowdown by the police.

De Blasio desperately needed an opportunity to show the police department he was indeed in their corner. At the end of the first month of the new year, a particularly jaw-dropping tabloid news story presented an opportunity.

The headline for the story in the *New York Post* read: *NYC gives machete-wielding thug $5K for menacing cops*. Police had shot the 24-year-old Brooklyn man involved in the incident after he waved an 18-inch blade at the officers. He sued the city for $3 million, and the city negotiated to pay him a $5,000 settlement, even though he pleaded guilty to menacing the officers.

The report of the settlement angered the top NYPD brass. Commissioner Bill Bratton said it was "outrageous" to pay the individual just to "make him go away."

That morning, during a breakfast speech, Bratton called out top city attorney Zachary Carter and the city Law Department, who are charged with defending most lawsuits against the police.

"Our cops work very hard trying to keep this city safe, and if they're not going to be backed up by the city law office, we need to do something about that," Bratton said.

To the police unions, this settlement was just proof positive of a bombastic argument that they'd made for years — that civil lawsuits against the NYPD were a short road to an easy payday for criminals. They contended that the city would rather just throw money at the plaintiffs and their attorneys to mitigate the potentially high litigation costs than defend them adequately. Hell, most of the time, the city didn't even tell the officers they were being sued, the unions claimed.

De Blasio reacted with indignation over the machete settlement.

"We should stand and fight in these lawsuits. These are frivolous lawsuits. They're just an attempt to scam the city for money," de Blasio told the press.

He said it was "not fair" to the officers involved in incidents like this who, according to the mayor, "didn't do anything wrong."

"[It's] some ambulance-chasing lawyers trying to make a lot of money," the mayor added.

In response, he promised the city would stop settling "frivolous" cases against the police. He blamed what happened in the machete case on a "broken policy" to settle cases too quickly and vowed to fix it.

De Blasio said that even before the publicity over the machete case, the administration had already planned to put more money into the Law Department to fight lawsuits. Unfortunately, the mayor acknowledged that it'll cost more money to fight the cases harder, but "it's worth it to end the madness."

The same day, one of the mayor's top deputies sent a letter to the police unions reinforcing the mayor's position on this. He wrote that the administration would not "coddle these ambulance-chasing lawyers anymore."

This dark tone from the mayor's office on settling civil litigation was a far cry from the pre-Gracie Mansion de Blasio. He had made settling the city's bitter fight over the stop and frisk litigation a signature part of his pitch to New York voters. The year before he was elected, he also spoke out in favor of ending the long-running civil case brought by the five men wrongfully convicted as teenagers in the 1989 rape of a female jogger in Central Park. The five men, who all spent between five and 14 years in prison as teens, claimed that their confessions had been coerced and that the police and prosecutors committed deliberate misconduct.

During the Bloomberg administration the Law Department continued to fight the Central Park case. During his 2013 campaign, de Blasio said the city should settle the lawsuit. "It's long past time to heal these wounds," he said. "As a city, we have a moral obligation to right this injustice."

The following year, during de Blasio's first year in office, the city settled the case and paid the men, who were commonly referred to as the Central Park Five, then, the Exonerated 5, a combined $41 million — about $1 million for each year they collectively spent in jail.

After the machete incident stirred up controversy, de Blasio made good on his promise to bolster the legal resources of the city to defend the NYPD. The Law Department added 30 more attorneys to fight lawsuits against the police specifically. Internally at the police department, the NYPD created a new 40-member unit called the Police Action Litigation Section, or PALS. This group of NYPD lawyers and investigators were tasked with assisting the Law Department in civil cases against officers.

The architect of the PALS program, Larry Byrne, the NYPD's deputy commissioner for legal matters, said that the machete affair alerted some in the city government to the issue with settling cases. But Byrne also backed up the mayor's claim that the idea to fight these cases harder was in the works before that particular settlement was reported.

In an interview with the *New York Times*, Byrne pulled no punches about the previous administration's approach to civil litigation. He claimed that under Mayor Bloomberg, the Law Department would offer settlements without fully investigating cases. Instead, they would offer what was known as a "nuisance value" deal to the plaintiff, Byrne said, which would be significantly less than the cost of taking a case to trial.

"Today, the taunt on the street is, 'Go ahead and arrest me because I'm going to file my lawsuit, and the city's going to give me money,'" Byrne told the *Times*. (Michael Cardozo, top Law Department attorney under Bloomberg, refuted Byrne's claim in the article, calling it "simply not true.")

Byrne was appointed the top lawyer at the police department in 2014. Before taking the job, he had a varied legal career that included private practice as a corporate defense attorney and a stint as a federal prosecutor. But his connection to the NYPD was deep and emotional.

Along with his father, who spent more than twenty years at the

NYPD, his brother Edward Byrne had been a New York City cop. In 1988, Eddie Byrne, who was a rookie on the force, was tragically killed. He was gunned down by Queens, New York gang associates on the orders of a crack kingpin while sitting in his squad car guarding the house of a witness set to testify in a drug case. The four conspirators in Byrne's death were convicted and sentenced to 25 years to life in prison. Decades later, when the killers came up for parole, Larry Byrne led a campaign against their release. As of 2022, none of the four men have been released from prison.

Before he died in December 2020, Byrne said that the NYPD and law department had been successful in the effort to "weed out" the frivolous lawsuits. Whether true or not, the weeding out has not made a deep dent in the annual payouts for NYPD misconduct lawsuits. That amount of money paid out each year for settlements by the city has remained staggeringly high at more than $200 million annually.

Nobody at the city ever suggested the Bah case was frivolous, but it was one of the lawsuits that the city wanted to fight.

"The sense was, from the beginning, the city was taking a very firm position that the officers did nothing wrong," said Debra Cohen, one of the attorneys representing Mohamed Bah's mother, Hawa Bah.

"They were dug in," her co-counsel, Randolph McLaughlin, added.

Asked if the mayor's declaration that he wanted the city to fight harder in some civil rights lawsuits impacted how the Law Department approached the Bah case, McLaughlin said, "We were caught up in that."

Mclaughlin and Cohen co-chaired the civil rights practice at the private New York City firm, Newman Ferrara LLP. Representatives for Hawa Bah brought them in after learning about their work representing the family of Kenneth Chamberlain, Sr., a White Plains, New York man who was killed by police in 2011 under startlingly similar circumstances to Bah.

On November 19, 2011, Chamberlain, 68, a former Marine with bipolar disorder, was alone in his apartment. His medical alert pendant mistakenly started to go off. When the pendant company couldn't reach him, they dispatched the local police to check in on him.

When they reached Chamberlain's apartment, the police claimed that they heard yelling inside. For 90 minutes, the officers tried to get Chamberlain to open the door. "I don't need you! I didn't call you!" he yelled at the officers. Chilling audio from the encounter revealed that one of the officers called him a "nigger" during the incident. An officer also seemed to taunt Chamberlain, telling him they needed to come in and use the bathroom.

The routine distress call turned deadly when officers finally entered the apartment. Like in the Bah case, the officers first tried to subdue Chamberlain with beanbag projectiles and tasers, but then an officer fatally shot him with a .40-caliber pistol. Police claimed Chamberlain was holding a knife, and they shot him in self-defense. No officers were criminally charged over Chamberlain's death. A decade after his killing, a lawsuit by Chamberlain's family was still ongoing.

Cohen and Mclaughlin took on the Bah case on "contingency." That meant that if their client didn't get paid, neither did they. "We take all the risk," McLaughlin said.

Because the city was not interested in a quick settlement in this case, Bah's attorneys got to take the depositions of at least some of the officers who responded to the scene that day. It was during deposition questioning that Det. Edwin Mateo altered the official story and said that he was hit with a taser by one of his fellow officers, which caused him to fall to the ground and cry out, "shoot him!"

"Mr. Bah wasn't stabbing you while you were on the ground, was he?" Bah's attorneys asked Mateo during his interview.

"No," he replied.

"When you said, 'He's stabbing me. Shoot him,' did you see Mr. Bah stabbing anybody?" they asked.

"No."

This account contradicted the NYPD's story after Bah was killed. On the night of September 25, 2012, the NYPD told the media that Bah stabbed Mateo and another officer, causing him to yell out, "He's stabbing me! Shoot him!" The police department had even provided reporters photos of the alleged knife lying on Bah's floor after the incident. Now, Mateo was admitting it was his own Emergency Services

Unit teammate's taser that caused the reaction that led to himself and two other officers shooting Bah.

Hawa Bah and her attorneys went public with the information from Mateo's deposition in the fall of 2015. It set off a new round of media coverage of the three-year-old case. One story in the *Washington Post* ran with the headline: *Did New York police lie about the death of Mohamed Bah?*

The Bah case turned into a bitter fight. And not just over the issue of Mateo's story changing. There were issues with the evidence in the case. Some of it had gone missing or might have been tainted in storage.

Initially, the city said it could not locate the clothes that Bah was wearing. According to the city, his clothes were "never vouchered" as evidence by the police. But Bah's attorneys said this wasn't true. They claimed that records showed that his clothes arrived at the medical examiner's office after his death.

The NYPD also moved the knife and the shirt worn by Mateo to an evidence warehouse in Greenpoint, Brooklyn, just four days before Hurricane Sandy hit the city. During the storm, runoff from the toxic Newtown Creek nearby contaminated the warehouse and ruined evidence from many of the cases stored inside. The city claimed both the knife and Mateo's shirt were contaminated during the storm and unavailable.

Bah's attorneys were incensed over the evidence problems in their case. As a new year approached, Cohen and McLaughlin informed the judge that they planned to go after "the strongest sanctions possible" for their counterparts at the Law Department. The city responded by calling the claims "outlandish and inflammatory."

McLaughlin didn't hold back in an interview with *The New York Daily News*. The killing of Bah was a murder, and the city was covering it up, he said.

"They're getting away with murder. The intentional shooting of an individual and then covering it up — that's murder."

8

THREE SHOTS IN EAST NEW YORK: THE POLICE KILLING OF DELRAWN SMALL

Delrawn Small spent July 3, 2016, at a pre-Fourth of July party with family and friends in the East New York neighborhood of Brooklyn. Small and his fiancé, Zaquanna Albert, and their kids were at the party for about eight hours that day before leaving at 11:30 pm. They ate, played cards, and drank rum punch while the children played with each other.

Small, his fiance, their three-month-old son, and his 14-year-old stepdaughter headed home at the end of the night. Along the way, a Nissan Altima cut them off, Albert later said. Small cut the wheel on their Kia EX, shifting lanes to avoid the other motorist, startling teenage Zaniah, who had her head on the baby's car seat in the back.

Behind the wheel of the Altima was 38-year-old Wayne Isaacs, an off-duty NYPD officer. Isaacs had just finished a four-to-midnight shift at the 79th precinct. He was on his way to a Fourth of July party in Queens. According to Albert, as Isaacs settled his Altima back into the right lane after swerving, they exchanged a look. The family in the Kia had no idea that Isaacs was a cop.

Delrawn Small was born and raised in East New York, Brooklyn. His mother had him when she was 16. He was the oldest of three children — his sister, Victoria, and brother, Victor, came after him. His mother died from complications of HIV when she was just 29 and Small just 13.

When his mom died, Small and his siblings went into the foster care system. "That was hell," Small's sister Victoria Davis said. Small, as the oldest, had to "navigate things for us" with foster care, she said. Her 13-year-old brother became the family's caretaker.

"The funny thing is, I thought he was an adult," Davis said.

As midnight on July 4, 2016 approached, the two cars came to a stop at a red light at the intersection of Atlantic Ave. and Bradford St. Small, enraged, unbuckled his seatbelt. Albert told her fiance, who had a hairpin trigger temper, to stay inside the vehicle. "Don't get out," she pleaded with him. "The kids are in the car."

Small got out anyway and walked across two lanes towards Isaacs' Altima.

"What the fuck is wrong with you? You cut us off. You could've killed my family," a furious Small said to Isaacs, clapping at him to show how pissed he was.

When Isaacs saw Small walking across the road, he could tell he was laser-focused on him. He later said he thought the man might have recognized him from an earlier arrest. Or he thought maybe he was a carjacker. The off-duty cop reached under his white t-shirt and unholstered his NYPD-issued Glock 26. According to Isaacs, when Small got to his vehicle, he reared back with his fist and punched Issacs in the face through the open driver's side window. Isaacs, a hand on his gun, raised his right arm and pulled the trigger. Isaacs fired a three-shot burst at Small, just like he had been trained to do at the Police Academy. Three bullet casings fell inside the car.

From the front seat of the Kia, Albert saw a spark. Small stumbled back and tried to grab a car in the next lane as it was driving by. He missed and tumbled to the ground. For a second, Small got up. Then, half hunched over, he stumbled and fell facedown between two parked cars.

One bullet hit Small in the stomach, another grazed his head, and a third hit him in the chest and pierced his aorta. Within a few minutes, Small was gone. EMS pronounced him dead at the scene.

After he shot Small, Isaacs drove the Altima forward a few feet then slammed on the brakes. He got out and walked towards the man he just shot, who was lying in a heap on the ground. Looking down at Small's body, Isaacs holstered his gun and flipped his white t-shirt over the weapon. The officer didn't assess Small's wounds or try to provide any medical assistance. After a few seconds, he just turned and walked back towards the Altima, which was idling on the street with the hazard lights on.

With Small bleeding on the side of the road, Isaacs pulled out his phone and called 911. He told the dispatcher, "I'm a police officer, and I was attacked." He said to send an ambulance. "It's an emergency."

In the background of the 911 call, Albert, who parked the Kia and ran towards Small, can be heard screaming, "Oh my god!" At no time did Isaacs tell the 911 dispatcher that he shot Small. He didn't even say there was a gunshot victim at the scene.

Victoria Davis and her 6-year-old son had just driven seven hours to North Carolina to see her aunt and have a mini-vacation down south.

Davis was in North Carolina for only a couple of hours when Albert called. Albert was screaming into the phone: "They shot him! They shot him!"

It took a few minutes of the chaotic call to realize Albert was talking about Small. Davis asked her brother's fiancé, "Where is he? What hospital did he go to? Let me speak with him." Albert hung up.

When Davis's phone rang again a minute later, her aunt snatched it from her. Davis saw her get silent, then just say 'OK.' Her aunt stepped outside the hotel they were staying at to continue the call. When she hung up, she told Davis, "Listen, you're going to have to be an adult and handle this."

"Handle what?" Davis said, frustrated. "Why is no one talking?"

"He died," her aunt said.

"Who died?"

"Delrawn is not here."

When it finally "clicked" what had happened, Davis sat on the concrete in the parking lot and sobbed.

In July 2016, Victor Dempsey was living in upstate New York. That night, he was out in the yard messing around with fireworks. His phone was going dead so he put it inside on the charger. Later on, Dempsey went inside to get his phone to take a video. He had so many missed calls and text messages. Many from people who he hadn't talked to in a while. Some leaving back to back missed calls. Other messages saying, "give me a call," "it's an emergency," and "pick up the phone."

Dempsey called back a cousin, Ali, who owned a family barber shop on the block where Small was shot. Ali was on the scene. When they spoke he didn't tell Dempsey all the details. Just that he needed to get to the city. He'd fill him in when he got there.

Dempsey wasn't really worried. He thought his brother was a really strong dude, an alpha male. They'd been involved in their share of neighborhood scuffles growing up. His brother always won, Dempsey thought to himself.

Dempsey is the baby of the family. When they were growing up, he said his older brother "became our father, he was our provider, protector, disciplinarian."

"He was the glue," Dempsey said about Small.

During the siblings' years in the foster care system, Dempsey said, "the only thing that was consistent was us bouncing around." He remembers foster care started when he was around five. Nobody had the space for all three of them. Dempsey and his sister, the younger ones, stayed together. Small was already a pre-teen. Dempsey said that sometimes Small would "land with us" but he wasn't always around. During these years the kids faced abuse from one of their foster parents. Dempsey said it ended up being up to Small to deal with that and protect his brother and sister.

"That kind of starts and finishes my opinion of who he was, he was more than a brother," Dempsey said.

When he got to Brooklyn in the early hours of July 4, 2016, Dempsey could see the police lights from three blocks down Atlantic Ave. As he walked to the scene of the shooting, he recognized a guy from the neighborhood, J.R. He saw Dempsey and said "there's Victor" in an eerie kind of way.

Dempsey got up to where the police had the street taped off. They wouldn't let him pass so he called his cousin Ali to come and get him. While he waited, he looked over and noticed a white sheet over a body on the street. That's when he started to lose it. He moved the tape and tried to get past the police. They grabbed him. Just then, his cousin ran over and grabbed him, too. Dempsey started asking, pleading with Ali, to tell him that his brother was in the hospital.

"I'm trying to get him to tell me that's not him under the sheet," he said. Finally, a cop in a suit told Dempsey that it was Small lying there in the street.

The official story that the NYPD put out that night was that Isaacs was sitting in his vehicle with the window rolled down when Small approached and repeatedly punched him in the head. According to the police, Small hit Isaacs in the face multiple times, and the officer "discharged his firearm during the assault." Small died at the scene, and Isaacs was transported to the hospital. The officer told police and EMS that night that Small "kept hitting me" in the lip.

That night, Commissioner Bratton said it was "much, much too early" to draw any conclusions. The NYPD acknowledged that some sort of "traffic dispute" occurred between the officer and motorist he shot. "We are comfortable, based on preliminary investigation, that it was an apparent road-rage incident that precipitated the events," Bratton said.

That week in the summer of 2016, a wave of deadly shootings involving the police dominated the national news cycle.

The day after Small was killed, an officer shot and killed 37-year-old Alton Sterling while trying to arrest him outside a Baton Rouge, Louisiana convenience store. Police were called to the store over a report of a man selling CDs who threatened somebody with a gun. When they got to the scene, they approached Sterling. Cell phone video captured by someone parked in the store's lot appeared online a few hours later. It showed officers tackling Sterling to the ground, then one of the cops pulling out his gun while kneeling on his back and shooting him.

One day later, another deadly incident of police violence in a different city was captured on video and went viral. In St. Paul,

Minnesota, 32-year-old Philando Castile and his girlfriend Diamond Reynolds were pulled over for a broken tail light. An officer approached the vehicle and asked for Castile's license and registration. He informed the officer that he had a licensed handgun in the car.

The agitated cop grew nervous and told Castile not to reach for the weapon. According to Reynolds, Castile was trying to retrieve his identification when the cop shot him. She live-streamed the aftermath of the incident on Facebook. Millions watched online as Castile bled to death in the passenger seat of their car.

The shootings set off protests against police violence around the country. On July 7, demonstrators gathered in Dallas, Texas, to march. Afterward, about 800 people were hanging out near the end of the protest route downtown. There were about 100 police officers present at the event. At around 9 pm, bullets started to rain down from above.

A sniper perched on the second floor of a parking garage overlooking the crowd unleashed round after round from an assault rifle. His targets were the cops assigned to police the demonstration. In the end, he killed five officers and wounded seven more along with two civilians.

Delrawn Small's death didn't get the national media coverage that these other tragic events did. The local media stayed on the story, though, which had more than its share of twists and turns that week.

Three days after he died, the *New York Post* ran a story about the owner of a nearby building who said his security camera captured video of the Small shooting. The building owner said that the footage showed Small "punching the shit" out of Isaacs. He said the footage showed Small throwing about four "big haymaker" punches. He said he planned to give the security tape to the police.

Small's criminal record was also leaked to the press and used to damage his character in the days after his death. The *Post* and other local tabloid media reported that he had been arrested 19 times and spent ten years in jail for multiple felonies, including attempted robbery, drug dealing, and assault.

Four days after the shooting, the press obtained a new video of the incident. It was footage captured by the security camera of an auto body shop. It was black and white and silent, but the camera captured a lot of what transpired at the intersection between Small and Isaacs. This video told a very different story about what happened.

"The video changed everything for us," Dempsey said.

The newly discovered footage showed Small approach the car. He appears to lean into Isaacs' Altima, and a split second later, he is thrown back by the gunshots. It is impossible to make out if he even throws one punch before he is shot. There certainly isn't enough time for him to punch Isaacs "repeatedly," as the police said, or throw four "big haymakers," as the other store owner claimed.

The media pointed out how this video contradicted the official NYPD story. The *New York Post* ran another story, this time reporting that Isaacs "waited just one second" before firing his gun. Small "barely has time to look the cop in the eye or even utter a word before Isaacs opens fire, causing him to stagger back," the story said. Three days after the video came out, the NYPD stripped Isaacs of his gun and badge.

That same day, Mayor de Blasio and Commissioner Bratton held a press conference on a different topic. The mayor and the commissioner called the media in to report that during the first six months of 2016, crime was significantly down across the board in the city. The mayor said that 2016 had seen the fewest shootings, robberies, and auto thefts of any first half of the year since the beginning of the CompStat reporting era in the 1990s.

"So, when you think about that, the lives of everyday New Yorkers are freer," de Blasio told the press. "They're more peaceful. They're less disrupted. And people have every reason to feel safer."

Despite the good news on the crime stats, the press conference was a tense affair. The police shootings of the past week that went viral online, coupled with the killing of officers in Dallas — the deadliest attack on law enforcement in the country since 9/11 — had put a spotlight on the frayed relationship between the police and those publicly protesting police violence in the street.

With tensions running high, some public figures weren't being especially helpful. The Sunday after the Dallas attack on the police, former New York City mayor Rudy Giuliani went on national television and accused Black Lives Matter, the driving force behind the protest movement, of promoting racism.

"When you say Black lives matter, that's inherently racist," Giuliani said in an interview on CBS's "Face the Nation." "Black lives matter. White lives matter. Asian lives matter. Hispanic lives matter. That's anti-American, and it's racist."

Giuliani was no stranger to divisive commentary. Before he became mayor, Giuliani helped whip a crowd of thousands of NYPD officers into a frenzy during a protest against Mayor David Dinkins' police accountability efforts in 1992. Speaking to a crowd of 10,000 cops, Giuliani told the officers, "The reason the morale of the police department of the City of New York is so low is one reason and one reason alone: David Dinkins!"

"The mayor doesn't know why the morale of the police department is so low," Giuliani continued. "He blames it on me. He blames it on you. Bullshit!"

After Giuliani and police union representatives spoke, the group of mostly white officers marched onto the Brooklyn Bridge, shutting down traffic, terrorizing motorists, and hurling racial slurs at Black people, including City Council members.

Years later, Giuliani would reprise this role of unapologetic hype-man for an angry mob on January 6, 2021. Speaking at a rally outside the White House protesting the results of the 2020 presidential election, Giuliani encouraged supporters of Donald Trump to engage in "trial by combat." Later that day, pro-Trump rioters marched from the rally to the US Capitol to stop the peaceful transition of presidential power after Joe Biden defeated Trump. Giuliani's legal representatives later said that he didn't mean for the insurrectionists to take his comments encouraging "combat" literally.

In the 2016 *CBS* interview, Giuliani made the accusation that the Black Lives Matter movement ignored crimes committed against Black people by other Blacks.

"When there are 60 shootings in Chicago over the Fourth of July and 14 murders, and Black Lives Matter is nonexistent," he said, "and then there's one police murder of very questionable circumstances and we hear from Black Lives Matter, we wonder: Do Black lives matter, or only the very few Black lives that are killed by White policemen?"

In New York, the press asked Bratton and de Blasio at their crime stats press conference about Giuliani's explosive remarks. Bratton first served as NYPD commissioner when Giuliani was in office in the 1990s. During this era, Bratton and Giuliani clashed, disagreeing about who deserved more credit for the drop in crime across the city. In July 2016, Bratton declined this opportunity to lower the temperature on the rhetoric and discredit his former boss's comments. Instead, he vented his frustrations about the rallies and the perception of police. "When I see marches...only on the issue of shootings by police...I say there's a different kind of bigotry because, like all prejudices, it is based on stereotypes and labels."

"We need to see police not as racists and bigots and murderers," an irritated Bratton said. "Unfortunately, some are. And we'll find them, and we'll deal with them."

A few weeks later, at the end of July 2016, after two-plus years on the job, Bill Bratton announced he was leaving his position as NYPD commissioner. Bratton said he planned to leave the department that September. As his successor, James O'Neill — the Chief of Department who had been pegged as Bratton's heir apparent — would be named the next police commissioner.

During his final months in the commissioner's chair, Bratton's signature policing strategy came under fire by the city's police department watchdogs. In June 2016, the NYPD's Inspector General (OIG) issued a blistering report that concluded that there was no correlation between the department's "broken windows" strategy of increasing enforcement of low-level, quality of life offenses and reducing violent crime. The OIG also found that broken windows disproportionately impacted communities of color.

Bratton fought back hard against the OIG's critique of his strategy. He said the report's methodology was bogus. "It is not an expert study," Bratton said in response. "It is deeply flawed. It is of no value at all."

Bratton also took shots at the people working in the OIG's office.

"I'm not sure of the quality of the researchers at the OIG," he said.

"The city spends a lot of money on staffing that. I think we have made it quite clear if you want to delve into these types of areas, you're going to need experts, not amateurs."

After the report came out, Bratton and the police department issued a counter-report titled "Broken Windows is Not Broken." This report said that the OIG report "betrays a complete ignorance" of how quality-of-life enforcement is done. To discredit the OIG's methodology, the NYPD brought in two leading criminologists who reviewed the inspector general's work. The criminologists concluded that the OIG's methods were "questionable" and cited "faulty statistical reasoning." They wrote that the OIG's analysis "is not strong enough to make valid causal conclusions regarding the relationship between the practices of the police and crime outcomes."

On a positive note in the rebuttal, one of Bratton's chosen criminologists, David Weisburd, commended the OIG. He wrote that its "recommendation that the NYPD should rely on a 'more data-driven approach to determine the relative impact of quality of life summonses and misdemeanor arrests on the reduction of crime' is certainly a very good one."

The rebuttal didn't offer empirical evidence that showed the NYPD's broken windows methods worked. In the end, this spat over whose analysis of broken windows was more accurate simply ended in a stalemate.

On his way out, Bratton took one more shot at the outside oversight of the police department.

In a *New York Times* op-ed that ran on his last day, Bratton wrote: "There are police reformers from outside the profession who think that changing police culture is a matter of passing regulations, establishing oversight bodies and more or less legislating a new order. It is not."

"Such oversight usually has only marginal impact," he continued. "What changes police culture is leadership from within."

The week that Delrawn Small was shot and killed, Mayor de Blasio called the incident "very disturbing" but said it was "hard to make out exactly what happened."

"We have to hear from the attorney general what his investigation reveals," the mayor said.

De Blasio was referring to a fresh approach to investigating police shootings in New York. About a year before Small was killed, in June 2015, Gov. Andrew Cuomo signed an executive order making the attorney general a special prosecutor in certain police killing cases in the state. Surrounded at the signing of the order by families of victims killed by police, Cuomo called it a "major step forward."

"A criminal justice system doesn't work without trust," he said.

The New York state attorney general at the time, Eric Schneiderman, had pushed the governor to give him this power after the local DA failed to indict the officer who killed Eric Garner in 2014. The following year, Cuomo met with families who had lost loved ones to police violence, including Eric Garner's mother, Gwen Carr, and the mother of Ramarley Graham, Constance Malcolm.

The mothers told Cuomo that the DAs couldn't handle these cases without conflict because they were close to the police. Cuomo, who served as New York's AG from 2007 to 2010, said at the signing that this order would "create an independent prosecutor who does not have that kind of connection with the organized police departments."

The DAs were not happy. The state's District Attorneys' Association called the order "gravely flawed." Brooklyn DA Ken Thompson told *The Observer*, "I am more than able to thoroughly and fairly investigate any fatality of an unarmed civilian by a police officer."

Two days before Cuomo signed the order, Carr and Malcolm authored an op-ed that ran in *The Daily News*. They claimed that Cuomo was backtracking on what he initially said he would put in place.

The mothers criticized the order he was planning to sign as stopping short by only allowing the AG to investigate cases in which the victim was unarmed. They pointed out that in some incidents, the initial police narrative will suggest that the victim was armed or dangerous when that wasn't the case, which could create an issue with which cases ultimately get selected by the AG.

When Cuomo signed the executive order, some of the family

members who were present hugged him. Hawa Bah, the mother of Mohamed Bah, offered a firm handshake to the governor instead. She told him, "I'll hug you when I get justice for my son."

In New York state, a person has the right to use deadly physical force if they reasonably believe that the assailant is using or about to use lethal force against them or commit a violent crime, such as rape or robbery. In most instances, you have to retreat if possible. Police officers do not have the same obligation when making an arrest or preventing an escape.

In the killing of Delrawn Small, even if he got a punch in that night when he confronted Wayne Isaacs in his car, it was debatable whether the officer shooting him three times was a justified response. But it would be up to a jury to decide if Isaacs's actions were reasonable that night. In September 2016, the New York attorney general charged Isaacs with second-degree murder and manslaughter. He became the first person charged by the attorney general's new unit on police killings. Isaacs was arrested and suspended from the NYPD with pay. He spent six nights in jail under protective custody at Rikers Island before posting bail.

If convicted of the charges, NYPD officer Wayne Isaacs faced 25 years to life in prison.

9

A LEGAL SAGA FOR FAMILIES: THE TRIALS OF RAMARLEY GRAHAM, MOHAMED BAH AND DELRAWN SMALL'S KILLERS

For the families of Ramarley Graham, Mohamed Bah and Delrawn Small, their pursuit of justice through legal channels took three very different paths. But all three instances underscore how daunting the process of fighting the city and the NYPD for justice and accountability can be.

The case of Richard Haste, the NYPD officer who fatally shot 18-year-old Ramarley Graham inside his Bronx apartment, became an example of how officers who kill can just walk away from the police department without facing full accountability for their actions.

First, the state criminal charges against Haste fell apart after a botched prosecution by the Bronx DA's office. Then, federal prosecutors decided against criminally charging Haste. In March 2016, U.S. attorney for the Southern District of New York, Preet Bharara, announced that he would not pursue the case. Bharara's office said in a statement there was "insufficient evidence" to reach the "high burden of proof required for a federal criminal civil rights prosecution." The statement said that "neither accident, mistake, fear, negligence nor bad judgment is sufficient" to charge Haste federally.

That year, Graham's mother Constance Malcolm wrote two letters to Mayor Bill de Blasio's office. In one letter, she asked the mayor to fire Haste and the other officers involved in the incident. A few months later, Malcolm once again called for the officers to be removed and requested details on the city's investigation into her son's death. She never heard from the mayor. Instead, she received one call from a deputy mayor who said they couldn't provide any information.

In September 2016, de Blasio's press office said in the statement on the Graham investigation: "The mayor has not spoken with any of the involved parties so as to avoid prejudicing the process." They added that the mayor supported the police commissioner's decision to "move forward" with a department trial against Richard Haste.

In January 2017, Haste was put on trial by the NYPD to decide whether or not he'd keep his job. It had been nearly five years since the officer killed Ramarley Graham. In the years since, Haste remained with the department on modified assignment. According to state pay records, during that time his salary grew by $30,000 to more than $94,000 from the regular raises he enjoyed.

Haste's department trial wasn't like a typical civilian trial held in any American courthouse. Instead, this was an administrative trial conducted by the NYPD. It was held in downtown Manhattan at One Police Plaza in the NYPD's trial room. The judge was a Deputy Commissioner of Trials who worked for the NYPD. The prosecutors came from the Department Advocate's Office, so they also worked for the NYPD.

There was no jury of Haste's peers. He didn't face jail time. The worst possible outcome for Haste was that he'd be fired from the police department. At the end of the case, the judge would recommend to the NYPD commissioner what, if any, penalty Haste deserved. And in the end, it was up to the commissioner to decide Haste's fate.

Also, because of Civil Rights Law 50-a, which kept police officer disciplinary information secret, the decision-making would be done behind closed doors and there was no guarantee that the public would know the outcome of Haste's case.

After Graham was killed, the NYPD's internal Firearms Discharge Review Board found the shooting justified. Therefore, the department was not charging Haste with unnecessary or excessive force. Instead, they opted to charge him with a violation of department procedures.

The department prosecutors built their case on the decision to chase Graham into his home. They said that once Graham went inside, he became a "barricaded suspect." At that point, officers were supposed to wait for the more trained Emergency Services Unit before anyone went in after him. Instead, Haste and his team kicked in the door and charged in after Graham.

NYPD prosecutor Beth Douglas said during the trial that Haste used "poor tactical judgment" when he entered Graham's apartment. She said he should've called for backup once Graham locked the door behind him. Douglas also noted that Haste never checked in with his sergeant before entering the building. "The rules are simple," she said. "Isolate and contain."

"Ramarley Graham was a son, a brother, and a friend," Douglas said. "The tactical failures of Police Officer Haste rest solely with him. The tragic death of Ramarley Graham could have and should have been avoided."

Constance Malcolm attended every day of the trial. She was joined in the small courtroom by various family and friends, including Gwen Carr, the mother of Eric Garner.

Haste's defense attorney, Stuart London, whose firm was retained by the Police Benevolent Association, said his client was being made a "scapegoat" over what happened. He said that any violation in protocol was the department's fault for not training its officers better.

Furthermore, London said his client was a "hero" for trying to get what he believed was a loaded weapon away from Graham and off the street. He noted that it was wrong for the department to subject officers to years of "second-guessing" over split-second decisions. And he suggested this all could've been avoided if Graham just followed Haste's commands.

"Show me your hands — that's all Ramarley Graham had to do," Haste's attorney said.

An Internal Affairs sergeant took the stand and testified about the department's Firearms Discharge Review Board report. The board had concluded that the shooting was "within department guidelines," the sergeant said. However, they also found that Haste used poor tactical judgment and recommended disciplinary action.

Several officers testified at the trial, including Haste's former partner, John McLoughlin, who kicked in the door before Haste rushed in and shot Graham. McLoughlin said he "one hundred percent" believed that "there was a man with a gun" inside the apartment. He said he was scared that day and was afraid to be shot. When the prosecutor asked him if his sergeant told him to kick in the door, McLoughlin said "no."

The sergeant who supervised the unit, Scott Morris, testified, too. Morris said he stood near the top of the stairwell inside Graham's building behind the officers that rushed into the apartment. Asked on the stand why he didn't call for the Emergency Services Unit, Morris said he didn't believe it was a barricaded suspect situation.

"We were in hot pursuit of an armed suspect. I thought we could handle it," Morris testified.

Morris said that after the shooting, Haste told him, "Sarge, I saw him reach," referring to Haste's claim that he believed Graham had a gun.

The last officer to testify at the trial was Richard Haste. He said that once they were in the bathroom, he yelled, "show me your hands," but instead, he saw Graham reach into his pants. "I thought I was about to be shot," Haste said. "I expected to be dead."

The police never found a gun inside the bathroom or anywhere inside the apartment. Instead, a bag of marijuana was found floating in the toilet.

Haste testified that after he shot the teenager he noticed Graham's grandmother, Patricia Hartley, and six-year-old brother Chinnor in the hallway. "Liar!" screamed a member of Graham's family after he made this claim suggesting that he didn't see them when he initially entered the apartment.

"I know what I did was justified in that I protected my life and my team, based on the information we had at hand," Haste testified. "I'm not pleased with the result."

Malcolm told reporters outside police headquarters that Haste was lying that he didn't see anyone in the apartment before shooting her son. "He doesn't have any remorse," she added. "Every day he comes to court, he have that stupid grin on his damn face."

After the trial, the department judge, Deputy Commissioner of Trials Rosemarie Maldonado, recommended firing Haste. She wrote in her report that Haste's decision to ignore department tactics was "repeated, flagrant, and avoidable."

"A reasonable officer in that position would have proceeded very differently," she wrote.

Haste learned about Maldonado's decision on Friday, March 24, 2107. He was told that Commissioner James O'Neill intended to follow through with the recommendation. Rather than let the department fire him, Haste walked into the NYPD's fleet services building in Queens and resigned that Sunday night. The next day, Haste gave an interview to a local TV station and said that he "chose to go out on my terms."

He said that he thought about the shooting "literally every day" but suggested that he believed he was being pushed out of the department for political reasons.

"It definitely had an air of not having to do with police work, but having to do obviously with powers above that — political nature of the job," Haste told a reporter from local TV station CBS2. "Which I understand. We work here, we have to have the public's trust, but to go for that solution seemed a little too charged."

Later that year, McLoughlin and Morris were also disciplined after making plea deals with the department. Morris was hit with failure to supervise charges. He was suspended for 30 days without pay and then allowed to resign. Like Haste, McLoughlin was accused of using poor tactics. He accepted a penalty of 45 lost vacation days and was placed on dismissal probation for a year, meaning if he committed even a tiny infraction, the department could dismiss him.

De Blasio said that the recommendation to fire Haste was "the right decision."

"Nothing can take away the profound pain left after his loss," de Blasio said about Graham, "But I hope the conclusion of this difficult process brings some measure of justice to those who loved him."

Malcolm put out a statement saying that the mayor and the police commissioner "should be ashamed of themselves" for allowing Haste to resign instead of firing him sooner. "This is just another example that the de Blasio administration doesn't care about justice and accountability," she said.

While she was infuriated with how Haste's case went and the result, part of Constance Malcolm always knew she was never going to be satisfied by what the department revealed during the trial. That was why she pursued an alternative channel to try to uncover more about what happened to her son. "I was determined to do everything in my power to get transparency," Malcolm said.

Three months before Haste's department trial, in September 2016, she filed an extensive Freedom of Information Law (FOIL) request with the NYPD for documents related to the killing of her son. By doing so, Malcolm was going up against one of the hardest, if not the most difficult, agencies in the city to pull information from.

A 2013 audit of 18 city agencies reviewed their responsiveness to FOIL. Each agency received a letter grade. The NYPD got an F. The author of the report was none other than the public advocate at the time, Bill de Blasio. In a press release accompanying the report, de Blasio said the city "is inviting waste and corruption by blocking information that belongs to the public."

The NYPD receives more than 1,000 FOIL requests every month. This request would be the first one Malcolm would ever make. "Before that, I didn't have any knowledge" about FOIL, she said.

To handle filing the request, she enlisted New York City civil rights lawyer Gideon Oliver. An attorney with a reputation for being particularly good at navigating New York's Freedom of Information Law, Oliver went to work to pry loose all that he could from the NYPD about the Graham case.

"Ramarley's family deserved access to every scrap of paper that could shed light on what led up to the police killing," Oliver said.

Oliver grew up the son of "lefty lawyers" upstate in Albany. His first job out of law school was for his father. "My dad taught me how to do FOIL work. That's an area of practice that I took from him," he said.

In an unusually long and detailed 24-page filing, Oliver sought the kitchen sink and more. From the Firearms Discharge Review Board's report to the radio transmissions made by the officers in Haste's unit to notes that police officials relied on when briefing the press in the immediate aftermath of the killing, Oliver and Malcolm wanted it all.

At a press conference to announce the FOIL request, somebody held a sign with Bill de Blasio's initial statement from after Graham's death, which read:

"Part of the healing process for the Graham family, and the city as a whole, derives from a fair, speedy and transparent investigation. That work should begin immediately."

During the press conference, Malcolm said that the mayor failed to make good on that promise.

The NYPD responded to Oliver and Malcolm and said that they needed 90 days to review the request before informing them if they'd be able to turn over any records. But it would ultimately take Oliver a year and a half of work — which included a lawsuit — to get the NYPD to turn over the records. In March 2018, the police department finally started turning over internal documents to Malcolm about her son's case. The records were both heartbreaking and revelatory.

The records showed that in the official police report, officers wrote that he struggled with Haste for his gun. Another document recording Haste's gun and the bullet he discharged recommended DNA testing on the weapon because the "perp" may have come in contact with it. This did not match up with what officials said in the days after Graham's death. Police Commissioner Ray Kelly had dispelled the myth that Graham and Haste had any sort of physical confrontation before he shot Graham. And he did so one day after the shooting.

One of the more shocking and infuriating documents for Graham's family was a second police report filed a month after his death. In that report, once again, the NYPD claimed that Graham "struggled" with Haste. Kelly had already knocked this down as misinformation. So it made no sense that the police were still filing reports a month later claiming that there was any sort of altercation between Haste and Graham.

For Constance Malcolm, the narrative being spun internally at the police department showed that the NYPD was trying to cover up what happened. Regardless of whether that's true or not, it is an undisputed fact that Haste did not get in a fight or scuffle or have any physical contact with Ramarley Graham before he shot him. And neither Haste himself, nor any other officer, testified at his disciplinary trial that anything like that happened inside the family's apartment.

The NYPD often claims that false statements and reports by its members are among the misconduct that it takes the most seriously. According to the department's Patrol Guide, any officer caught making a false statement can be fired from the department. Yet, it appears the NYPD never investigated or charged anyone internally for the incorrect information about an alleged struggle in either the initial police report or the one filed a month after Commissioner Kelly dismissed that false narrative.

After she and Oliver won the FOIL fight against the NYPD, Malcolm's painful legal battle with the City of New York pretty much ended. She didn't get every shred of paper that they requested. The department successfully withheld certain documents about the officers because of the 50-a law that shielded police records from the public.

While she knows she's fortunate to have had the people in her corner to help her navigate the process, Malcolm said that she felt families of victims "shouldn't have to learn about these things" — like how to sue over a FOIL denial — "to get answers."

"Most people don't have access to lawyers like I did, they don't have the resources," she said. "They shouldn't have to fight in the streets for transparency. That's crazy."

Hawa Bah's legal fight over her son's death shows that even when you win in court it's not a simple process to hold the police accountable.

After her son Mohamed Bah was killed, she sued the city and the police in federal civil court. For five years the case was litigated, then in November 2017 it finally went to trial.

Most of the witnesses who testified at trial were cops that were there the day Bah was shot and killed inside his apartment.

An NYPD sergeant who fired his Taser testified that he remembered seeing the wires from his stun gun touching the shoulder of one of the cops who shot Bah, Detective Edwin Mateo, who then fell to the ground and cried out for his fellow officers to shoot Bah, yelling, "He's stabbing me! Shoot him!"

It was undisputed that three officers fired their guns inside Bah's apartment. The autopsy had determined that the deadly shot to Bah's head came from a Glock handgun. Two of the shooters had Glocks that day: Det. Mateo and another officer. During the trial, however, both denied shooting Bah in the head.

Lieutenant Michael Licitra defended his actions as the supervisor at the scene. Inside the building, Licitra perched on a step leading to the landing of Bah's building floor. He instructed the team to "go" during the standoff, and the officers rushed into the apartment. He pointed out during his testimony that he did not command his officers to shoot Bah. When Mateo called out to shoot, Licitra said, there was no time for him to order them to do otherwise.

Detective Mateo's testimony at trial was a mess of confusion and contradiction.

He was called as a witness by Bah's attorneys. Initially, he reiterated what he said during his deposition: Bah was not stabbing him when he called out, "shoot him!"

"So you did say at some point when you were on the ground say 'shoot him, he's stabbing me,' right?" the attorney asked.

"That's correct," Mateo responded.

"And at that point, Mr. Bah wasn't stabbing you, was he?"

"He was advancing at me."

"Was he stabbing you, sir, at that moment when you were on the ground?

"No."

Bah's attorney then asked Mateo, "when you said, "shoot him, he's stabbing me," he wasn't stabbing anyone at that time, was he?"

"He was advancing right towards me," the detective said.

Bah's attorney pressed Mateo. "The question is at the time you said, "shoot him, he's stabbing me ..."

"I can't recall," he said.

This last answer raised some eyebrows in the court. In questioning during his deposition taken before trial, Mateo answered "no" when asked if Bah was stabbing anyone when he cried out, "shoot him!" Now, he was saying he couldn't remember.

During cross-examination by his attorney from the city Law Department, Mateo again changed his story about what happened.

"Can you just explain to the jury, on September 25, 2012, why did you shoot your weapon?" his attorney asked.

"On the evening of September 25, 2012...the reason why I shot my weapon, discharged my weapon, was I was in fear for my life, my partner's life as well, and I was in a fight for my life."

The Law Department attorney followed up. "So just what was it that you saw or observed that caused you to employ your firearm?"

"I observed Mr. Bah coming at me, and he was stabbing me. He was stabbing my vest, my lower torso area."

Det. Mateo fired five shots inside Bah's apartment. He testified that after he fired the first two shots, Bah was still moving towards him. And when he fired the third shot, he said Bah was falling to the ground. He said he couldn't recall if Bah had dropped to the ground when he fired the fourth and fifth shots.

Bah's team called well-known forensics pathologist Dr. Michael Baden to testify. Arguably the country's most famous pathologist, Baden had investigated 20,000 deaths in his career, including Eric Garner, Martin Luther King, Jr., Nicole Brown Simpson, and John Belushi, to name a few. In this case, he meticulously laid out the details of the shot that killed Mohamed Bah.

Baden said the bullet entered Bah's head behind his ear and traveled at a downward angle before exiting through his neck. Baden added that the stippling — black soot ejected from the muzzle of a gun — on Bah's forehead showed that it had been fired at close range, from two feet away or less.

In Baden's opinion, the gunshot to the head was most likely fired when the shooter and Bah were both on the ground. The analysis reinforced the plaintiff's theory in the case that Bah had fallen and Mateo, lying on his side, shot him in the head from close range.

At the end of the trial, the jury ruled in Hawa Bah's favor. They awarded her $2.2 million in damages to be paid by the city. On top of that, they took the rare step to find both Detective Mateo and his supervisor, Lieutenant Licitra, liable in Bah's death. The officers weren't obligated to pay any money towards the damages. But the two cops would now have an official court judgment against them on their records for the rest of their lives.

Even though they lost the trial, the city Law Department wasn't done fighting the case. The judgment against the two officers was a sticking point for the city. They filed a motion asking the judge to overturn the jury's verdict on a judgment of the law. They were basically asking Judge Kevin Castel to say that the jury got it wrong.

At a hearing on the motion in May 2018, the city's attorneys argued there was "no evidence that disputes Mr. Bah posed a threat of death or serious injury at the time Mateo fired." They requested that the jury's verdict — and the $2.2 million payout — be thrown out and a new trial ordered.

Judge Castel pushed back on the city's request, pointing to the inconsistency of Mateo's testimony at trial. "Isn't a jury entitled to say, 'I don't believe this guy? I don't believe this guy because he has contradicted himself?'" Castel said in court.

A few days later, Castel delivered his ruling. On Licitra, the judge noted that on its verdict sheet, the jury said it concluded that he "reasonably believed, even if mistakenly, that Mr. Bah was in urgent need of medical assistance when Mr. Bah became silent inside the apartment."

"Before he authorized entry, he understood that Bah was in need of hospitalization, had a large kitchen knife in hand, and had been largely unresponsive in the apartment for about 45 minutes," the judge wrote. "Hindsight would have taught a different lesson if Bah had seriously injured himself during further delay." The judge said Licitra's actions were "objectively reasonable."

On the contrary, in Mateo's case, the judge wrote that the jury found that he "did not have a reasonable belief" that Bah posed a serious threat once he fell to the ground. The judge reasoned that it violates "a clearly established right" if "the final shot to the head that killed Bah was fired at close range while Bah was lying wounded on the ground after being previously shot multiple times by the officers."

He overturned the judgment against Licitra. But the judge let the jury's judgment against Mateo stand. However, Mateo still kept his job.

The city filed a notice of appeal which dragged the case out for nearly another year. Then in March 2019, about six-and-a-half years after Mohamed Bah's death, the city agreed to pay his mother $1.9 million, about $300,0000 less than the jury awarded her at trial.

———

THE MURDER TRIAL of Officer Wayne Isaacs for the shooting death of Delrawn Small was the first case brought to trial by the New York attorney general's special prosecuting unit dedicated to police killings that was created after Eric Garner died.

Following the governor's executive order in 2015 establishing the unit, predictably the police unions opposed its creation.

"Given the many levels of oversight that already exists, both internally in the NYPD and externally in many forms, the appointment of a special prosecutor is unnecessary," Patrick Lynch, the president of the PBA said. "The rules of law apply regardless of who is investigating a case, but our concern is that there will be pressure on a special prosecutor to indict an officer for the sake of public perception, and that does not serve the ends of justice."

By the start of Isaacs' trial, the unit had investigated eleven other cases. Six were closed, while five others remained open. The team also declined to investigate more than 80 other cases. Isaacs' prosecution was the first case they brought to trial. So this was the unit's chance to show on a courtroom stage, and in the face of criticism from the police unions, how good they were. The stakes were high.

Prosecutor Jose Nieves said he knew it was going to be a "tough case" to convince a jury to convict Isaacs.

"Going into it, we knew it was hard," he said. "I think the majority of people want to trust the police."

The courts give police officers tremendous latitude when it comes to using deadly force. In case after case, juries have acquitted cops who killed because the officers claimed they perceived a threat in the heat of the moment and made the split-second decision to fire their weapon and take somebody's life. However, one thing that made the case against Wayne Isaacs unique was the judge told the jury to treat the NYPD officer like any other civilian.

The state of New York requires regular people to use a parallel level of force when faced with a threat. So that meant the jury assigned to hear the case against Isaacs had to believe that firing three shots at Delrawn Small was reasonable self-defense.

Demographically, the twelve-person jury that would decide Isaacs' fate in Brooklyn criminal court was made up of five Whites, five Blacks, one Hispanic and one Asian. There were five men and seven women. In the courtroom, family members and loved ones of Small packed the rows. They were joined by family members of other victims of police violence like Gwen Carr, and organizers and activists from the movement for police reform. The judge told one spectator wearing a shirt with "Black Lives Matter" written on it in large lettering to turn his clothing inside out during the trial.

Supporters of Isaacs also attended the trial. Along with members of his family, a group of NYPD officers representing the Police Benevolent Association came to court. The PBA group filled out a whole row behind the table Isaacs was sitting at with his attorneys. The officers donned blue and white police jackets, which, unlike the shirt with a Black Lives Matter logo, the judge didn't seem to have an issue with.

Serving as Isaacs' primary defense attorney was Stephen Worth, a partner at the firm Worth, Longworth, and London, LLP, or WLL. For the past two decades, Worth's firm held the retainer from the PBA, which paid the law firm more than $5 million a year. They defended New York City cops in criminal and civil actions, as well as during internal disciplinary cases. Name a well-known case involving the NYPD over those past two decades, and WLL had probably been involved in it. For example, Worth's partner Stuart London represented former NYPD officer Richard Haste after the killing of Ramarley Graham. And at the time of the Isaacs trial, London was also representing Daniel Pantaleo in the Eric Garner case. Worth himself had defended officers criminally charged in cases like the NYPD killing of Amadou Diallo and the brutal assault of Abner Louima by police officers inside a precinct bathroom.

The prosecution told the jury that Isaacs' shooting of Small was a "brutal and deliberate act." Nieves said during his opening statement that the officer's actions were not consistent with someone acting in self-defense. He said that Isaacs never tried to diffuse the situation by identifying himself as a police officer. Nor did he try to avoid the confrontation by just rolling up the car window or driving away. Instead, when Small approached him, Isaacs "pulled out his gun, pulled the trigger three times, and killed Delrawn Small in the blink of an eye."

"Then he strolled over to his body, took a look, and walked away," Nieves said.

He said that instead of trying to render aid to Small, Isaacs "coldly" walked back to his car and called 911 "to allege he was attacked, punched, as Delrawn Small laid on the concrete in his own blood."

The prosecution leaned on the fact that mere seconds passed during what transpired on the street that night. Nieves told the jury that even if they thought that Small hit Isaacs, the altercation between the two men was far too quick to justify Isaacs' drastic response to pull out his gun and start shooting.

"There was absolutely no time for anything to happen that would legally justify this defendant's decision to pump three bullets into Delrawn Small that night," Nieves told the jury. "Even if you believe Delrawn Small may have thrown a punch at this defendant."

Isaacs' defense team made the argument that his response was appropriate given his profession. His attorney told the jury the officer "acted professionally" and used his weapon "as he was trained to."

"Police officers are trained to shoot in three-shot bursts and then assess the situation, and that's exactly what he did," Worth said.

Isaacs testified that while he was parked at the light, he noticed a "big guy" coming at him. "You could tell he was upset with me," Isaacs said. On the stand, he denied that he had cut Small off earlier while driving. "That never happened," he said.

Along with video of the shooting, the jurors also viewed footage of the two cars going back for blocks before the intersection where Small got out of his car. Jose Nieves said that it was clear from the footage that the drivers were "engaged in something."

"We felt it was clearly a mutual entanglement, a combat situation," he said.

Isaacs testified that, as he removed his gun from his holster, he was unsure "what was going on or what was going to happen."

He said that Small punched him through his window, which he said was already rolled down before the confrontation.

"He came and said, 'I'm gonna fucking kill you,'" Isaacs testified. "I turned my body to the left...he struck me right away" on the cheek. He said he feared for his life and believed he had to "stop the threat."

"At that point, I thought I was going to lose my life," he said. "Delrawn Small struck me. That's the only reason I had to stop the threat of me losing my life."

The prosecution questioned Isaacs' testimony that his window was already rolled down while he was driving. During his closing argument, prosecutor Joshua Gradinger showed a blown-up poster image of Isaacs' car from a few blocks before the location of the shooting. In the picture, there's a reflection coming off Isaacs' driver side window.

"The window is up," Gradinger told the jury.

The prosecutor told the jury that Isaacs was "less than forthright with you about that window being down." He told the jury that the officer couldn't claim he acted in self defense because he rolled his window down as Small approached him.

"He lowered his window for one reason, to kill...that's murder," Gradinger said.

At the end of the trial, the judge instructed the jury to consider whether Isaacs' actions at that moment were reasonable. The judge reminded them that the state is required to prove beyond a reasonable doubt "that the defendant was not justified" in his use of force. He also instructed the jury that Isaacs could use his police training as long as he perceived a threat.

The video footage at the center of the case does not show to the naked eye if Small threw a punch or not. However, some of the jurors who heard the case said that they saw a punch. In an anonymous interview with the *New York Times* after the trial, two jurors said that the jury watched the video on a laptop zoomed in on Small and the driver's side window of Isaacs' car. "His head kind of goes all the way down," one of the jurors said. "Then you see his shoulder come up very clearly, and strike forward."

On the day the verdict was announced, Small's sister Victoria Davis walked into the courtroom, and it felt different. She looked around at the court officers standing around the perimeter of the room. There were more of them. She felt like they knew what was about to happen.

The jury acquitted Isaacs of the charges. As the jury foreman read the not guilty verdict, supporters of the officer clapped. Those on the other side of the courtroom wept. "He got off!" somebody yelled angrily. A red-eyed Isaacs turned and hugged his wife and embraced his attorney.

When she heard *not guilty*, Victoria said her body told her to "run." She got up and started to leave. A court officer yelled at her, "sit down!" She thought, "I can't. I have to run." She managed to get outside. But when she entered the hallway, she fainted.

The judge thanked the jury for their service. He turned to Officer Isaacs and said, "Only you know what exactly happened out there. So no one's passing any judgment, and let's try to hope that we have no further incidents like this in the future."

"I guess that's the only thing I can hope for," the judge added.

Wayne Isaacs became the sixth officer in the US criminally charged in a fatal shooting to avoid conviction in 2017. The other examples included a St. Louis police officer who shot and killed Anthony Smith in 2011 and was acquitted in September 2017. A Tulsa police officer killed Terrence Crutcher in 2016, and a jury acquitted him in May 2017. A University of Cincinnati cop who killed Samuel DuBose had two mistrials, the most recent in June 2017. A Milwaukee police officer who shot and killed Syville Smith in 2016 was also acquitted in June 2017.

Just as in the Isaacs trial, a video was a significant factor in the case over the police killing of Philando Castile, which also went to trial in the summer of 2017. In the case against the officer that shot Castile, it was what hadn't been captured clearly on camera that dictated the outcome. Neither the police dashboard camera nor the Facebook livestream by Castile's girlfriend after the fact showed the moment of the shooting. With the crucial moment missing, the trial became a *he said, she said* event. The officer testified that he feared that Castile was grabbing for a gun when he reached for his glove compartment during the traffic stop. Castile's girlfriend maintained that he was trying to pull out his identification to give to the officer. In June 2017, the Minnesota cop who killed Castile just two days after Small died was acquitted.

Nieves said losing the Isaacs case was "disappointing."

"I respect the jury's verdict," he said. "I still believe it was a proper prosecution."

Looking back on the case, Nieves thought he understood why the jury came to its conclusion, even if he didn't agree with it. He said that while looking for witnesses and talking to people in the community, many didn't find Isaacs' reaction unreasonable.

"They thought, 'When you go after somebody, you get what you get," Nieves said. "But that's not the law."

Outside the courtroom on the day of the verdict, Small's brother Victor Dempsey spoke to reporters. He thanked the prosecutors and said they had laid out a good case. "Goes to show the system is not for Black people," he said. "I don't care how we look at it."

A year after the trial, the NYPD quietly closed its internal investigation and said that Isaacs did not violate its use of force guidelines. He was restored to full duty.

10

"ANYTHING BESIDES AN EMPTY HAND THERE, I'M SHOOTING HIM.": HOW THE COPS WHO KILLED MIGUEL RICHARDS WERE PROTECTED

On the afternoon of September 6, 2017, Glenmore Carey, the landlord of a building on Pratt Avenue in the Bronx, placed a 911 call. He said that he hadn't heard from one of his tenants in a while and he was concerned.

31-year-old Miguel Richards rented a small room in an apartment on the third floor of the building. Carey described Richards to the police as a strange guy who didn't talk much and kept to himself. Originally from Jamaica, Richards moved into the apartment a few months earlier. Back home, he was studying information technology at a community college and an exchange program brought him to New York to finish his degree.

Richards was supposed to pay his rent every week but he hadn't paid in two months, the landlord told the 911 dispatcher. The dispatcher requested that the police conduct a wellness check at the address. NYPD officers Mark Fleming and Redmond Murphy from the 47th precinct got the job. It didn't sound like an urgent situation so the officers didn't rush to Pratt Ave. On the way, they stopped at a bank so Fleming could get some money. They also stopped for pizza at Patrizia's on Katonah Ave. a couple blocks from the apartment building. Fleming ordered a large pie to go then they drove to a dead-end a few blocks away from the job.

Murphy placed a call to the landlord while Fleming ate. Murphy asked Carey if he heard or smelled anything from Richards' room. He said no. The officers thought it might be a DOA situation or maybe Richards skipped town. About an hour and a half after the 911 call came in, Murphy and Fleming arrived at Pratt Ave.

Carey took Fleming and Murphy up to the third floor. He directed the officers down the hall to Richards' door. The door was locked. Carey said he had a friend who could pick the lock and went to get the person. They returned with a screwdriver and popped the door open. Inside, there was a man standing in the corner next to his bed. He had on dark sunglasses. He wasn't moving or saying anything. He just stared back at the officers standing in his doorway. His body was turned slightly so the officers saw just his left side. His right hand was behind him and hidden from their view by a black backpack on his bed. In his left hand, he held a small black knife with a 4-inch blade. It was Miguel Richards.

The officers drew their guns. They told Richards to drop the knife. "Put that knife down...put your hands up dude," Fleming said to Richards. "I don't want to shoot you. Put your hand up and drop that knife."

"My man, put that down. This is not going to end well for you if you don't put that down," he said.

Officer Murphy was focused on what might be in Richards' right hand, which he couldn't see. Murphy asked him repeatedly, "What's in the other hand?"

Standing down the hall, Carey called somebody on a cell phone who knew Richards. He put the person on speaker phone and handed it to Fleming. The officer slid the phone across the bedroom floor towards Miguel. "Talk to your dude," Fleming said to Richards. More time passed and Richards continued to just stare back at the officers in the doorway.

Officer Fleming radioed his boss, NYPD Sergeant Howard Roth, and said they had a man over here at Pratt Ave. with a knife who won't drop it. He told Roth to get over here now. He also requested over the radio another police unit with a taser. He confirmed that they were dealing with an 'Emotionally Disturbed Person,' or EDP.

Fleming said over the radio he didn't want a lot of cops showing up and making the situation worse. "We just need one unit with a taser. We don't need a whole bunch of guys coming over here," Fleming said.

Officers Matthew Hartnett and Phelim O'Rourke from the NYPD Emergency Services Unit (ESU) were patrolling the area and monitoring the 47th precinct's radio channel. They heard the call come out for a taser. Hartnett had one on him so they threw on the lights and siren and headed for Pratt Ave. Officer Jesus Ramos from the 47th precinct and his partner Officer Marcos Oliveros also heard the call come out. Ramos was armed with a taser so they started to make their way towards the scene, too.

Inside the apartment, Murphy and Fleming continued to try to get Richards to drop the knife and put his hands up. As minutes passed, Fleming's commands became more forceful. He told Richards he's "seconds away from getting shot if you don't tell us what's in your other hand."

"Do you want to die?" Fleming said. "I don't want to shoot you man, but I will if you come at me with that knife, you hear me."

The NYPD Patrol Guide outlined the department's procedures for dealing with mentally ill or emotionally disturbed people. The department's policy said the "primary duty of all members of the service is to preserve human life." It said that officers can use force if the person "is dangerous to himself or others." The policy stated that deadly force should only be used as "a last resort to protect the life of the uniformed member of the service assigned or any other person present."

The policy also noted that if the EDP is "armed or violent" that NYPD officers will not attempt to take them into custody "without the specific direction of a supervisor unless there is an immediate threat of physical harm to the EDP or others present."

"If an EDP is not immediately dangerous, the person should be contained until assistance arrives," department policy said.

After ESU officers Hartnett and O'Rourke arrived at Pratt Ave. they made their way upstairs. When they got inside the apartment they saw Murphy and Fleming with their guns drawn, laser-focused on the man standing stationary inside the bedroom. Just then, Murphy thought he finally caught a glimpse of Richards' right hand. He saw the outline of a small silvery object in his hand. He believed it was a gun. Murphy announced to his fellow cops that Richards was holding a knife *and a gun!* Hartnett told Fleming and Murphy that he and O'Rourke were going to go downstairs and "suit up" with their protective gear. Fleming thought to himself, if Richards raises his right hand and there's anything besides an empty hand there, I'm shooting him.

As they were heading back outside, the ESU officers saw Officer Ramos and his partner making their way upstairs. Inside the apartment, Ramos took out his taser and approached Richards' doorway. Inside the room, he saw Richards, just standing there with a "cold" stare on his face — not moving or saying anything. Officer Murphy told Ramos he might have a gun.

Ramos asked Fleming, "You want me to drop him?"

"Hit him," Fleming responded.

As Ramos began to raise the taser he thought he saw Richards make a sudden movement with his right arm. It startled Ramos and he jumped back. He tried to center the red dot from his taser on Richards' body. Just then, Ramos saw a red light hit his shield and reflect up into his eyes. Murphy and Fleming saw the red light on Ramos too — they thought he was about to get shot. Ramos squeezed the trigger on the taser. At the same time, Fleming and Murphy squeezed the triggers on their handguns, firing eight rounds each at Richards.

Ramos fell back through the doorway. "Ramos, you good?" Murphy asked, thinking he might be shot. "I'm good," Ramos responded.

Inside the room, Miguel Richards lay bleeding on the floor, face-down. His left hand was still holding the knife. Fleming told him one last time to "drop it," then he stomped on Richards' hand and he finally let go of the knife. Ramos' partner, Officer Oliveros, ran into the room and cuffed Richards, who was barely clinging to life. Fleming began to search for the gun.

Outside the building, Hartnett and O'Rourke were pulling their gear out of their trunk when they heard the shots ring out. The noise of the rounds going off subsided after a few seconds. They put the rifles and shields they were grabbing back into their vehicle and picked up a medical bag then went back upstairs. When they got back inside the apartment, Hartnett pulled Richards away from the bed to try to give him medical aid. Hunched over him on the ground, Hartnett saw Richards gasping for air. He took one breath and that was basically it. The EMS team that showed up a few minutes later pronounced him dead at the scene.

Fleming canvassed the room, telling his colleagues that the gun had to be around here somewhere. He asked them if they saw anything under Richards, in his pocket, or under the bed. Nobody had spotted a gun. On the ground next to Richards was a dresser. Fleming shined his flashlight under it and said he saw a small silver imitation pistol with a laser-pointer on it. "Looks like a toy," Fleming said.

In 2017, the NYPD launched an initiative to outfit its officers with body cameras while on patrol. Richards was the first person fatally shot by the NYPD whose death was captured on body cams. A week after his death, Police Commissioner James O'Neill announced that he was releasing some of the footage.

The police unions opposed this decision. PBA President Pat Lynch said that releasing the body cams violated Civil Rights Law 50-a and would set a dangerous precedent that would expose officers to a "very real and substantial risk of harassment, reprisals, and threats to their safety."

In a note to NYPD officers, O'Neill said they were releasing the video because the department "is committed to being as transparent as possible."

"In the vast majority of these cases, we believe that body-worn camera video will confirm the tremendous restraint exhibited by our officers," O'Neill said.

The NYPD put out a 16-minute video of the shooting, which was a compilation of footage from the officers at the scene. The department was later forced to release its complete footage to a group of attorneys led by the New York Lawyers for the Public Interest who sued for all the videos and won in court.

Richards was also the tenth person killed during a mental health episode by the NYPD since Mohamed Bah in 2012. In a lawsuit filed by Richards' family against the NYPD and the city, they wrote, "It was apparent, or should have been apparent" to the officers that Richards "was experiencing a mental health crisis and/or was emotionally disturbed."

The lawsuit claimed that the NYPD officers violated department policy for how to handle an EDP. The attorneys cited other police killings by the NYPD of New Yorkers suffering a mental health episode — including the death of Bah — as evidence that the NYPD can't seem to train their officers to follow the department's own rules when it comes to responding to people in crisis.

"This isn't a case of differing versions — you can see it with your own eyes. Fleming points his gun and threatens a clearly terrified, frozen young man who is standing in his own bedroom," Daniel McGuinness, attorney for the Richards family, said in 2022. "Fleming gets louder and more aggressive over time, escalating the situation without a single word or movement from Miguel. It's difficult to imagine a worse response."

McGuinness called Fleming's decision to "send in a junior officer to 'take him'" when he told Ramos to tase Richards "truly unfathomable" considering that Fleming knew that the ESU officers who were trained to handle EDPs were downstairs and would be back momentarily.

"The fact that Fleming is still an NYPD officer is not just a slap in the face to Miguel's family, but a threat to all New Yorkers," McGuinness said. "The next officer involved in a similar situation won't be considering the NYPD Guidelines anymore than Fleming did. He'll be thinking about how Fleming handled this situation and the fact that he faced zero consequences despite killing Miguel."

Early on in his mayoral tenure, Bill de Blasio announced he was creating a task force on Behavioral Health and Criminal Justice. One of the goals of the task force was to address "how the criminal justice and health systems can work together better to ensure that we are reserving criminal justice resources for the appropriate cases and deploying treatment and other proven effective remedies to interrupt those needlessly cycling through the system." In December 2014, the group announced an action plan, which included a plan to provide 40 hours of crisis intervention team (CIT) training to NYPD officers.

At the time, CIT units were growing in popularity at police departments around the country. The origin of CIT tracks back to the 1980s in Memphis, Tennessee. In 1987, Memphis police were called to a public housing project where a young man was reportedly threatening people with a knife. When the man refused to put it down, the officers shot and killed him.

The police faced a torrid of criticism over how they handled the incident. It turned out the man had a history of mental illness. Also, the victim was Black and the officers were White.

In the wake of the tragic incident, the Mayor of Memphis reached out to local advocates from the National Alliance On Mental Illness and other stakeholders, including the police department. The group set out to come up with a new approach to how police responded to individuals in mental health crises. What they came up with was the MPD Crisis Intervention Team. CIT later became known as the Memphis model.

The Memphis model recommended that departments train 25% of its officers in crisis intervention. Under the model, the specially trained CIT officers would be used to respond to individuals in crisis, rather than SWAT or Emergency Services Units. The training included spending time with people who experienced mental illness to learn first-hand about their challenges. It also included intensive training in verbal de-escalation.

In January 2017, the city's Office of the Inspector General (OIG) released a report that evaluated the first 18 months of the NYPD's adoption of CIT training. The report said that since the start of the program approximately 4,700 NYPD officers completed the CIT training, only about 13% of the force. The OIG report also found that the NYPD had not set up a system to ensure "CIT-trained officers are consistently assigned to calls involving people in mental distress." OIG also found that the department had "no dedicated personnel" to coordinate its CIT efforts. Furthermore, OIG criticized the NYPD for not updating its policies for how to deal with people experiencing a mental health crisis.

"NYPD's current policies for responding to people in mental crisis focus on containment, placing individuals into custody, and tactics for dealing with potential violence from a person in crisis," the report said.

In the meantime, more EDPs died during encounters with the NYPD. A *ProPublica* report found that during the first three years of the NYPD's CIT training program, at least nine people were killed by the NYPD while experiencing a mental health crisis, including Miguel Richards.

The problem with police killing mentally ill individuals has persisted on a national level. A *Washington Post* analysis found that between 2015 and early 2022, more than 7,000 people were killed by the police. Of that group, at least 22% — more than 1500 people — of those killed were experiencing a mental illness. A study in 2015 by the Treatment Advocacy Center found that people with untreated mental illness were 16 times more likely to have a fatal interaction with the police.

At the same time, some cities around the country were finding success adopting a non-police model for responding to mental health calls. For example, in Eugene, Oregon, the Crisis Assistance Helping Out on the Streets initiative, or CAHOOTS, operated as a mobile crisis intervention program staffed by the local White Bird Clinic, a non-profit provider of medical and mental health services that focused on helping underserved communities.

Established over three decades earlier, CAHOOTS was designed to provide a non-police response to the majority of the city's mental health emergency calls. CAHOOTS dispatched two-person teams of crisis workers and medics to respond to 911 and non-emergency calls involving people in behavioral health crises. By 2022, CAHOOTS was responding to over 20% of the city's total 911 calls without the police. Over the first 32 years in operation, CAHOOTS responded to as many as 24,000 calls a year without a single person or staffer ever being seriously injured. Across the US, similar non-police emergency response programs were being established in cities like Denver, Oakland, Olympia, Washington, New Haven, Connecticut and San Francisco.

In New York, advocates started to grow louder in their calls for a similar non-police strategy to dealing with people in mental health crises. In the Summer of 2021, the de Blasio administration launched the Behavioral Health Emergency Assistance Response Division (B-Heard) program, which aimed to create the city's first non-police response program. Launched as a pilot in Harlem, B-Heard gave 911 dispatchers the ability to send teams of mental health professionals and emergency medical technicians out on calls rather than the police. But data from the initial pilot, which operated in only three NYPD precincts, found that the police still responded to the overwhelming majority of EDP calls. In the first three months of the pilot, 911 operators routed just 23% of mental health calls in the pilot zone to B-HEARD teams. The remaining 77% of calls were sent to the police.

In December 2021, the last month of de Blasio's time as mayor, a coalition of advocates filed a class action lawsuit alleging that de Blasio and the NYPD had violated the civil rights of New Yorkers by sending the police, rather than trained mental health professionals, to respond to people in crisis. They were joined in the lawsuit by a handful of New Yorkers who alleged they or a loved one were harmed by the NYPD during a mental health call.

The lawsuit claimed that the city's "systemic failure to provide safe, appropriate, and immediate responses to New Yorkers experiencing mental health crises" violated the Fourth and Fourteenth Amendment rights of New Yorkers, as well as the American Civil Disabilities Act.

"Despite the myriad civil rights violations suffered by those with mental disabilities at the hands of the police, and despite the desperate need for reform, New York City has discriminatorily and unconstitutionally continued to use armed police officers as first responders to mental health crises," they wrote in the complaint.

In the case of Miguel Richards, the NYPD's Force Investigation Division (FID) started interviewing the officers who responded to Pratt Ave. at around 2 am that night. A group of FID investigators spoke to the Emergency Services Unit cops, Sgt, Howard Roth, the supervisor in charge of the cops that shot Richards, and others who responded to back up the officers inside Richards' apartment.

FID also reviewed all the body-camera footage. It showed the standstill negotiations between Fleming and Murphy with Richards, trying to get him to drop the knife and put his hands up. The police body cameras also captured Officer Ramos coming into the apartment and firing his taser at Richards. Other police footage showed officers ducking for cover behind doors and up against the walls in the apartment during the shooting.

The FID was created in 2015 by Commissioner Bratton after Eric Garner was killed. Bratton established FID at the NYPD as part of a package of new tools he was adopting from the Los Angeles Police Department, which he previously ran from 2002 to 2009. The new division was given a significant purview of investigatory responsibilities at the NYPD. FID was tasked with investigating all firearms discharges by members of the force, plus all incidents where a person in police custody died or was seriously injured and likely to die. A few years after it was established, FID was also given the responsibility of investigating all cases of suspected officer suicide.

The Force Investigation Division is a bit of a black box in terms of what's known publicly about how it does its work. For each case, FID's findings are reviewed by the First Deputy Commissioner's Use of Force Review Board. The board makes a determination on whether the actions of the officers were proper or not — and whether any disciplinary actions against any officer is warranted. That recommendation travels up the chain to the final decision-maker on all disciplinary matters, the NYPD commissioner. But these records — the FID reports, the recommendations of the board — don't get shared with the public.

Ramos, Fleming and Murphy weren't interviewed by FID until months after the shooting in January 2018. They were each accompanied by a PBA lawyer and union delegate to the interviews. Murphy and Fleming also spoke to the FID investigators about six months later for follow-up questioning.

Ramos told the investigators that when he arrived inside Richards' apartment he asked Officer Fleming what to do because Fleming was the "senior cop" at the scene. Ramos confirmed to FID that he asked Fleming if he wanted him to "take him down" and he said yes.

The investigators asked Ramos what made him want to go into the room at that point and take Richards into custody as opposed to waiting for the ESU officers to come back to the apartment.

"I could see he had the knife and I had the taser, I mean, they asked for somebody with a taser to take him down, I was there and I decided to go into the bedroom," Ramos said.

The FID investigators asked Fleming and Murphy why they didn't broadcast to a wider police radio channel that they had an EDP that was armed with a knife.

Fleming said that they didn't want a "flood of police cars to be coming over" and "over eager" officers coming in and alarming the person.

"I've seen it plenty of times in my career where cops that don't know what's going on show up and, you know, making matters worse than helping," he said.

"We've done knife jobs before, and usually if you start going over the air saying that somebody's got a knife, you're going to have people flying over," Murphy told investigators. "We never really — we kind of handle things on our own usually."

"We thought we'd be able to handle it once the taser arrived," Murphy added. "We'd tase him and that would be the end of it."

FID concluded in its report that the officers' use of deadly force was justified. However, FID also concluded that Murphy and Fleming violated the department's EDP policy by not waiting for supervisor approval before attempting to take Richards into custody. FID's findings were presented to the Use of Force board, which was chaired by NYPD First Deputy Commissioner Ben Tucker. In September 2018, the board concluded that it agreed with FID that Murphy and Fleming violated EDP policy. The board recommended that the two officers face disciplinary charges for the alleged misconduct. That recommendation went up the chain to Commissioner O'Neill who gave it his stamp of approval a few weeks later. But then, a few months later, something changed.

Terence Monahan always wanted to be a New York City police officer. His grandfather became a New York City police officer back in 1927. His father joined after World War II. He joined the force in 1982. "This is something that has been in my family," he said.

He worked a lot of beats during his career. One of the positions he looked back on most fondly was serving as commanding officer of Manhattan North back in the mid-1980s in the height of the crack-era in New York City. He loved working narcotics. By the time he retired in 2021, after 39 years with the NYPD, he'd risen through the ranks to Chief of the Department, the highest uniform member on the police force. It took him more than 36 years to reach that rank.

"Obviously being Chief of the Department is a tremendous accomplishment," he said. "It was exhausting, you don't sleep a lot."

On the day that the Firearms Review Board went over the Richards case, Monahan said that he wasn't available. He was on vacation. But as a Chief of the Department he was on the board and was supposed to get a vote. The First Deputy's office was supposed to check with him to make sure that he was available but they didn't, Monahan said. He said it was an "incomplete board" without him. "I didn't get to voice my vote."

On Christmas Eve 2018, Monahan wrote a memo to O'Neill saying that he disagreed with the board's recommended discipline in the Richards case.

Monahan wrote that "although there were some tactical decisions that could have been made differently it was a chaotic scene that occured in a confined space" and the job "appeared to transition to a firearm job." In his memo, he did not recommend that Fleming and Murphy face charges for violating EDP policy. The only infraction the officers committed, according to Monahan's assessment, was not showing up to the job in a timely manner.

"They delayed getting to the job, held the job," Monahan said later. But on how they handled the job on the scene, he said, "after watching the body cams a million times, though you would have liked them to have waited, they had a gun pointed at them and had to take some sort of action."

After hearing from Monahan, Commissioner O'Neill informed the board that he had revised his decision on Murphy and Fleming's misconduct. The commissioner directed that Fleming and Murphy should only receive a lesser internal charge — a Command Discipline A — for not showing up to the job faster. As a penalty, they lost 3 vacation days each. In the end, they were not charged with violating the department's EDP policy.

The only discipline that the officers who killed Miguel Richards received was a slap on the wrist because instead of responding immediately to the 911 call they went to get pizza.

11

THE NYPD FILES STASHED AT THE LIBRARY: TWO CIVIL RIGHTS ADVOCATES AND THOUSANDS OF SECRET POLICE DISCIPLINARY RECORDS

In the spring of 2016, the *New York Daily News* reported that Daniel Pantaleo had a history of misconduct while working at the NYPD. He had been disciplined in at least one incident involving an illegal frisk of a Staten Islander that took place two years before the fatal encounter with Eric Garner. The *Daily News* reporters learned this information because a record of Pantaleo's misconduct and subsequent discipline — better known at the NYPD as a 'personnel order' — had been printed out, posted on a clipboard, and hung on a wall inside police headquarters.

A few weeks after that news broke, Legal Aid attorney Cynthia Conti-Cook learned that copies of these police personnel orders weren't just being briefly tacked to a wall where they might by chance catch the eye of a diligent reporter or two. Rather, scores of these records were being filed and stashed away at the city's Municipal Library, located just across the street from City Hall. She decided to make the short walk over from the Legal Aid office and brought along her paralegal, Julie Ciccolini.

Ciccolini came to New York to attend college at New York University. She came from the suburbs of Central Massachusetts where the police presence was "really minimal."

"Never in my life had I engaged with the police. I moved to New York at 18. Now I see them on every corner," she said.

Around this time, the NYPD was stopping and frisking people more than ever. In 2011, the police stopped a record 685,724, a 14% increase from the year before. Ciccolini said that when she moved to New York, she learned that police "enforce whatever social control is desired."

When Eric Garner was killed, Ciccolini felt that she had to do something. After graduating from NYU, she got a job at the Legal Aid Society in early 2015. Technically, she was hired as a paralegal. But the plan was to work with Conti-Cook and try to document information about the New York police officers arresting Legal Aid's clients.

"I really didn't know what to expect with the position," Ciccolini said.

Ciccolini and Conti-Cook worked two doors down from each other. They were a good match. Conti-Cook had been on a quest for police misconduct records that predated the Garner killing.

The duo went to work trying to build an online database of NYPD misconduct. Ciccolini didn't have a computer science background, her focus in school was in the social sciences — applying sociology and psychology to the real world. But she taught herself about databases and database design on the job. Ciccolini said the job felt "empowering." She thought it was a "creative approach" to police accountability work.

When they got to the New York City Municipal Library in the summer of 2016 they couldn't believe what they found. The clerk handed them a healthy stack of binders of NYPD disciplinary records.

The information in these binders opened a new door for the team. Ciccolini had spent some time attending the NYPD disciplinary trials at police headquarters. She later trained a team of interns to go to the hearings, too. But back in those days, there was no trial calendar, so they would show up at One Police Plaza before 10 am, see if anything was on the docket, and if there was a trial that day, they would sit in the trial room and take notes. But they never learned the final outcomes of the cases they observed because the penalties were decided by the commissioner behind closed doors.

But now, here in front of Ciccolini and Conti-Cook in these binders was an absolute trove of information about what penalties NYPD officers were being given for misconduct. They started taking photos with their cell phones. Then they thought: what are we doing? That's going to take forever. Ciccolini had the idea to come back with the new portable scanner that they recently acquired. Later on, they sent over the interns to scan and scan some more. However, the records they found were written in free-flowing language, meaning it was hard to clean up and impossible to code.

The Legal Aid team spent a part of the summer going back and forth to the library, scanning the pages of the binders. Conti-Cook said that while their interns were scanning there was "some harassment from the librarian about the noise."

"I think the librarian even called Legal Aid," she said.

In the meantime, Conti-Cook was waiting for a response from the NYPD on her Freedom of Information Law request for all NYPD disciplinary records dating back to 2011. In the FOIL, she indicated that for years the NYPD posted the information she was after on the clipboards they hung inside the stationhouses and headquarters.

In August 2016, the NYPD denied her FOIL request. The department officials thanked Conti-Cook for the heads-up about the process with the clipboards. The NYPD said it had made a mistake putting that information out publicly. Upon review, they realized those releases violated Civil Rights Law 50-a, the department said. They announced that they would cease posting the information. Mayor de Blasio backed the decision.

In October 2016, the mayor's office quietly proposed an amendment to 50-a. In a press release posted to the city's website on a Friday afternoon, de Blasio's administration said it supported changing the law so that the Civilian Complaint Review Board could release disciplinary information related to the cases it prosecuted in the NYPD trial room. However, this accounted for just a fraction of the discipline that the department doled out. The CCRB was only authorized to investigate certain types of cases. And even fewer of those cases resulted in a trial — most resulted in plea agreements.

In December, Legal Aid filed a lawsuit over the FOIL denial for the NYPD's disciplinary records dating back to 2011. This new lawsuit came as the public defenders were also waiting to learn the fate of the city's appeal over a judge's decision to release Pantaleo's CCRB disciplinary history to Legal Aid.

But the debate over whether to release Pantaleo's files was about to become a more complicated affair.

In the spring of 2017, the liberal-leaning website ThinkProgress published a report showing that, from 2009 to 2014, Pantaleo was the subject of seven CCRB complaints containing 14 allegations of misconduct. The CCRB found enough evidence to substantiate four of the claims. However, the only discipline that Pantaleo faced was the loss of two vacation days.

Pantaleo was the subject of far more allegations than the majority of the 36,000 NYPD officers on the force. Using about ten years of CCRB data, ThinkProgress found that only 1,750 current officers — less than 5% of the total force — had received as many CCRB complaints as Pantaleo.

The report said that an unidentified CCRB employee leaked the files to ThinkProgress. The city would later conduct an investigation which led to the leaker being forced to resign.

Months later, the Court of Appeals would rule in the city and Pantaleo's favor denying Legal Aid access to the officer's disciplinary records. Legal Aid called that decision "regrettable but not a surprise" because of the leak of his record to ThinkProgress earlier in the year. The courts also blocked the release of all the NYPD disciplinary records dating back to 2011 that Legal Aid sought.

In the fall of 2017, Conti-Cook and Ciccolini met with myself and Kendall Taggart, who were working at BuzzFeed and reporting on NYPD misconduct at the time. During the meeting at Legal Aid, the disciplinary records they had collected from the library came up. Initially, Conti-Cook and Ciccolini were unsure if they would be able to share the records with BuzzFeed, but they said they would think about it.

Ciccolini and Conti-Cook met with others at Legal Aid to decide what to do with the files. They knew they didn't want to just release them themselves. The police unions would seize on that.

"We knew the police unions would make it about Legal Aid," Conti-Cook said.

"Some of it was fear, some of it was because we don't have time to deal with the police unions and jeopardize our project," Ciccolini added about the decision not to publicly release the files from Legal Aid. She said they believed that the unions would have come out and said something like, "There goes the defense attacking the police again."

"It would have tainted the findings," Ciccolini said.

One day in October 2017, Ciccolini sent an email to the two Buzz-Feed reporters she'd met with earlier that fall with a spreadsheet attached. Inside the document were rows and rows of secret NYPD misconduct records. The multiple columns included officers' names, misconduct offenses and charges, and penalties faced. Some of the entries used vague cop lingo to describe offenses as simply "abuse of authority," "failed to supervise," or "discourteous to a supervisor." But other entries were remarkably more descriptive, such as this one: "While Off-Duty, Did Place Her Child In Fear For His Life By Threatening To Stab Him, While Pulling A Knife Out Of A Kitchen Drawer."

Ciccolini said that they manually typed out all the details for each personnel order from the PDF files that they scanned from the library. In total, the cache contained over 2,000 secret records for more than 1,800 officers from the years 2011 to 2015.

The files contained hundreds of entries for officers who had received a vaguely described penalty: dismissal probation. According to the NYPD Patrol Guide, when an officer is put on dismissal probation, "the member is dismissed from the Police Department, and he or she acknowledges the dismissal in writing." But the department would always delay those dismissals for one year. During that probation period, if the officer committed more misconduct — any misconduct, no matter how minor — they could be kicked off the force, no questions asked. But, if they kept out of trouble for a year, they kept their job.

This meant that officers given the penalty of dismissal probation had committed misconduct severe enough to be fired by the NYPD. Some of the conduct that had warranted dismissal probation in the files Legal Aid shared with BuzzFeed was brutal — including beating people during arrests, and domestic abuse of spouses and partners. Some of it was shocking in other ways and included lying in court and falsifying statements on warrants and criminal complaints.

From a journalism perspective, there was a major issue with the data: each entry included no more than a paragraph about what type of misconduct occurred, so additional sources would be required to fully understand each incident. And because of 50-a, it was likely, if not guaranteed, that requesting more information from the city would just lead to a denial from the NYPD.

The lack of details in the files was not a complete road block, however. Many of the officers named in the disciplinary files and the misconduct could be matched to civil rights lawsuits against the NYPD. These court documents helped fill in the narrative for the particular incidents and, importantly, provided the names of alleged victims of police abuse to reach out to.

Another source of information that could be linked to some of the secret disciplinary files were the annual reports by the anti-corruption board the Commission to Combat Police Corruption (CCPC).

The CCPC had been around since the early 1990s. It was created following a highly-publicized scandal in Brooklyn's 75th precinct. Officers from the precinct were making up to $8,000 a week by ripping off some drug dealers and providing protection for others. The revelation embarrassed the police department and the city as a whole, so in the wake of the scandal Mayor Dinkins appointed Judge Milton Mollen to investigate in the summer of 1992.

The Mollen Commission found that the department was incapable of policing itself. Mollen found the police department's top officials to be "willfully blind" to drug-related corruption. "We find as shocking the incompetence and the inadequacies of the department to police itself," Mollen said when he released his report in 1994.

One of the Mollen Commission recommendations was to create an independent agency to investigate corruption within the police department. Mollen said the body should have subpoena power to legally compel the NYPD to produce documents. The City Council agreed and started to move to create such an agency, but incoming mayor Rudy Giuliani ended up blocking that approach. As an alternative, by executive order, he created the Commission to Combat Police Corruption, which was staffed with just a handful of lawyers and not given subpoena power.

Each year, the CCPC issued a report that looked at specific serious incidents of police misconduct. The CCPC, which was made up of attorneys working as volunteers, evaluated how the NYPD handled the wrongdoing within its ranks. It was debatable whether the CCPC has had much impact on corruption at the department since there have been multiple corruption scandals since its inception.

Seemingly every year, the CCPC found examples of the NYPD going easy on cops that were caught lying — an offense that the department's own Patrol Guide said warrants termination. Year after year, the commission made the straight-forward recommendation that the NYPD follow its own rules and terminate the cops that it catches lying. But then the following year, another CCPC report would end up raising the same issue: too many lying NYPD cops kept their jobs.

In their reports, the CCPC anonymized the NYPD officers it wrote about — typically referring to someone as something like "Officer #1." However, the CCPC case studies also contained dates and details of incidents. This meant that some examples from the CCPC reports that corresponded both in terms of unique details and time frame could be matched to the misconduct in Legal Aid's cache of secret disciplinary files.

For example, in one of the reports the CCPC wrote about an officer who struck somebody in the head with his baton, opening up a gash on the man's head that needed stitches, while taking him out of a police car at a Bronx station house. The use of force against the man happened after the officer and the victim got into an argument because the police refused to investigate the man's claim that his teenage friend was groped by another person, the CCPC wrote.

In their report, the commission wrote that the officer should have been fired. The details of what happened matched one of the disciplinary records in the secret files. Instead of firing him, the department put the officer, Raymond Marrero, on dismissal probation.

In March 2018, BuzzFeed's first big story on the files hit. It identified 300 NYPD officers who had beaten people, lied, or committed other fireable offenses, but instead of being kicked off the force they had been put on dismissal probation.

The reporting caused quite a stir in New York City. Two days after the story broke, the mayor and top police officials held a press conference. Their main reasons for this press conference were A.) a snowstorm bearing down on New York City was poised to drop 8-12 inches on the city, and B.) the mayor and the police commissioner wanted to tout the latest very good crime numbers. The report on the secret NYPD disciplinary files showing that at least 300 cops committed fireable offenses and weren't dismissed from the department, however, dominated a good portion of the Q&A.

Some of the reporters there that day wanted to know what the mayor thought about the police secrecy law, Civil Rights Law 50-a. De Blasio called it a "bad law." He said that for years he'd been pushing for it to change. But he stopped short of saying it needed to be repealed. NYPD Commissioner James O'Neill also didn't call for 50-a to be repealed, but said that the NYPD's disciplinary system "has to become more transparent."

"There are many things we do well at the NYPD. We fight crime well, neighborhood policing is going well," O'Neill said during the press conference. "Letting people know about our internal disciplinary process — that's not something that we do very well at all."

A month later, BuzzFeed published an online database of all the secret NYPD disciplinary records from Legal Aid. Along with the database, a new story revealed some of our most shocking findings from the data. For example, the files showed that at least 250 NYPD employees faced accusations of using excessive force, threatening someone, getting into a fight, or firing their gun unnecessarily. Some faced only minor penalties. For instance, a handful of school safety agents each lost five vacation days after using excessive force against students.

The files in the new database also showed that of the more than 100 NYPD employees who were accused of lying on official reports, under oath, or during an Internal Affairs investigation, only a handful were fired, while others were docked anywhere from a few days to a month of vacation time. These penalties occurred despite the fact that the NYPD's rules instruct that, barring exceptional circumstances, officers who lie about a "material matter" must lose their jobs.

The BuzzFeed database was searchable so that the public could enter an officer's name and find out if he or she had a history of misconduct. At the time in the spring of 2018, it was the first and only online database of NYPD misconduct.

In the days leading up to the publication of the database, the police unions publicly attacked BuzzFeed, despite the fact that both the police department and the unions were given a heads-up in advance about the publication of the database and what it would contain. The PBA declined to comment or have anyone at the union be interviewed about the files. Instead, its president, Pat Lynch, publicly released a letter that he sent to the police commissioner asking him to internally investigate the leak of the records.

In the letter, Lynch wrote that BuzzFeed were in possession of secret NYPD disciplinary files that "likely have been stolen or misappropriated from the NYPD." He told the commissioner that BuzzFeed intended to publish the entirety of these "stolen Confidential files" online and this needed to be stopped.

"In the interest of our members' safety, a goal which we assume the department shares, we demand that the Department and City immediately take all possible steps to prevent BuzzFeed's disclosure of stolen Confidential Files including, but not limited to, seeking an injunction in court," he wrote.

The investigation and court injunction Lynch requested never happened — not that looking internally for a leaker would have led anywhere. Unbeknownst to the PBA, it wasn't an officer inside the police department who provided BuzzFeed with the disciplinary records. However, since at their request, the sources of the files were kept secret by BuzzFeed, very few other people knew the reality either.

Of course, in reality, an intrepid lawyer, her paralegal, and their interns had simply walked over to the library and found the information in dusty old binders.

BuzzFeed kept reporting on the NYPD and its disciplinary system through the rest of 2018, as did other outlets. For example, that spring, Joe Goldstein at the *New York Times* published a series on NYPD officers getting away with lying, including "testilying" in court. Goldstein's reporting revealed that since 2010, of 81 cases in which the Civilian Complaint Review Board found an officer had lied, the NYPD brought up "false statement" charges against just two cops.

In one instance, the *New York Daily News* revealed that a Queens detective had made up fake witnesses to close grand larceny cases. When the department found out, the *Daily News* learned, the commissioner punished the detective by docking just 20 vacation days. After the story was published however, he was forced to retire.

Commissioner O'Neill must have noticed all this not-so-great press, because in June of 2018, he appointed a three-person independent commission to audit the NYPD's entire system of discipline.

It consisted of two former U.S. Attorneys, Mary Jo White and Robert Capers, and a former federal prosecutor and judge, Barbara Jones. All three were well known players in American law enforcement.

White was probably the most celebrated of the group. She was the first woman appointed as U.S. Attorney for the Southern District of New York. Serving as Manhattan's top federal prosecutor, she prosecuted major terrorists and financial criminals during her tenure from 1993 to 2002. She tried and won cases against those who carried out the 1993 World Trade Center bombing. She also won the convictions of four followers of Osama Bin Laden after the 1998 East African Embassy bombing. Later on, President Obama appointed her chair of the Securities and Exchange Commission.

Former Brooklyn U.S. attorney Robert Capers had previously brought cases against drug lord Joaquín "El Chapo" Guzmán. He also oversaw the indictment of nearly 30 FIFA soccer officials before he left Brooklyn's federal prosecutor's office.

Barbara Jones, a former Manhattan federal judge who served 16 years on the bench, spent time as the chief of the Organized Crime Strike Force unit in Manhattan's federal prosecutor's office. As a prosecutor, she won convictions against some of New York's most reputed mobsters of the 1970s and 1980s, including members of the Bonnano crime family in cases that were later made famous in the movie "Donnie Brasco."

O'Neill said that the panel would spend months and investigate every aspect of the department's disciplinary system — from the internal investigations, to the department trials, to how he as commissioner, who had the final say on penalties, determined how to punish officers.

The unions were not pleased. PBA President Pat Lynch said, "This new panel will undoubtedly increase the pressure on the NYPD to mete out unjustly heavy-handed discipline, further damaging police officers' morale and due process rights."

The panel spent seven months going over the disciplinary process, soup to nuts. They spoke to many key stakeholders in the disciplinary process. They also interviewed members of the public who had personally been harmed by the NYPD or who had loved ones who had been harmed. Constance Malcolm, mother of Ramarley Graham, told the panel she fought "tooth and nail" for six years to obtain any information regarding the disciplinary cases against three officers involved in her son's death.

In the end, while the panel found the NYPD's disciplinary process to be "robust and fair," it also found the department's process to be plagued by "a fundamental and pervasive lack of transparency."

"The public confidence in the department to hold its own accountable depends on its openness and candor," Mary Jo White said at a press conference to announce the release of the group's findings.

The panel made a number of recommendations about how the NYPD could improve, including calling for the department to develop a disciplinary matrix with penalty guidelines similar to the criminal court system, which should be made public, and doing a better job of punishing lying cops. The panel cited the repeated call-outs over the years by the Commission to Combat Police Corruption that the NYPD failed to crack down hard enough on cops not telling the truth.

In addition, the panel called for the NYPD to "upgrade and integrate its disciplinary record-keeping and case management systems" to better monitor misconduct case outcomes and trends.

On the shroud of secrecy created by New York's Civil Rights Law 50-a, the panel said that the department should "strongly support" legislation to change the law. "The current law keeps the public in the dark about police discipline, breeds mistrust, and reduces accountability," they said in the report.

The final findings were disappointing to some. At the time, Cynthia Conti-Cook said she didn't think the panel made the "strong recommendations" that she and other advocates for police reform felt were necessary to bring "wholesale change" to the NYPD disciplinary system.

Conti-Cook later reiterated that she thought the NYPD and the city of New York didn't make any "major reforms" in the wake of Eric Garner's killing and the reporting in the media by BuzzFeed and others on the NYPD's disciplinary system. By contrast, she said, look at what happened after Laquan McDonald was killed in Chicago.

In October 2014, about three months after Eric Garner died in New York, 17-year-old Laquan McDonald was shot and killed by Chicago police officer Jason Van Dyke. The Chicago Police Department claimed Van Dyke opened fire on the teenager because he was advancing towards him and other officers with a knife and ignoring commands to drop his weapon.

It would take thirteen months and a lawsuit by a freelance journalist for the city to release video of the shooting captured by a police cruiser dashcam. That video, released in November 2015, showed that Van Dyke in fact shot McDonald as he had his hands raised in the air. He continued shooting him after he fell to the ground. In total, Van Dyke shot the teenager 16 times.

Van Dyke had an extensive history of documented citizen

complaints — 20 in total, according to a database compiled by the non-profit journalism group Invisible Institute, who obtained the information after a lengthy battle with the Chicago Police over a Freedom of Information request for misconduct records. Researchers from the University of Chicago determined that Van Dyke had more complaints than 94% of all the cops on the Chicago PD. Yet their research found Van Dyke had faced no discipline over the years. The revelations begged the question: shouldn't twenty complaints prior to the shooting have set off some red flags about Van Dyke?

In the aftermath of the McDonald killing, the Chicago police chief was fired and the state's attorney lost reelection. Van Dyke became the first on-duty Chicago police officer convicted of murder in nearly 50 years. The mayor of Chicago at the time, Rahm Emanuel, also didn't seek another term.

While the reporting on the NYPD didn't have the same sort of direct impact on the police department or the mayor's administration compared to Chicago, it did keep police discipline at the forefront of the conversation about public safety in New York City in 2018.

The publication of the BuzzFeed database, which consisted of 2,000 police misconduct cases, also dispelled a major talking point by the police unions: It showed that making police misconduct data public would not lead to retaliation against individual officers. None of the named officers who had been punished had been harassed or attacked.

It would remain to be seen how the NYPD would follow through on the reforms proposed by Mary Jo White and her team. But in the short term, the department's disciplinary system was destined to be on a very public display yet again. The disciplinary trial of Daniel Pantaleo was scheduled to start in just a few months in May 2019. And that long-awaited tribunal would finally decide if the officer who put Eric Garner in a fatal chokehold years earlier would be fired or keep his job.

12

PANTALEO ON TRIAL: THE LONG AWAITED DISCIPLINARY DECISION

In the spring of 2019, the NYPD finally put Daniel Pantaleo on trial for his job. It had been nearly five years since Eric Garner died when the trial got underway. That long passage of time complicated the department's case against Pantaleo.

For one thing, the statute of limitations on bringing department charges against Pantaleo had been blown entirely. New York state prohibits bringing standard misconduct charges against officers more than 18 months after an incident occurs. Had Pantaleo's departmental trial happened within that time frame, and it was proven that he used a prohibited chokehold against Garner, it might've been enough to get Pantaleo fired, considering the department's ban on the maneuver. But, because they were well past that 18-month window, the prosecution had to prove by a preponderance of the evidence — meaning the judge had to be convinced that there is a greater than 50% chance that the claim is true — that he committed at least one criminal offense in the case.

With that high bar in front of them, the CCRB — the prosecutors in the case — sought to convince the department judge presiding over the tribunal that Pantaleo committed assault in the third degree, a misdemeanor, and intent to strangle, a felony. The added requirement to prove some level of criminality made the case against Pantaleo far from open and shut.

A department disciplinary trial against Pantaleo was never going to happen within 18 months of Garner's death. Four months passed between Garner's death and the Staten Island DA's decision not to charge Pantaleo criminally. After that, the city made it clear that it would wait for the Department of Justice to decide whether to bring federal civil rights charges against Pantaleo before moving forward with any internal case.

Just days before the Staten Island DA's announcement, Commissioner Bratton told the press, "We have completed our investigation, our administrative investigation, we are ready to proceed with it."

But Bratton said that after consulting with the U.S. Attorney General and federal prosecutors in Brooklyn running the federal investigation, the police department "effectively stopped our investigation until they complete their investigation."

That federal inquiry languished at the DOJ through the end of Barack Obama's administration and into Donald Trump's presidency. The DOJ had its own statute of limitations to contend with — the federal prosecutors had to decide to bring charges or not by the fifth anniversary of Garner's death in July 2019. With that anniversary approaching, the city finally decided to move forward with the internal case against Pantaleo in the spring of 2019.

Just days before the trial was scheduled to begin, Mayor de Blasio discussed the decision to move forward. He also cast blame on the DOJ for the delays in its process.

"I know the Garner family and they have gone through so much and they're still waiting for an answer from the Justice Department but we finally got to the point of saying to the Justice Department, the NYPD is going to go ahead with its disciplinary process," de Blasio said on WNYC's The Brian Lehrer's show on May 10.

"I don't know if the Justice Department is ever going to act .... I'm astounded, and it went over two administrations without any resolution, but we owe it to the people of the city and the Garner family to get to whatever resolution a court process brings and that will happen this year," he said.

On what if any penalty he thought Pantaleo should face from the department, de Blasio said, "It's not my place to pass judgment. It's a full trial that needs to take place and once and for all have closure this year on this case."

Over the years, he had declined to say whether or not he believed Pantaleo should be fired, and the mayor wasn't going to offer that opinion now, just days before the officer faced a department trial.

Inside City Hall, the mayor's senior staff was engaged in constant planning related to Panteleo during the spring and summer of 2019. Whether he was fired or not fired, de Blasio's team was preparing for both scenarios. Each morning the mayor's staff met in the Green Room at City Hall at 9 am. All senior staff attended — the chief of staff, the first deputy mayor, de Blasio's press secretary, and others. The mayor was briefed afterwards. It was supposed to be a meeting on the issues of the day but the daily gathering transformed into essentially a planning meeting on Pantaleo.

There were worries among the mayor's staff that the police commissioner might strike a middle ground — let Pantaleo resign and keep his pension. But there was also a confidence that Commissioner James O'Neill was the type of leader that would in the end move to terminate Pantaleo if that's what the judge in the case recommended. And to the mayor's staff, there was no question that they believed that's what should happen.

For years, some of de Blasio's closest staffers wanted him to come out and just say Pantaleo should be fired. But the mayor was being advised by the city's Law Department not to comment on the process and risk Pantaleo using it against the city in a potential lawsuit to get his job back. Thus, the city and the mayor's official position became that they would just stay the course, not say anything and wait for the Department of Justice to conclude its investigation before moving forward.

This frustrated and exhausted some who worked closely with de Blasio. Some of his staff were telling the mayor to stand up and just say:

Pantaleo should be fired. After that, if Pantaleo wants to take the city to court, wrap us up in a lawsuit, so be it. But the city's top attorney Zach Carter was insistent. We defer to the federal prosecutors from the Eastern District of New York and we wait.

"It's not an overstatement that Zach Carter called the shots," one former City Hall staffer said. "He was driving the bus on this and de Blasio was being wholly deferential. Carter thought the best way to handle this was to let it play out."

As the years went by and the public waited to see what Pantaleo's fate would be, the mayor never wavered on the position that they were waiting for the federal investigators to wrap up their investigation.

"He really tried to stay within the boundaries. He was not swayed by the optics," former de Blasio press secretary Freddi Goldstein said.

Eric Phillips, another former de Blasio press secretary, said the position of the Law Department "put the mayor in a terrible position."

"There's no doubt he should have overruled his lawyers on Pantaleo," he said.

"Looking back at it. The mayor should have put his foot down and said no, we're going forward with the NYPD disciplinary prosecution," Phillips said. On the DOJ, Phillips said he thought de Blasio should have told them, "If that affects your case, well that sounds like a 'you' problem."

Leading up to the trial, the police union further complicated things by suing to challenge the CCRB's jurisdiction in prosecuting the case. The PBA claimed that there was evidence that the person who made the initial complaint to the CCRB was not an eyewitness. Instead, they believed that the complainant, identified in the complaint as "Jada Wilson," watched an online video and called it in the next day. Their proof, they claimed, was that this person got specific details of the incident wrong. For example, according to the lawsuit, Wilson said that officers choked Garner with a nightstick and that three officers — not two — arrived on the scene on Bay St. Then, when the CCRB tried to contact Wilson to investigate, she never called them back.

In part, the lawsuit represented the police union's latest maneuver in a decades-long campaign against the CCRB. In the press, PBA President Pat Lynch called the city agency "anti-police." The PBA also called for the CCRB to be reigned in as the agency had gained the ability to prosecute more and more of the most serious cases against officers in recent years. However, the state court shot the union's efforts to derail Pantaleo's trial down — a big win for the CCRB.

The trial began on a cold, rainy Monday in New York City. Despite the elements, about two dozen people gathered along with Garner's mother, Gwen Carr, outside One Police Plaza in downtown Manhattan. "These are just tears from heaven," Carr said to the crowd outside police headquarters.

"Eric is crying from heaven because he sees his mother and his family still out here trying to fight for justice for him."

More hardship had befallen the family in the years since Eric Garner died. His daughter Erica, who emerged as one of her father's most tenacious fighters for justice after his death, died at Christmastime in 2017 at just 27 years old. The family said she suffered a heart attack brought on by asthma.

After Eric Garner was killed, Bratton promised to retrain NYPD officers on best practices for using necessary force. He vowed that the Garner incident would be remembered as a catalyst for systemic change at the NYPD. But as Pantaleo's trial approached, the department's success in this area was also being questioned.

The NYPD spent $35 million after Garner's death to retrain its officers on physically restraining suspects. A new multi-day training program was created that focused on teaching proper use of force procedures at the department. During the program, one day was devoted to teaching officers the proper takedown techniques to use against suspects, with an emphasis on avoiding the neck.

Some of the officers said that the additional training was a waste of time. In 2015, a high-ranking police official told the *New York Post* that 8 out of 10 officers who underwent the training gave it a negative review. The official said that the training lacked real-world tactics, and instead, many officers fell asleep during the dull, eight-hour lectures.

On May 13, 2019, inside the trial room on the fourth floor of One Police Plaza, the trial of Daniel Pantaleo began. The prosecutors from the CCRB laid out for Deputy Commissioner of Trials Judge Rosemarie Maldonado, the department judge presiding over the court, why they believed that Pantaleo acted "reckless" and "gave his victim a death sentence over loose cigarettes."

"This officer didn't let go even after Mr. Garner fell to the ground," CCRB prosecutor Jonathan Fogel said. He said Pantaleo applied pressure to Garner's neck for 15 seconds as he pleaded, "I can't breathe," while another officer said, "He's down."

"Eric Garner's pleas for air is ignored. Instead of giving aid, this officer buries this man's face in the ground," Fogel said. He called it a "lethal dose of deadly force."

During his opening statement, Fogel paused for effect for 15 seconds to show the length of time the prosecutors claimed Pantaleo choked Garner.

Pantaleo's defense attorney, Stuart London, argued that Garner died because of his poor health. He said that Garner's chronic asthma made him "a ticking time bomb," which "set these facts in motion by resisting arrest."

London quoted Garner saying, "I'm tired of it. It stops today," claiming that statement showed Garner resisting. He pointed out that the officers spent 10 minutes trying to reason with Garner before Pantaleo touched him.

"Had he accepted the summons, he would be here today," London said of Garner.

The attorney had made similar arguments in the disciplinary case of the officer who fatally shot Ramarley Graham in 2012, Richard Haste, who he also defended. At Haste's department trial, London argued that all the 18-year-old Graham had to do was follow the officer's orders to "show me your hands," and he would be alive. In addition, as he said about Haste, London said Pantaleo was being made a department "scapegoat" in this case.

The defense also contested the claim that Pantaleo used a banned chokehold against Garner. Instead, London told the court that Pantaleo used a "seatbelt technique" taught at the Police Academy.

Ramsey Orta, the friend of Eric Garner who filmed the video of the arrest that went viral, testified by video from an upstate prison. He was serving time for gun and drug charges at the time.

Orta testified that he had run into Garner at a KFC restaurant that afternoon. The two continued to "the stoop" next to the beauty shop on Bay St. They hung out, talked football, and made plans to go to Buffalo Wild Wings later that evening, Orta said.

Orta said that he "knew for a fact" that Garner wasn't selling cigarettes that day as the NYPD had claimed. He said that while they were on Bay St., another person from the neighborhood called "Twin" came up to them and asked for a cigarette. He said that he gave Twin a dollar "to take to the store." After he walked away, according to Orta, another man punched Twin in the face, and a fight broke out between the two. He said Garner immediately jumped up and broke up the fight, telling them to "take it up the block." That was when the unmarked police car rolled up, Orta said.

During his testimony, the prosecution played Orta's cell phone video. Garner's family watched from the front row of the trial room. After a little while, both Garner's mother and his sister Ellisha left in tears.

Orta testified that after Garner lost his balance and fell to the ground, Pantaleo put his arms "around" his neck. He said that he saw Pantaleo "trying to interlock his fingers" as he held Garner. "He kept saying, 'I can't breathe, I can't breathe,'" Orta said at trial. "Then I saw his eyes roll back, and that was it."

The bulk of the testimony at the trial came from other NYPD officers. In particular, Lieutenant Chris Bannon's account offered context on how the NYPD's enforcement strategy factored into the case.

Bannon, a Special Operations Lieutenant for the 120th precinct in Staten Island, said he attended a meeting at police headquarters on "quality-of-life" offenses in March 2014. During the meeting, Bannon was shown a photo of a man selling cigarettes on the street in the area of Bay St. near Tompkinsville Park. He said at the trial that he was tasked with addressing "the condition" by the top NYPD brass.

After this meeting, from the end of March through mid-July, the NYPD made multiple arrests in the neighborhood for illegal cigarette sales. Eric Garner was arrested twice during this period, once while in possession of 24 cigarette packs without New York State tax stamps and another time when he was holding six packs.

On the morning of July 17, 2014, Bannon said he was driving by the intersection of Bay St. and Victory Boulevard when he observed about ten men "huddled" together. He testified that he did not observe any illegal cigarette sales but believed the group's gathering suggested that such a transaction might be taking place. He said he immediately called Sergeant Dhanan Saminath at the precinct and told him to send the Quality of Life Coordinator, Officer Justin D'Amico, to check out the scene. Bannon said that a second officer should accompany D'Amico. Saminath selected Pantaleo, who was just finishing up lunch.

Bannon was asked to read the text messages he sent to Saminath after being told Garner might have died. When he read the text where he wrote, "Not a big deal. We were effecting a lawful arrest," in response to Saminath telling him Garner was "most likely DOA," others in the courtroom audibly gasped.

Bannon testified that he was not dismissing Garner's death with his "Not a big deal" comment. Rather, he said he was trying to comfort his officers. "My reasoning behind that text message was not to be malicious. It's to make sure the officer knew [he] was put in a bad situation," Bannon said. "To try to bring him down to a level where you put him at ease."

Later, the prosecution asked him if he thought Eric Garner was put in a "bad situation."

"I don't know how to answer that," he responded. "I don't know if he was or wasn't."

Officer Justin D'Amico testified he was about 100-200 feet away from Garner when he claimed he witnessed the cigarette sale. During cross-examination, the prosecutor challenged this, claiming the officers were more than 300 feet away.

"Would it surprise you to learn that the actual distance is 328 feet?" CCRB prosecutor Suzanne O'Hare asked D'Amico. "More than a football field?"

D'Amico said that distance might be correct.

He said that during the 10 minutes that he and Pantaleo argued with Garner in the street, the officers remained calm as Garner grew "irate." D'Amico said he was trying to calm him down using "verbal judo."

D'Amico testified that he initially believed Garner was faking his medical condition when he appeared to lose consciousness on the sidewalk. During his testimony, O'Hare asked him about trying to stand Garner up after Pantaleo got off him, and they had placed him in handcuffs.

"You did that because you believed he was playing possum?" O'Hare asked.

"Yes," D'Amico said.

D'Amico rode with Garner in the ambulance that day. Along the way, the ambulance pulled over to wait for a paramedic with a defibrillator. The paramedic boarded the ambulance and began to perform CPR on Garner. At the hospital, emergency room staff took over CPR. A short while later, Garner was pronounced dead.

What D'Amico said he did when he got back at the station house raised eyebrows during the trial. Back at the precinct, he continued to process the arrest of Garner. On the online arrest form, D'Amico listed a felony charge against Garner. For that charge to be appropriate, prosecutors would have had to prove that Garner illegally sold at least 10,000 cigarettes. Under the field labeled "force used," D'Amico entered "no."

At trial, D'Amico confirmed that Garner did not possess enough cigarettes to warrant the felony charge. He said that Garner had about 100 cigarettes on him when he was arrested. In the end, the complaint form filed against Garner listed a misdemeanor as the most serious offense.

The prosecution showed D'Amico a series of stills from the video of the incident. He never said on the stand that Pantaleo put Garner in a chokehold. After displaying one image where Pantaleo has his arm around Garner's throat, prosecutor O'Hare asked D'Amico: "Officer Pantaleo still has his arm around Mr. Garner's neck?"

"It was around his body," he responded. "Upper body."

Pantaleo's Police Academy instructor, Sergeant Russell Jung, was also called to testify. He backed up the defense's argument that Pantaleo's takedown was a "seatbelt maneuver," not a chokehold. But in a blow to the defense's argument, Jung said that he had not taught Pantaleo the seatbelt grip during his 2006 training.

The Academy instructor also generated groans from some in the courtroom when he said, "There's a million maneuvers we do in the street that we're not trained to do."

The NYPD's Internal Affairs Bureau (IAB) investigators revealed they had found quite the opposite when they investigated Pantaleo's conduct. In their probe of the Garner incident, IAB investigators interviewed 16 civilians and 21 uniformed witnesses, including Pantaleo. Deputy Inspector Charles Barton, commanding officer for the IAB group investigating the case, testified that he requested that charges be filed against Pantaleo in January 2015.

In a memo, Barton requested a charge against the officer "for violation of Patrol Guide 203-11, 'Use of Force,' in that he placed Eric Garner in a chokehold." But neither the Department Advocate's Office, the NYPD's internal prosecution unit, nor the CCRB acted on Barton's recommendation at the time.

While this revelation that the NYPD's own people — not just external investigators at the CCRB — found misconduct boosted the prosecution's case, it also raised more questions about why it had taken so long to bring charges against Pantaleo.

For one, Barton's testimony that he recommended charges less than six months after the incident suggests that Pantaleo could have been charged with a chokehold by the department within 18 months — alleviating the issues with the statute of limitations. Instead, they waited over four years to put him on trial, despite concluding he used a maneuver that the department claims to have banned.

The two sides' expert medical testimony was a contentious affair in the courtroom. Dr. Floriana Persechino, senior Chief Medical Examiner for the New York City Medical Examiner's Office, was called to testify. She performed the autopsy on Eric Garner after his death. In 2014, some of Dr. Persechino's findings were released to the media. In the report, she ruled that the cause of death was: "Compression of neck (choke hold), compression of chest and prone positioning during physical restraint by police." Persechino also found Garner's asthma, obesity, and high blood pressure were "contributing conditions."

In a dramatic moment at the trial, London ripped up a copy of Persechino's report. He called the medical examiner's findings "worthless, completely worthless."

On the stand, Persechino said that Pantaleo "set into motion a lethal sequence of events." She noted that Pantaleo caused Garner to have an asthma attack when he put him in a chokehold during the arrest. As the prosecution displayed a series of autopsy photos for her, the medical examiner used a laser pointer to show ruptured blood vessels in his neck muscles that she said were caused by compression of Garner's neck.

Persechino agreed with London and the defense that the chokehold was not the sole cause of Garner's death, as her report had indicated. However, she pushed back when he pointed out that no external bruising was found on Garner's neck, and the bones and cartilage in his neck were not fractured. She said that forearms, being soft and broad, do not necessarily leave marks. She added that she had only seen fractured bones in a minority of choking and strangling cases.

The defense called its own medical expert to refute Persechino's findings. To the annoyance of the other side, it delayed the trial by three weeks due to the witness's schedule. On June 5, Michael Graham, a chief medical examiner for the city of St. Louis and professor of pathology at St. Louis University, arrived at One Police Plaza to give his testimony.

Graham said that after viewing the cell phone video, it was his opinion that even though Garner "probably felt he couldn't breathe," that "the fact is he could breathe." Graham believed the fact that Garner was talking during the incident backed this argument up. He went on to say that in his opinion, "it was heart disease exacerbated by his interaction with law enforcement" that caused his death.

The next day, the final day of the trial, London announced that his client would not testify. Instead, a transcript of Pantaleo's interview with IAB investigators was entered in the record. London said that Pantaleo would not take the stand because the outstanding Department of Justice investigation was still ongoing. He expressed concern that there was an assistant U.S. attorney from the Eastern District of New York observing the department trial in the audience. "It's disconcerting that the U.S. attorney was here, but we have nothing to hide," he said. After London said Pantaleo wouldn't testify, the U.S. attorney left the courtroom.

During his interview with Internal Affairs, investigators asked Pantaleo what the department's policy on chokeholds was. He replied, "That we are not supposed to use them."

Investigators then asked him what he believed constituted a chokehold. Pantaleo said, "you take your two hands, and you're choking their throat or if you use your forearm grasped with the other hand, and you pull back with your forearm onto the windpipe preventing him from breathing."

Investigators found Pantaleo's answer to be incomplete. So he was asked to read the definition of a chokehold from the NYPD's Patrol Guide. Investigators then asked him if he had used a chokehold on Garner. "No, I did not," he replied.

When the investigators were done interviewing him, Pantaleo's attorney asked him to explain the positioning of his left forearm around Garner's throat as they were moving away from the window and down to the ground. Pantaleo said, "I was able to push him forward to now where I landed with my feet up in the air behind me and only one arm around his upper area, I believe close to the throat, but his throat area was in the crook of my elbow."

His attorney asked if he was "pressuring the neck" at this point. Pantaleo replied, "There was no pressure to the neck. It was pretty much me just laying on him, preventing him from trying to get back up on all fours."

The investigators played the video for Pantaleo during the interview. They showed him a segment where his arm was around Garner's neck, and his hands were locked together. He admitted that his one arm was "holding onto" his other arm during this segment. But he once again denied using a chokehold.

After 14 witnesses over six days of testimony, the trial was over. Prosecutor Suzanne O'Hare said during her closing that the CCRB recommended a penalty of "termination without his pension" for Pantaleo.

Pantaleo, his defense attorneys, Garner's family, the prosecutors from the CCRB, and a world of interested observers that had followed the saga were left to wait for the judge to make her recommendation. Ultimately, Pantaleo's fate lay in the hands of NYPD Commissioner James O'Neill, who had the final call on whether or not to punish the officer. But first, O'Neill would get a recommendation from Judge Maldonado.

The speculation of when she would present her decision to O'Neill began. Stuart London said that he thought Maldonado's recommendation might come before the July deadline for the DOJ to file federal charges, which was a little over a month away.

On July 16, 2019, the Department of Justice announced it was declining to file federal civil rights charges against Pantaleo. Federal prosecutors in Brooklyn met with the family and informed them of the decision on the day before the fifth anniversary of Garner's death. After the meeting, Gwen Carr told the press in frustration, "The DOJ has failed us."

"The streets of New York City are not safe with them walking around. Five years ago, it was me. It was my family. Today or tomorrow, it could be your family," she said.

On the fifth anniversary of Eric Garner's death, demonstrators marched around City Hall and police headquarters. "This makes my heart smile," Carr said, addressing the rally.

There were other rallies around New York City that day, too. A group marched from the Staten Island ferry terminal to Bay St. And others gathered that night in the driving rain in front of Pantaleo's house, chanting: "He needs to be scared everywhere that he go! We will find you Pantaleo!"

Over a month passed since the department trial had ended — and no word yet from the judge on Pantaleo's fate.

On the morning of May 16, 2019, while the Pantaleo trial was going on downtown, Mayor Bill de Blasio and his wife, Chirlane McCray, walked into the midtown Manhattan studio of "Good Morning America" for a nationally-televised interview. That day, de Blasio was announcing his bid for President of the United States of America.

At the time, de Blasio was the 23rd candidate to enter the crowded Democratic field of hopefuls vying for the chance to take on President Donald Trump in the general election. In announcing his candidacy, de Blasio pumped up his accomplishments as mayor, like universal pre-K and raising the minimum wage. He also claimed that as a fellow New Yorker, he was best suited to take on "Con Don," as he referred to Trump on *GMA*.

Nevertheless, de Blasio's campaign never gained enough traction where one could argue that he was ever a serious contender for the presidency in the 2020 election. However, he did garner the minimum amount of support to earn himself a spot on the crowded debate stage with other top candidates in the Democratic Primary.

On July 31, 2019, de Blasio took the stage at the second night of debates in Detroit, Michigan. As he delivered his opening statement, people in the crowd interrupted him with chants of, "Fire Pantaleo!" The mayor forged on through his remarks, but when Sen. Cory Booker began his opening statement, the shouts of "Fire Pantaleo!" started up again. Other candidates seized on the issue. New York Sen. Kirsten Gillibrand said that if she were mayor, she would have fired Pantaleo. "He should be fired. He should be fired now," she said.

After the debate, de Blasio put out a tweet about the interruption. "To the protestors in the audience today: I heard you. I saw you. I thank you."

"This is what democracy looks like and no one said it was pretty," he said.

The media asked the mayor after the debate about the state of the Pantaleo case. He promised that the "Garner family is going to get justice in the next 30 days." Two days later, the judge who presided over Pantaleo's department trial delivered her decision.

If you scroll to the bottom of Judge Rosemarie Maldonado's decision in the case, you'll learn very quickly that she recommended that the NYPD fire Pantaleo. But, if you dig deeper into the 47-page document, you will also find that the judge's words reflect the complexity of her conclusion.

For one thing, she agreed with Pantaleo and his defense team that some of the officer's initial actions when he took down Garner did not rise to the level of recklessness necessary to prove the charges against him. For example, she did not fault Pantaleo for trying to avoid breaking the glass storefront window during the scuffle with Garner on the ground.

"It is important to underscore that, initially, [Pantaleo] did not seek to gain compliance of the subject by setting up for, or by using, a prohibited chokehold," she wrote.

"Instead, he originally attempted to handcuff a larger individual who was resisting arrest by executing two maneuvers sanctioned by the Department," the judge said.

In analyzing the expert medical testimony, Maldonado called the city's medical examiner's testimony "exceptionally qualified and unbiased" while calling the defense's rebuttal by the medical examiner from St. Louis "self-serving" and "without substantiation."

The judge credited the city medical examiner's testimony that Pantaleo's use of a chokehold caused internal bruising and hemorrhaging in Garner's neck. She wrote that the physical injury and "substantial pain" rose to a level that met a threshold associated with an actual Penal Law violation, not just a violation of department rules. She added that she agreed with the city's medical examiner that Pantaleo's "recklessness" contributed to Garner's death.

Maldonado said that she found the city medical examiner's testimony to be a "cohesive, fact-based and reasoned summary of medical findings that support a conclusion." She said the testimony supported the argument that Pantaleo's chokehold "was a significant factor in triggering the acute asthma attack which contributed to [Garner's] tragic death." She added that she agreed with their medical conclusions that Garner was not in any "apparent physical distress" until Pantaleo "put his forearm around his neck."

The judge did not give a kind assessment of Pantaleo's statement in his internal affairs interview. She said that she found his denial that he used a chokehold "implausible and self-serving." On the credibility of Pantaleo's statements of what happened, the judge said his answers had "questionable reliability." In truly damning analysis, she wrote that she found Pantaleo's explanation of his actions "untruthful." She added that she regarded Pantaleo as "disingenuous" when he viewed the video and denied using a chokehold.

Maldonado also discredited the testimony from Pantaleo's fellow officers who were on the scene. Regarding their observations of Pantaleo during the encounter, Maldonado noted that several officers testified that they were not focused on the position of Pantaleo's arms on Garner. She called this testimony "unhelpful or unreliable."

In finding he acted recklessly, the judge noted the numerous times that the police department informed Pantaleo that chokeholds were prohibited without exception, including during his training and in the Patrol Guide that every officer is issued. Furthermore, she pointed out that Pantaleo himself acknowledged that chokeholds were not to be used in his interview.

Maldonado wrote sternly in her report that the NYPD's prohibition on chokeholds is "unequivocal" and "absolute." She cited the NYPD's training materials which refer to them as potentially "deadly," noting that the ban was in place explicitly to "reduce the possibility of in-custody deaths."

This "absolute" prohibition may have been true on paper when Pantaleo placed Garner in a chokehold in 2014. However, two years after that, Commissioner Bratton changed the rules on chokeholds. In June 2016, the department updated the Patrol Guide. The section on "department prohibitions" said that NYPD officers "shall not" use a chokehold. However, the updated guide included a note saying that the department would review any incidents of prohibited force on a case-by-case basis, and "under exigent or exceptional circumstances, the use of the prohibited action may have been justified and within guide-lines." In short, the supposed blanket ban on chokeholds was no more.

Ultimately, taking all the factors argued at trial into consideration, Maldonado ruled that the CCRB proved its case to satisfy the high threshold of establishing all of the elements of Assault in the Third Degree. Thus, the judge found Pantaleo guilty of the first charge in the case.

Despite her many criticisms of the defense's case, Maldonado cleared Pantaleo of the second charge. She wrote that the prosecution failed to establish that Pantaleo acted with intent to strangle Garner and impede his breathing.

Here the judge focused on why Pantaleo was there, and his intent, which she said was to arrest Garner. She noted that Pantaleo did not "target" Garner but rather was ordered to Tompkinsville Park by a supervisor to investigate the situation. She called Pantaleo's initial attempt to arrest Garner "lawful" and said that his first attempts to handcuff Garner — by grabbing his wrists and elbow, and then by taking him down from the rear — were moves sanctioned by the NYPD.

"Undoubtedly, [Pantaleo's] forearm moved up" to Garner's neck and "remained there in a prohibited chokehold as they fell to the ground," the judge wrote. "Within the context however the tribunal is not persuaded that [Pantaleo's] intent, even when his hands were clasped, was to impede Mr. Garner's breathing."

On the judge's recommendations in the Pantaleo case, former CCRB Chairman Fred Davie said he respects the findings, but doesn't agree that there was justification for the stop. "I think there's considerable evidence that the officers were pretty far away, when they saw Garner, maybe selling loosies," he said.

From 2017 until 2021, Davie served as chair of the CCRB. Civil rights work had been embedded in his character from a young age. Born and raised in North Carolina, he came of age as the civil right movement was maturing in the 1960s. In 1965, he tried to integrate a local amusement park, Stowe Park, in Belmont, North Carolina. Davie was just 9 years old.

"There were about 12 of us, oldest was 13, came from vacation bible school," he said. "We wanted to go to the park and it wasn't a Tuesday."

Right on the sign it said that Tuesday was the day reserved for "coloreds," he said.

When they tried to go in they were escorted out. The park closed that day. After their "visit," he said, Stowe Park closed in 1965 and it did not reopen until 1978 after it had been sold to the City of Belmont. And by then, the entire town, at least all public accommodations, were racially integrated.

On the decision to stop Garner in the first place in July 2014, Davie said, "My read, [the officers] went to the scene, with a presumption, instead of acting on what was going on, which was basically nothing," he said.

"As I understand it, they had been required to take some action in that area," Davie added, regarding enforcement against the illegal sale of cigarettes. "But none of that was going on, when they supposedly saw something from a football field away."

"While I respect the judge herself, the reading of the facts, I would choose to disagree about the justification for approaching in the first place," he said.

While noting that this case is "singular in its facts," in her report, Maldonado said that Pantaleo's case had a "strikingly similar set of circumstances and medical issues" to another case. The judge said that case also involved an NYPD officer who used a "forbidden chokehold" on an arrestee who died from "neck and chest compression with chronic asthma as a contributing factor." She didn't name it, but Maldonado was referring to the well known case of former NYPD officer Francis Livoti.

On December 22, 1994, 29-year-old Anthony Baez and his three brothers were playing football in the street at around 1 am outside their parents' home in the South Bronx. Two NYPD cruisers were parked nearby.

During the game, an errant pass hit one of the police cars. After a second ball again struck one of the NYPD vehicles, Officer Livoti got out and started yelling at the brothers, ordering them to go home. They decided to ignore him and play on. So Livoti stepped out of his car again and placed Baez's brother David under arrest for disturbing the peace. Livoti told David he would be spending Christmas on Rikers Island.

Baez, who was home visiting from Orlando, Florida, protested his brother's arrest. After Livoti put David in the squad car, he pushed Baez onto the sidewalk and attempted to handcuff him. Baez resisted, crossing his arms around his chest. That's when Livoti wrapped his arm around his neck. He held it there for over a minute while Baez's father, who had come outside, begged Livoti to let up. Baez fell limp and died.

Unlike Pantaleo, Livoti was charged in criminal court. Two years after the incident, a Bronx judge acquitted him on negligent homicide charges. But in 1998, Livoti was found guilty in federal court of violating Baez's civil rights and sentenced to seven years in prison. At sentencing, the judge pointed out that there had been nine earlier complaints of brutality against Livoti. The judge said those complaints should have been enough "to alert those in charge to the fact that Mr. Livoti should be off the streets, if not off the force."

"The Police Department let him remain on the streets, knowing that one day a real tragedy would occur,'" the judge added. Ultimately, Livoti was dismissed from the police department for using a prohibited chokehold against Baez.

Baez's death was a spark in the city that helped ignite the activist movement against police brutality that continued through the death of Eric Garner and today. His mother, Iris Baez, waged her own battle for justice after her son's death. Years later, she attended Pantaleo's trial at One Police Plaza, sitting alongside Garner's family and comforting Gwen Carr when the autopsy photos or video footage became too much for her to bear.

In her report, Maldonado said the judge's recommendation that Livoti be terminated was warranted and said that she had reached the same conclusion in Pantaleo's case.

She wrote that there "is only one appropriate penalty for the grave misconduct that yielded an equally grave result — [Pantaleo] can no longer remain a New York City Police Officer."

Under the City Charter, the final decision on Pantaleo's punishment belonged to the police commissioner. Two weeks later, on August 19,

2019, Commissioner O'Neill announced that he accepted the judge's recommendation. O'Neill fired Pantaleo. He became the first officer fired over the use of an illegal chokehold since Livoti.

At a news conference, Mayor de Blasio said, "Today, we have finally seen justice done."

The mayor, who went to great lengths over the years not to publicly weigh in on what should happen to Pantaleo and instead repeatedly called out the Justice Department for slowing down the process, took one more shot at the DOJ on how they handled their investigation of Pantaleo.

"The place that we had turned for generations to, the place that was synonymous with making things right *failed us*, the United States Department of Justice, absent and unwilling to act even to come to any decision for five long years," de Blasio said. He went on to praise the NYPD's disciplinary process for acting "fairly and impartially."

"Our attorneys did a phenomenal job," former CCRB chair Fred Davie said, adding, "Everybody knows it took so long."

On de Blasio's reaction after Pantaleo was fired, Davie said he was "pretty disappointed he didn't say anything at all about the CCRB, no thank you to the CCRB." He said he let that be known to City Hall, calling it a "pretty big oversight."

The PBA held its own press conference to counter the message from city officials that fair justice had been done. Pat Lynch said that rank-and-file officers were outraged and "brokenhearted" over the decision. He called for the governor to remove de Blasio and O'Neill. "There's no confidence for the leadership at City Hall and One Police Plaza," he said. "The leadership has abandoned ship and left our police officers on the streets, alone."

Lynch went on to accuse O'Neill of choosing "to cringe in fear of the anti-police extremists, rather than standing up for New Yorkers who want a functioning police department, with cops who are empowered to protect them and their families."

"With this decision, Commissioner O'Neill has opened the door for politicians to dictate the outcome of every single NYPD disciplinary proceeding, without any regard for the facts of the case or police officers' due process rights," Lynch said. He said that the commissioner will "wake up tomorrow to discover that the cop-haters are still not satisfied, but it will be too late."

"The damage is already done," Lynch said.

Following his firing, Pantaleo sued in state court to get his job back. His lawyers argued in the suit that his termination was an excessive punishment that was "shocking to one's sense of fairness." Two years later, in May 2021, a state appeals court panel of five judges ruled against him. The panel wrote that there was "substantial evidence" to support the NYPD's conclusion that Pantaleo "recklessly caused injury to Eric Garner by maintaining a prohibited chokehold for nine to ten seconds after exigent circumstances were no longer present, thereby disregarding the risk of injury."

While reports had begun to trickle out in the days leading up to Pantaleo's firing that O'Neill would follow through on Maldonado's recommendation to terminate him, many were interested to see what the commissioner would have to say about reaching his decision. O'Neill himself had served as a uniformed police officer for 34 years before being anointed as commissioner. At the press conference announcing his decision, he talked about how policing was "in my DNA."

"I can tell you that, had I been in Officer Pantaleo's situation, I may have made similar mistakes," he said.

He noted that he wished Garner had not resisted arrest when D'Amico and Pantaleo stopped him. "Every time I watched the video, I say to myself, as probably all of you do, to Mr. Garner: 'Don't do it. Comply.'"

He continued, "To Officer Pantaleo: 'Don't do it.' I said that about the decisions made by both Officer Pantaleo and Mr. Garner."

O'Neill said he made the "very difficult decision" in the past few days. But he had known since being appointed commissioner that he would at some point have to deal with the situation. "I've been thinking about this since I was sworn in as police commissioner," O'Neill said.

He said that he accepted that there would be blowback over his decision. "I've been a cop for a long time," he said. "And if I was still a cop, I'd probably be mad at me — 'You're not looking out for us.' But I am."

That afternoon, O'Neill put out a tweet seemingly to attempt to cool the situation. "We recruit from the human race," he tweeted. "We're not perfect. But, the next time you're walking down the street and you feel safe, thank the N.Y.P.D."

Outside police headquarters, an energetic Gwen Carr proclaimed that day, "I'm not stopping this fight...I'm out here for the long run." She reiterated her call for the other 11 officers on the scene that day to be held accountable. "They all need to lose their jobs," she said. Ultimately, only one other officer, Sergeant Kizzy Adonis, would face department discipline. The first supervisor to arrive on the scene, Adonis, pleaded guilty to a charge of failure to supervise and was docked 20 vacation days by the NYPD.

Standing in front of signs that said "FIRED" with Daniel Pantaleo's picture underneath, Carr spoke into the mic, addressing the now-former cop. "Pantaleo, you may have lost your job, but I lost a son," she said.

"You cannot replace that. You can get another job, maybe at Burger King."

13

MELEE IN MOTT HAVEN: A NEW WAVE OF PROTESTS AND A BRUTAL CRACKDOWN BY THE NYPD

On May 25, 2020, Minneapolis police officer Derek Chauvin killed George Floyd, a 46 year-old former high school football star, by kneeling on his neck for over 9 minutes. Bystander video captured Chauvin refusing to get off Floyd while he cried in agony "I can't breathe!" and "Mama!" Onlookers pleaded with the cop to get off him. Chauvin just stared back at them while keeping his knee on Floyd's neck.

All over the country, people flooded the streets to express their anger, frustration and disgust over Floyd's death and the decades of police violence against people of color that preceded it. In New York City, the demonstrations lasted over a week.

The first couple of nights of protests in New York City brought out huge crowds. But several demonstrations were marred by a mix of police violence, destruction of property, and looting.

On May 28, during the first night of protests in Union Square in Manhattan, police pushed, shoved, and pepper sprayed protesters. The officers hit people with their batons and knocked others over with their bicycles. The next night in Brooklyn, an officer riding in the passenger seat of a moving police cruiser opened the car door to knock down a person in the street. Nearby, NYPD Officer Vincent D'Andraia approached a female protester and hurled her to the ground after calling her a "fucking bitch." The victim, Dounya Zayer, said she suffered seizures after having her head slammed to the pavement.

One night later, near the intersection of Flatbush and St. Mark's Avenue in Brooklyn, protesters blocked the path of a police car with an NYPD barricade. Some in the crowd began to throw plastic water bottles and garbage at the car. The NYPD officers responded by driving two cars directly into the crowd. Several people were knocked to the ground as one of the police cars rammed into the barricade.

During some of the demonstrations, bad actors threw bricks through storefront glass windows while protesters pleaded with them to stop. Looters infiltrated the crowds and ransacked dozens of stores in neighborhoods like the Soho shopping section of lower Manhattan, in Brooklyn around the Atlantic Terminal, and on Fordham Road in the Bronx.

That week, Mayor Bill de Blasio also faced one of his more bizarre and personal clashes with a police union boss. Union president Ed Mullins used the Sergeants Benevolent Association Twitter account to publish the private information online — or as it commonly known on the internet, dox — the mayor's daughter, Chiara de Blasio. In a tweet from the official SBA account, Mullins posted Chiara's personal information and address after she was arrested during a protest. Mullins referred to the mayor's daughter as a "rioting anarchist."

The tweet about the mayor's daughter was just one example of attacks made by Mullins on social media in 2020. Some of his other Twitter missives from the SBA account during this time were filled with discriminatory and hateful language. A few weeks prior to the protests, he called the city's health commissioner Dr. Oxiris Barbot a "bitch" after it was reported that she clashed with the police department over a request for 250,000 masks for officers during the Covid-19 pandemic. Before Mullins spouted off on social media, the *New York Post* reported that Barbot told Chief of Department Terence Monahan, "I don't give two rats' asses about your cops," in response to the mask request from the department. She later apologized.

Also during 2020, Mullins called openly gay city councilman and congressional candidate Ritchie Torres a "first class whore" on Twitter after the lawmaker called for an investigation into a possible police work slowdown. "He[sic] we go America this is what a first class whore looks like RITCHIE TORRES," Mullins tweeted.

The day after the tweet attacking his daughter, de Blasio called Mullins' action "unconscionable," while noting that his daughter "was acting peacefully" during a protest.

"I admire that she was out there trying to change something she thought was unjust," he added.

By Sunday morning on May 31, more than 345 people at demonstrations had been arrested over the course of three nights in New York City. The NYPD said that 33 officers had been injured and more than 40 cop cars damaged. The next day, New York Governor Andrew Cuomo and de Blasio made the decision to institute a curfew in New York City. It was the first time since 1943 that the city was put under curfew. The officials claimed the curfew would allow the police to use their resources to respond to the looting taking place in the city. When the looting continued after the curfew announcement, de Blasio changed the start time from 11 pm to 8 pm. But while this isolated bad behavior occurred downtown and in shopping districts around the city, it was places like Mott Haven in the Bronx that would face the brunt of the coming curfew crackdown.

On June 4, 2020, a group of about 300 people gathered in the Mott Haven section of the South Bronx. This gathering was organized by an activist collective known as FTP. The shorthand FTP stands for a number of things — "free the people," "for the people," as well as "fuck the police." The rally, called "FTP4," was promoted online with fliers featuring illustrations of a man jumping over a cop car and a police cruiser on fire. The NYPD would later suggest that they saw these images as a provocation. However, FTP's promotion included a manual asking attendees to refrain from "hooliganism," to not bring weapons or engage in any violence, and to "follow the people from the hood" during the rally.

Despite the relatively modest size of the gathering in Mott Haven (some protests that week around the city numbered in the tens of thousands), the NYPD sent a large police presence to the event. At least 100 officers were dispatched to the Bronx, including dozens of high-ranking "white shirt" officers, according to a report by the Human Rights Watch.

30-year-old Brett Bates moved to New York City from Pensacola, Florida in 2015. In 2020, Bates, who is White, attended several of the protests in New York City after George Floyd was killed. He walked over the Brooklyn Bridge with thousands of demonstrators that week. He also narrowly avoided getting hit by one of the police cars that drove into protesters on a Brooklyn street, running away from the stampede after he heard the screams.

He learned about the FTP4 rally in Mott Haven on social media. He liked the organizers' "grassroots, power of the people, more militant message." He had not protested yet in the Bronx. So he traveled to Mott Haven alone from his neighborhood in Ridgewood, Queens to attend.

Dan Edelstein was also living in Ridgewood, Queens. For years, he had "strong feelings about political equality and police accountability." Edelstein, who is White, grew up in the Bay Area in California and was living there when Oscar Grant was killed by police on the platform of an Oakland train station. A friend of Edelstein involved in housing activism heard about the Mott Haven protest and a handful of their friends decided to go up to the Bronx on June 4.

Krystin Hernandez, a Latinx person born and raised in the Bronx, grew up in the Soundview section on the East Side of the borough along the 6-train line. In 2020, Hernandez was studying law at CUNY Law School in the city. They also volunteered as a legal observer with the National Lawyers Guild at protests around New York City. On June 4, they volunteered to legal observe in the Bronx and Hernandez and their husband went over to Mott Haven.

James Lauren, who is White, was working as a registered nurse in an emergency room in a hospital in New York City. They were in contact that week with others about the need for medics at the protests. "There's a loose informal way of people talking," Lauren said. Whenever Lauren had a free night or day and knew there was a need, they would be there.

Lauren arrived at the Mott Haven protest before the march started dressed in scrubs with a mask over their face. They carried a clear backpack filled with water, gauze, tape, and cardboard to make splints. The backpack had a red cross on it. Nothing too elaborate but enough to provide light medical attention if necessary.

When Bates got to the Bronx he noticed that the protest wasn't huge. There were only around a few hundred people there. At the spot where they were gathering, known as The Hub, there were people playing drums, some speeches happening, and folks handing out leaflets, ear plugs and masks. He also noticed that there were a "ton of cops."

Edelstein said some of the speakers at The Hub talked about how there haven't been that many protests in the Bronx despite the fact that the area had been "put upon by the NYPD" for years.

"They basically said 'We want Bronx natives and people of color leading the chants, leading the protests, we're happy to have your support, don't make it about you,'" Edelstein said. He found this message refreshing. He had been at some of the earlier protests in Manhattan where he saw people "posing aesthetically" and questioned whether some demonstrators' support was sincere. While watching the speakers at The Hub, he noticed cops on the roofs of the surrounding buildings.

The group started its walk through the neighborhood. As they combed through Mott Haven, there was "a lot of support from onlookers," Bates said.

The people in the neighborhood were excited to see the group. The march went through the Patterson Houses, a public housing project in the heart of Mott Haven. "It was cool to be doing this thing, engaging, people thinking it was an exciting thing to see," Edelstein said.

For a while, the march proceeded with "virtually no interaction with the police whatsoever," Hernandez said.

Lauren was stationed at the rear of the march, a few feet behind the demonstrators. They stayed focused and vigilant on people's safety. Lauren knew that even when the marches seemed to be going smoothly, there was always the potential for things to turn more serious. The cops were making Lauren nervous. Their radar was always up when the police were around.

As 8 pm approached, the marchers turned down 136th street. Just then, Bates noticed a group of cops in "black militaristic gear" that he had never seen before. They were swiftly biking down the sidewalk on the left flank of the group in an "organized battalion," he said. Bates could sense they were "moving in formation to do something." This was not just trailing or monitoring by the police.

"This was more active than reactive. Kind of executing something," Bates said.

To handle crowd control the NYPD deployed its Strategic Response Group, or SRG, to Mott Haven. The SRG was initially created as a specialized 350-officer unit by NYPD Commissioner Bill Bratton several years earlier.

At a January 2015 luncheon in midtown Manhattan put on by New York City's Police Foundation, Bratton said that the department was in need of an "elite" unit trained in "advanced disorder control." Noting the recent terror attacks in Paris and Mumbai, Bratton said the SRG would focus on anti-terror, active shooter scenarios, and large-scale crowd and protest control.

He immediately faced backlash from activists and civil liberties groups for his intentions to use the heavily-armored officers who trained daily in anti-terror tactics to police protests. Shortly after Bratton laid out his plan, James O'Neill, his number two at the department at the time, walked back the strategy and told the media that the Strategic Response Unit will "not be involved in handling protests and demonstrations." O'Neill said that the unit will be focused on anti-terror work.

This proved to be a hollow promise from the department. That same year in 2015, the SRG played a major role in policing Black Lives Matter demonstrations, using aggressive arrest tactics on protesters. Within a year of its creation, the SRG also doubled in size and its budget grew from $13 million to nearly $90 million.

As 8 pm neared on June 4, 2020, the Mott Haven marchers continued down a hill on 136th street towards the intersection of Brook

Avenue. When they got to the bottom of the hill, they came upon a line of cops blocking the street. The call came out for White allies to move to the front of the group and put their bodies between the cops and the rest of the demonstrators. Both Bates and Edelstein moved to the front.

Bates was face to face with the line of cops that was blocking the marchers. He started to notice a "pressure from behind us." He said that he and the others in the front of the group tried to communicate to the protesters behind to "stop pushing." But then the group learned that it was actually cops in the back of the group "pressing in, pushing."

The police started to play a recording ordering the protesters to disperse. But even if the protesters wanted to leave, there was no way for them to do so. The demonstrators were kettled; trapped between a line of officers in the front of them and behind them. Some people begged the police to just let them leave. The officers refused.

Medics like James Lauren were trapped in the kettle too. "I was in the back, they were lined up in a wall blocking any exit," Lauren said. Lauren was immediately arrested and pulled to the side of the street. They were zip tied and forced to stand there and watch as the police descended on the crowd of protesters.

On the scene in Mott Haven was Kenneth Rice, a sergeant with the NYPD Legal Bureau, a unit who assists NYPD officers in departmental legal matters. He got on the bullhorn. Rice announced that legal observers could be arrested. "They're good to go," Rice said.

Krystin Hernandez told the police, "I'm an essential worker." They pulled out attestation of essential services documents they had printed out and tried to show the officers. The police swatted the papers out of Hernandez's hand. They kept repeating "I'm an essential worker." Then a cop lifted Hernandez up, slammed them to the ground, and cuffed them with zip ties.

Different officers yanked Hernandez up off the ground. They felt pain in their upper body. Fortunately, their shoulders hit the ground before their face did. Fearful of what might happen next, Hernandez said they screamed out "call my mom!" into "the abyss," hoping that their husband would hear.

A fanny pack Hernandez was wearing busted open and their

personal belongings flew out onto the pavement. A cop picked up Hernandez's stuff and gave back the fanny pack. The forms stating that they were an essential worker stayed on the ground. The officer who recovered Hernandez's notebook and other belongings told them, "I'm sorry, mama, I'm sorry."

On the night of June 4, Chief of the Department Terry Monahan said he was in his car in the vicinity of the 40th precinct. It had been among the busiest weeks of his career. He said he had slept just "two hours in the past 72."

Monahan said it's a "common misperception" that he was on the scene in Mott Haven when the arrests began. "I was in the general area, I responded over there, probably around 8:20, got the radio transmission," he said. When Monahan got to the scene he said he made the decision to "cut" the arrests of the legal observers.

After they were taken into custody, Hernandez was led to the bottom of the hill. Their mask was gone. The other folks lined up on the sidewalk had lost their masks as well. At some point, the police started to pick out the legal observers one by one, separating them from the larger group. The officers took pictures of their IDs and badges from the National Lawyers Guild. Then the cops let the other legal observers go. An officer cut their zip ties and told Hernandez, "You should go, and you're not going to get a second chance" to leave.

But instead of leaving, the legal observers went back to work. They got the contact information of the arrested protesters being loaded onto buses, hoping to help them if they needed legal assistance later on.

Inside the kettle, the cops in front of Bates started telling the protesters, "stay back, don't come at us." The protesters, with their arms linked, tried to tell the police they were getting pushed from the back.

Marco A. Carrión, Commissioner for Community Affairs in the de Blasio administration, went up to Mott Haven on the day of the protest. He was from the Bronx originally and had lived in the area. He was there for his job but was also curious what the protest in the neighborhood would be like.

As the Commissioner for Community Affairs, part of Carrión's job was to be de Blasio's eyes and ears in the streets during protests. The two had a close relationship. The mayor saw himself as working in a similar unit under Mayor Dinkins. After Eric Garner was killed in 2014 and massive protests started up around the city, Carrión and de Blasio worked with organizers to try to help the demonstrations run smoothly. This work included efforts like providing the protesters safe passage over the Verrazano Bridge to Staten Island. "I think it was really smart," said Carrión. "That all came from the mayor."

The summer of 2020 was different. This was not the Garner protests. There was a lot less of an understanding and a willingness from city officials and the police to work with protesters. Instead, the NYPD adopted a zero tolerance attitude towards the protesters.

"From the police standpoint, with Garner there was an attitude that people are upset and have a right to protest," Carrión said. "With Floyd, for the police it became you have a short leash, we're going to warn once, twice, then make an arrest."

For the mayor, in 2020 it became more about what the people were doing and less about police action. When Carrión would report back to City Hall about what was going on in the streets, he noticed there was less concern about whether the NYPD were being violent. He found that when he did report police brutality the mayor was not accepting what he was saying. "It was less about police accountability, more about accountability of people," Carrión said.

As the Mott Haven march approached the NYPD's 40th precinct station house, Carrión noticed there were dozens of federal agents, wearing flak jackets and armed with automatic weapons, stationed outside the building. This federal law enforcement personnel was not something that de Blasio asked for. Rather, the Trump administration had sent them to New York to coordinate with the NYPD. Carrión split off from the march and tried to figure out who these feds were so he could report back to the mayor's office.

When Carrión caught up with the march he noticed a police helicopter starting to circle low in the area. He knew this was a police tactic to disperse people. Because he stopped at the precinct, Carrión was behind the line of police that had formed at the rear of the protest. There was another line of cops at the front of the group, penning them in. He knew that several members of his staff that he brought along that day were trapped inside the kettle that the NYPD created. Just then, police started to move in.

His staff were calling him frantically. They told him the NYPD had released a chemical agent to disperse the crowd and there was nowhere for them to go. His team was telling him they were afraid there's going to be a stampede. At the same time, Carrión was on the phone with First Deputy Mayor Dean Fuleihan about what was happening at the 40th Precinct. He told the First Deputy he needed to get his people out.

In the front of the group, Bates desperately tried to keep holding his ground. He said that the cops kept ignoring them, acting like they couldn't hear what the protesters were telling them, while continuing to warn them not to come closer, repeating over and over "don't come at us."

"One or two people got pushed or ended up a little too close" to the police line, and "they just started batoning people," Bates said. To his right, he could see cops had climbed on the hood of a car parked on the side of the street and started swinging their batons at the kettled demonstrators.

Their linked arms began to break apart. Bates heard screaming all round him. But he couldn't move. "I just know that I'm about to get fucked up," he said. Then he felt the blow to the crown of his head.

"It was like a movie, I hear that high pitched sound and then everything becomes muffled," he said.

He was tackled to the ground by the police. Blood started running down his forehead from the blow to the head. A couple of cops pushed his face into the ground and zip tied him.

Standing on the sidewalk in zip ties, Lauren saw people trapped in the street with bleeding head wounds. They asked the police a couple of times if they would let them provide medical assistance to those who needed it, but the police refused.

Dan Edelstein was also penned inside the kettle, his girlfriend Zoe to his right. Things were getting tighter and tighter and they were shoulder to shoulder. To the cops in front of them, they started asking "where do we go?" They pleaded with the police, "Let us leave, we'll leave." The officers just stared back with their batons out. As the group got jostled and pushed with nowhere to go, the goal became to just stay on their feet.

Edelstein was a couple rows back from the very front. He was trapped by cars parked on the sides of the group that prevented them from getting to the sidewalk. Suddenly two people fell in front of him. Thinking they were about to get trampled, he went forward to pick them up. This brought him right up to the police line.

Police began to pull at Edelstein and hit him with a baton. A cop on the sidewalk reached over a car and pepper sprayed the crowd. Then three cops climbed onto the car and began swinging at them with batons from above. Edelstein was struck in the head and a gash opened up. Some people who lived on the block had come outside onto their stoops. They were aghast. Edelstein looked in the eyes of a woman who was crying as she watched him and the others get beaten.

Edelstein was knocked to the ground. He laid there, face to the pavement with two or three people on top of him, making it hard to breathe. He locked eyes with someone else at the bottom of the pile. "I'm staring at this person in this weird dark cave and we're looking at eachother like, 'this is fucked up,'" he said.

When he managed to get up, the cops grabbed him, threw him to the ground and zip tied him. He spotted his girlfriend laying next to him in zip ties. For a few minutes they just laid there and tried to console each other, telling each other it was over and they were OK.

Edelstein asked for some water to wash the blood and pepper spray off his face. Other people around him started telling the police to get him a doctor. A nearby medic asked the cops to let her treat him, but they refused. After about 30 minutes, they brought Edelstein to the side of the road and let the medics work on him. They cleaned his head, rinsed out his eyes, and opened up his jeans to see if he broke anything. EMS who responded to the scene of the crackdown loaded Edelstein onto a gurney and the police handcuffed him to it. Finally, he was put in an ambulance and taken to Lincoln Hospital.

Marco Carrión tried to get inside the kettle himself. He'd put his body on the line multiple times that week. He helped pour milk into the eyes of somebody who was gassed outside Barclays Center. He was on the phone with the mayor while just a few feet away a NYPD van was being lit on fire outside of Fort Greene Park. Eventually, Carrión was able to get his team out. Thankfully, they were carrying badges and had found an officer that let them out of the kettle.

In the hours and days after the crackdown, Carrión spoke to people who lived on the block. "Everyone said nothing happened, the police just moved in."

Medic James Lauren was loaded into a van and taken to a police precinct where they were held in jail for a number of hours. Inside the precinct, the conditions were dirty and crowded. Most of the people arrested from the protest had protective masks because of the pandemic, Lauren said, but the officers inside the station did not. Lauren said they were "lucky" to be one of the "first people to get out" that night.

At the hospital, Edelstein remained handcuffed. Two cops stayed with him while the doctors worked on him. His hand was broken, his knee messed up from the baton blows and he couldn't walk. He needed staples in his head to close up the gash. At around 11 pm, six cops walked into the hospital room. They removed the cuffs and handed Edelstein a summons for a curfew violation.

In total, the NYPD arrested 263 people in Mott Haven that night, more than any single protest in New York during the George Floyd demonstrations. After their arrests in the Bronx, some protesters began an odyssey between jails in multiple boroughs. They were stuffed in cells that were only meant to hold a few people with dozens of others. For some, the zip tie handcuffs were too tight, cutting off circulation and causing nerve damage to their hands and wrists. If the mask they wore as a Covid-19 pandemic precaution fell down they were unable to lift it back into place because they were zip tied. Some of the arrestees were held for nearly 24 hours and reported not receiving any food or water. Most were charged with curfew violations or unlawful assembly, a Class B misdemeanor punishable by 90 days in jail and up to $500 in fines.

In Mott Haven, Brett Bates was loaded onto a Corrections Department bus with other protesters. His face was streaked in blood. He had worn work goggles because he heard they would protect his eyes if he were maced or pepper sprayed. But the blood that had run down his face had pooled inside them. He asked the cop that zip tied him to take them off for him. The officer said no. As more blood started to pool inside he shook his head to try to shake them off. After a few minutes of pleading, an officer finally removed the goggles. Along with the wound to his head, Bates had scratches on his face and bruises on his arms and wrists from being shoved into the pavement by the police. Others on the bus were yelling about how tight their zip ties were. Some people were in tears. Their hands were turning blue.

They drove the group from the Bronx to Queens Central Booking. When they got to Queens, Bates said, they just sat in the parking lot while the police figured out "how to deal with all of us." They weren't given any water. The air conditioning seemed like it was on only sometimes. He ended up sitting on that bus for more than five hours.

The corrections officers who drove them to Queens started "talking shit" about the NYPD, Bates said. They looked at him and his face. "This guy with the bloody face is going to be a lawsuit," Bates recalled one of the officers saying.

Every once in a while, a cop would come on the bus and one or two people would be taken off. Then more time would go by where nothing happened. The group was told that the NYPD were trying to find the arresting officers. It seemed like "a bunch of people got arrested, thrown in a bus, taken to Queens, and they don't know how to find the cops to put their name on this," Bates said.

A couple of different cops looked at Bates' face. The first cop took a picture but didn't ask him if he needed medical attention. An hour later, another cop asked him if he wanted medical attention. He said he was not sure. He thought if he could get processed quickly and avoid being brought to the hospital in handcuffs that would be a good thing. Later on however, thinking that he didn't know if he had a concussion or not, he told the police that he wanted some medical attention but they ignored him.

Hours passed. A corrections officer made another comment that nobody wanted to be the cop who "puts their name" on Bates because he looks like a "poster for police brutality." Hours into the whole ordeal, an officer finally came to bring Bates in to be processed. The officer didn't look like the one who put him in zip ties. Maybe he was the guy who hit him on the head? Bates would never find out. He did learn that the cop who took him off the bus was named McNulty — the same name as a cop on the television show, *The Wire*.

They brought Bates inside the jail. He still hadn't seen his face yet. But as he was being walked to the cell he saw people reacting to him. He heard somebody ask the officers escorting him in a whisper, *'what the fuck did you do to this guy?'*

He was put in a cell with about a dozen other people. His face was covered in dried blood and he was worried that his wound was infected. There were twelve other people in the cell with him and no airflow. He got his zip ties off but wasn't given any water or a chance to use the bathroom. He asked if he could clean the caked-on blood that had run down his forehead and dried on his cheeks. Other people in the cell yelled to the cops, *'Hey! Help this guy!'* They ignored that, too. One officer finally responded, telling Bates to use the bathroom in the cell, which was just a toilet, no sink or faucet. Bates just took a seat next to the toilet and waited to be processed.

A couple hours later, they finally took Bates out of the cell. Suddenly, all the officers were being very nice to him. And Bates, who is "cursed with politeness," just followed their instructions.

"They were weirded out," Bates said about the police inside the booking station. "Almost like a little sheepish, a little bit worried about what was going on."

When the officers went to take a mugshot, the camera wouldn't work. At first, it couldn't recognize a human face because of all the blood.

Ten hours after he was hit in the head with a baton on 136th street in the Bronx, Bates finally walked out of the Queens station. When he walked outside, he was met by people working jail support, a group of volunteers who helped to make sure that when protesters were let out of jail they got home or to a hospital for medical attention. He called those who met him outside the Queens station "the best people in the world." It was 6 am. He figured they would have gone home by now. A doctor with the group looked at Bates' head. The wound was too deep for him to help Bates on the street. He needed to go to the hospital.

Somebody from jail support drove Bates to the hospital. When he walked into the emergency room he was still covered in blood. The doctors cleaned out the wound and put three staples in Bates' head. He told a nurse what happened to him. She was very sweet and almost started crying. She told him that on TV they make it look like the protesters do "all this," meaning the violence in the streets during the demonstrations.

14

THE END OF THE POLICE SECRECY LAW:
REPEALING CIVIL RIGHTS LAW 50-A

On May 29, 2020, New York State Senator Zellnor Myrie decided to attend a protest happening in downtown Brooklyn near the Barclays Center over the death of George Floyd. He chose what he was going to wear carefully. Initially, he was going to go in all black, but changed his mind, instead putting on a "bright ass neon" green t-shirt with 'Senator Myrie' written on the back in big, black letters.

Myrie went down to the protest with another elected official, Diana Richardson, the Assemblymember from Brooklyn's district 43 that included the Crown Heights section that Myrie lived in and represented. At first, things were going well. He talked to constituents. He had moments of solitude and reflection in between the chanting and marching. As a state senator, he was also acting as a liaison between the protesters and the NYPD. He spoke to some of the higher-ups from the police department on the scene and told them, "I'm here, just so you know."

At around 8 pm, a group of cops with bikes from the NYPD Strategic Response Group started to form a line in front of the protesters. The police instructed the demonstrators to retreat down the street. Myrie began to comply with the order. But as he was walking, he felt a bike being jabbed into his shoulders and back.

Myrie was born and raised in Crown Heights. It was just him and his mom in a small, rent-controlled apartment. For work, his mom went around the neighborhood and sold beauty products to hair salons. Later on, she opened a jewelry store on Flatbush Ave. He said everyone in the neighborhood knew her which meant they knew him, too. This meant there were watchdogs all over the neighborhood that helped keep an eye on Myrie.

During the 1980s and '90s when Myrie was growing up, the neighborhood had its share of crime and gang activity. On his walks home from school, he would take his big blue coat and put it in his book bag so "not to draw attention" to himself. His mom was strict about who Myrie hung out with and wouldn't let him be outside after dark, which he hated.

The first time that Myrie lived anywhere outside of New York City was when he attended law school at Cornell University upstate in Ithaca, New York. During his second year of law school, Myrie got a teaching job at the Auburn Correctional Facility. The prison was a five hour drive from New York City, but Myrie was shocked to learn when he walked into the prison classroom that "75% of my class was from Brooklyn."

"Here I was, 200 miles away, so many of my neighbors were here," he said. Myrie thought "something is very wrong with this picture."

After Cornell, he moved back in with his mom in Crown Heights. He got a job at the white shoe law firm Davis Polk but also stayed active in local politics in his community. On election day 2016, he was working in Crown Heights doing election protection and making sure that voting for people in his neighborhood went smoothly. That night, he was in the war room with the rest of the team watching the results come in. He remembers that as it started to sink in that Donald Trump was going to win, people started to leave. "I remember just walking out, being in a state of shock," he said. He also thought: "What am I going to do about it?"

One day before, the Democratic state senator who represented Myrie's district, Jesse Hamilton, announced that he was going to join the Independent Democratic Caucus, a rogue group of Democrats that caucused with the Republicans in the state senate and effectively handed the GOP the majority. "I remember being so incensed," Myrie said.

Over the years, Myrie had worked with local members of the City Council and community board doing both legislative and media work. He maintained a number of relationships in Brooklyn political circles. So he started reaching out to his contacts about Hamilton, saying "somebody has to challenge this guy."

Everyone he talked to would say this was a despicable choice by Hamilton to join with the Republicans. But some of his contacts were weary of the idea that someone could take him on. They told him that Hamilton had been in the community for a long time and, importantly, will have a lot of money to spend.

Since nobody was going to step up, he started considering what it would take for him to run. He reached out to political contacts and started talking about policy ideas. He wanted to run on housing. He had done work with the local tenants' association and knew the way to change the rent laws was through the state legislature. He also believed that Hamilton was "in the pocket" of big real estate. The people he reached out to told him your ideas are cute but that to make a serious run you need to raise $100,000.

Myrie reached out to everyone he ever knew to raise money. He was relentless on the phone, emails, texts. He didn't raise $100,000, but he got close – he raised about $97,000. Close enough he said where people told him he was "no joke."

In September 2018, Myrie defeated Hamilton in the primary. He was one of a handful of new candidates during the election cycle to take out Democratic senators who had joined forces with the Republican side. He went on to easily win in November's general election. And within his first two years in office, Myrie would have a role to play in the state's most high-profile police reform effort in recent history.

A few years earlier, in May 2015, at a public hearing of the New York State Assembly, Camille Jobin-Davis, assistant director for the New York State Committee on Open Government, an organization that evaluates and provides advice on public access to government records, said it was their recommendation to do away with Civil Rights Law 50-a. Jobin Davis said the law "defeats accountability, increases public skepticism, and foments distrust."

"The effect of 50-a ... is to make the public employees who have often the greatest power over the lives of New York residents the least accountable to the public," she said. "So long as 50-a remains on the books, other efforts to increase police accountability that have been proposed are less likely to be effective."

Jobin-Davis said that "outright repeal" of the law would "serve as a positive step toward increasing transparency in law enforcement."

Assemblymember Daniel O'Donnell, a representative from Manhattan, was sitting in the chamber that day listening to Jobin-Davis. This was the first time that O'Donnell heard about the law. As she spoke, he wrote down in his notes: *What is 50-a?*

"I went and researched it. I thought this is a problem," O'Donnell said.

He put in two bills — a bill to repeal and a bill to modify the law. Both went nowhere. The police unions "vehemently opposed" his proposals, he said. And he couldn't get support because many of his colleagues counted on contributions from the unions. That wasn't an issue for O'Donnell.

"Fortunately, for me, I didn't get any money from the police unions," O'Donnell said.

He thought "they didn't give me money last year, they weren't going to give him money this year." So he kept pushing the bills, but they languished.

Neither the governor or New York City mayor were any help to O'Donnell, he said. Mayor de Blasio was "paying lip service" with some "lame proposals" to reform the bill. And the governor never "uttered the words" about getting rid of 50-a.

O'Donnell said de Blasio's aides came to him with a few ideas. "His people would come to me, show me proposals like, why don't we only release the records after two years," he said. "I thought, 'what's the point of that?'"

The mayor's team also presented O'Donnell the idea of only

releasing substantiated complaints. O'Donnell thought this was a flawed idea, too. For example, he cited a report that showed the NYPD had 2,000 complaints of racial profiling and they failed to substantiate even a single complaint.

"2,000 racial profiling complaints, zero substantiated, which tells me the process they're using is bogus," he said.

Myrie was also in favor of getting rid of 50-a. When he talked to colleagues in the legislature about changing the law, he said the reticence to act wasn't limited to the Republicans on the other side of the aisle from him. He said that many constituent communities viewed police officers and the "nature of their job" as so dangerous that we need to be "equipping them with as many tools as possible" to do the work. "50-a was viewed as such a thing," he said, even though he disagreed. But law enforcement had been very effective at presenting the law as something that, if it went away, would "hinder their ability to keep people safe," he said.

The activist coalition, Communities United for Police Reform (CPR), had been pushing for years to reform the NYPD disciplinary system. In 2012, one of the coalition's original goals was to change the NYPD system for discipline so that the commissioner no longer had the ultimate power to decide if penalties were handed down. But Joo-Hyun Kang, the former director of CPR, said that they realized that there wasn't going to be a "good model, workable model to do that." CPR also discovered that there was a clear lack of public knowledge that "systemic police violence" doesn't get punished, she said.

It all came to a head in 2015 and 2016, when the NYPD pivoted and decided to change its policies on releasing disciplinary information. After that, the issue of 50-a became more front and center for CPR's advocacy. Still, it was difficult during that time to get the public and legislature to pay attention to why police reformers saw this as a problem.

"It's a technical thing involving the Freedom of Information Law," Kang said about the disclosure of disciplinary records. "You asked the average New Yorker, they don't know about FOIL."

The activists spent years making trips to Albany to push for the repeal. Some legislators told them they were crazy, that it was never going to happen. However, the increased press coverage about the NYPD disciplinary system helped the advocates make their case to the lawmakers. In 2018, articles like the BuzzFeed investigation revealing that more than 300 NYPD officers had committed fireable offenses and kept their jobs, while their disciplinary records remained a secret, became part of the talking points on CPR's visits with legislators. That press coverage made it easier to help people understand how perverse the system was, Kang said.

At the same time, the police unions continued to push back against changing the law. In April 2019, SBA President Ed Mullins authored an op-ed in the *New York Post* arguing against the repeal of 50-a. In the article, Mullins wrote that repealing the law would lead to egregious violations of officers' privacy.

"This common-sense privacy protection ensures that our neighbors in uniform can do their jobs without activists and lawyers weaponizing information taken out of context, including complaints and disciplinary proceedings, to hamstring law enforcers and first responders," he wrote.

In a stroke of irony, Mullins, the vitriolic Twitter mouth-piece of his union, decried the dangers of social media's influence in society as a reason to uphold 50-a.

"With the social media mob mentality that now shapes our civic discourse, this protection is more necessary than ever," he wrote.

In October 2019, the state senate's Codes Committee held a hearing on 50-a and the possibility of repeal. As far as committees go, Codes can be highly influential. It reviews hundreds of bills each legislative session and has jurisdiction over all aspects of criminal justice policy. However, not all bills get a hearing so this was a big deal. Mothers from the movement for police reform and representatives from the various police unions in the city attended the hearing in Lower Manhattan. Myrie, who was on the Codes Committee, commended his colleague and committee chair, Sen. Jamaal Bailey for holding that hearing. "Had that hearing not happened," he said. "50-a [repeal] doesn't happen."

"The state legislature doesn't just have that kind of hearing for everything," Kang said. "It was smart to do because none of the police unions could say they didn't have a chance to weigh in."

The advocates for repeal felt that momentum was building and the senate hearing showed how "baseless the union's argument was," Kang said.

Speaking at the hearing, Eric Garner's mother, Gwen Carr, said that 50-a made it "impossible to truly fight for justice for Eric."

For years she failed to obtain the disciplinary history of the officer who choked her son, Daniel Pantaleo. And after Pantaleo's department trial, which led to him being fired, Carr was denied access to the full trial transcripts because of the 50-a law.

"It's been five years since my son's murder, and there's been a widespread cover-up," Carr said.

Ramarley Graham's mother Constance Malcolm called for the senate to "be Ramarley's voice" and repeal the law. She too had battled with the NYPD and the city to release information about her son's death and personnel records of the officers involved. And it took her years in court just to get some of the information.

"I had sleepless nights. I still worry every day about my other son, who was 6 at the time, as he watched his brother murdered by officers," an emotional Malcolm told the committee. "I don't want to have to bury another son."

Daniel O'Donnell, the Assembly Member who had proposed the bill to repeal 50-a four years earlier, pointed out that the lawmaker who crafted the original law in the 1970s himself said that it was flawed.

"The Republican senator who wrote 50-a before he passed away said, 'We never intended it to be like this,'" O'Donnell said.

When it was their turn to speak, the law enforcement union representatives tried to play defense. Lou Matarazzo, the former president of the Police Benevolent Association, told the committee "there's a total misconception for what 50-a does and does not do." He noted that if an officer has a handful of civilian complaints that was "not a hell of a lot," especially when some cops make hundreds of arrests on the job.

Paul DiGiacomo, vice president of the New York City Detectives Endowment Association, which is the union for NYPD detectives, said,

"There's no other profession in the world that has as much oversight" as the NYPD. DiGiacomo argued that "drug dealers and gangs" make civilian complaints to "keep the police away from them."

When it was his turn to speak, Myrie addressed a union argument that the officers who make the most arrests receive more complaints. He said the unions' position that this "somehow diminishes the complaints" is "weak."

"If you had two restaurants, one that was opened from 9 to 5, and the other was opened from 9 to 9 — but the 9 to 9 restaurant got more complaints than the 9 to 5, you wouldn't say, 'well, you're opened four hours more, you had more availability, we're not going to validate any food poisoning complaints.' Doesn't make sense."

Matarazzo at one point directed his frustration and criticism at the lawmakers, questioning how much they cared about the police.

"I wonder how many people in this room remember the last police officer that got killed," he said. "Anybody remember his name? Does anybody remember the last three names? I dare say not."

Senator Jessica Ramos from Queens replied, asking Matarazzo if he knew the names of the last three people killed by the NYPD.

"Garner, Bell, and the third one I do not know," Matarrazzo replied. The actual three names were Kawaski Traiwick, Antonio Williams and Nasheem Prioleau. Matarazzo's incorrect response was booed by the audience, some who held up simple signs on white pieces of paper that said "PBA LIES" in black block letters.

"That's the thing about pointing fingers and not being open to having a sincere conversation about what repealing 50-a really means for communities of color," Ramos said to Matarazzo. "I'm a little admonished by your testimony because it comes across as if you think that because you wear a badge you are better than us."

On the day of the hearing, the de Blasio administration put out a statement that reiterated the mayor's position that he was in favor of changing the law, but not repealing it.

"The Mayor has been vocal in his advocacy of 50-a reform," a spokesperson for de Blasio said in a statement. However, the administration felt the law "must balance transparency and safety" for law enforcement.

Expected to speak that day were representatives from the CCRB and the NYPD, but that never happened. A few days after the hearing, the *New York Post* reported that the mayor blocked the representatives from the city from testifying at the hearing. He vehemently denied the claim and blasted the *Post* in a radio interview with WNYC, saying that the tabloid is not a "fact-based publication" and "they will say anything they want all the time."

Former CCRB chair Fred Davie said the report that he was blocked by the administration from speaking at the hearing was not accurate. Rather, he said that there was a conversation between himself and City Hall that went "back and forth" about whether or not someone from the CCRB or the NYPD would testify at the hearing.

"No one knew what it meant, to have one agency on one side and another agency on another side" of the issue, Davie said. "Nobody knew what the implications were" of presenting that point of view. Davie said that everyone agreed that he would not testify.

"It was a collective decision in the end," Davie said. "And we understood that the NYPD wouldn't testify either."

"I did not feel blocked. I felt like we cooperated in a joint decision," Davie added.

But a couple days later, he tweeted from his personal Twitter account that 50-a should be repealed. "I took it upon myself to say that I thought 50-a should be repealed," Davie said. He said the rest of the board was in "vast agreement" with me. "That created some agita at City Hall," he said about the tweet.

"I did it out of conviction with the vast support of the board," Davie said. "I would not have gotten out that far without the backing of the board."

After the hearing, a number of state senators called for the bill to repeal 50-a to be brought up early in the next legislative session. But that never happened. Things got very quiet regarding repeal after that hearing. This is not uncommon. Bills languish in committee all the time, and "don't move unless there is broad consensus that this is something that will pass," Myrie said.

"I'd say that like a number of policies that don't get across the finish line, it's hard to know why," Myrie said.

Even after the hearing, 50-a repeal was still a controversial matter, Myrie said. "In order to break through you had to have that extra push," he said.

But little did he know at the time that the following year in 2020, in the midst of 50-a repeal and other police reforms getting the "extra push" needed to move in the legislature, that he would personally endure a violent episode of police brutality.

As the SRG cops jabbed their bikes into Myrie's back outside the Barclays Center, he turned around and said, "why are you doing this? We're listening." He tried to shield himself with his arms as the cops continued to push him. He thought this was "escalating way too quickly." He turned around again. That's when he saw an officer holding a canister and got hit with an orange stream of pepper spray. The sharp pain was a truly indescribable feeling. He was blinded and couldn't see. All he heard was an officer say, "cuff him."

Multiple NYPD officers grabbed Myrie. They pulled his arms behind his back. He had gotten separated from his fellow lawmaker, Assemblywoman Diana Richardson. He screamed for her, "Diana! Diana!" Little did he know at the time that just a few feet away from him Richardson had been hit with pepper spray as well. Some fellow protesters saw her and pulled her over to the sidewalk to deal with the after-effects. Myrie wasn't as lucky.

The cops forcibly pushed Myrie to the ground and zip tied him. When they picked him up, he was crying in pain and calling out for medical attention and yelling "what is happening?" Nobody told him anything.

The police took him over to the sidewalk and put him in a line of people with others that had been detained. He was still in a state of shock. While he was waiting in the line, an officer recognized him. The cop got one of the NYPD higher-ups and they clipped Myrie's zip ties.

He sat down on the curb and waited for Assemblywoman Richardson to find him.

Sitting on that curb, Myrie's shock subsided into a blend of negative emotions – confusion, anger, depression. It was a level of fear and vulnerability that he was not familiar with. At the same time, he was aware that had he not been a state senator he probably wouldn't have enjoyed that privilege of being pulled off the line of people about to be arrested.

That night when he got home he tweeted a photo of himself riving in pain, ooze from the pepper spray dripping down his face, as the police put him in zip ties. A lot of people were reaching out but he didn't feel like talking to anyone. One of the people who contacted him was Mayor de Blasio. The mayor left him a voicemail but Myrie never called back. "I had no interest in speaking with the mayor that night," he said.

"I wasn't interested in hearing apologies. Because the police department has been able to run this city, unencumbered," he said. "They have not been challenged."

He added, "There are too many people who don't have my platform" who were harmed during the protests "who don't get that call."

For five years, the bill to repeal 50-a went nowhere in the legislature. Until George Floyd was killed. After that, a groundswell for the legislation began in the summer of 2020.

"The day after, the family of George Floyd, and everyone in the country, knew the disciplinary history [of Derek Chauvin], that was public record — the city and an outside group kept their own list," Assemblyman Daniel O'Donnell said. "In contrast to the family of Eric Garner, who knew nothing."

After Floyd's death, O'Donnell began to "bang the drum" for 50-a repeal again amongst his colleagues in the legislature. "But then, and this was not my doing, it became *the* issue," O'Donnell said.

He recalled going to a rally in Harlem and seeing "young 19-year-olds" holding up signs saying 'Repeal 50-a.' O'Donnell approached them and asked them "'what's 50-a?'" — and they knew exactly what the law was. They asked him, "Are you going to vote for it?" He replied, "well, I wrote it."

On the last Saturday in May, Gov. Cuomo was asked about the law during his daily briefing on the Covid-19 pandemic. He stopped short of endorsing outright repeal. But he said that if the legislature passed a bill he would sign it immediately.

"I would sign a bill today that reforms 50-a," Cuomo said. "I would sign it today. So the Legislature can now convene by Zoom, or however they do it, pass the bill, and I will sign it today. I can't be clearer or more direct than that."

"For us, that meant we needed to mobilize right away," Kang said. "Cuomo said he would do it."

Momentum was building rapidly. By June 5, New Yorkers had sent more than 100,000 emails and placed over 20,000 phone calls to lawmakers pushing for the repeal of 50-a, according to CPR.

Some lawmakers were noting how rare it was to see such an aggressive and well organized push to get a law passed. State Senator Brad Hoylman tweeted on June 2, "My office has gotten 1,987 emails and counting today," along with a photo of his inbox showing dozens of emails with the subject line: *Repeal 50-a.*

"'Repeal 50-a,' what a horrible name," Kang said. "The hilarious thing to me, the week before it passed you had people like Mariah Carey and Rihanna calling for it. Something as wonky as 50-a crept into the national consciousness."

"We were able to take advantage of what the moment provided," she added.

CPR went into negotiations with the legislative staff for the Senate leadership. There were disagreements to work through and the police unions were still pushing for carve outs that would keep certain information secret. In the final repeal bill, only the addresses of officers were mandatorily omitted.

"I do think that some of the negotiations happened really quickly," Kang said. But it wouldn't have been possible without the years of work that CPR put in.

"We literally gave them the language," for the final bill, she said.

On the day of the repeal vote, Sen. Myrie spoke in the chamber. He said he showed up to Albany that day "looking wild."

"I hadn't had a haircut because of Covid," he said. "That's not usually how I show up to the chamber."

In fact, that day was the first time he put on a suit since the pandemic began. And for the first time ever, Myrie, who is "a big sneaker person," wore Jordans to the vote. He felt empowered and like he was "being my authentic self."

"We have heard from some folks that our grievances against police brutality and our attempt to rid it out of our police department are us taking advantage of a political moment," he said to begin his speech.

Myrie continued: "Some people have said that it isn't a real grievance. That this is not happening here in New York. You are taking advantage of what's happening around the country — and you're only doing it now."

He listed off some of the New Yorkers who have been killed or brutalized by the police over the years, including Eleanor Bumpurs, Abner Louima, Amadou Diallo and Eric Garner.

"So you're right. This is the moment. We are tired," Myrie said. "There has been no consequence for the brutality against our people."

He added that because of the shield of 50-a he had no idea if the officer who pepper sprayed him outside the Barclays Center protest 12 days earlier "has a history of excessive use of force."

"That is what this bill is about. It is about the history. We have seen brutality go unanswered. This isn't an attack. This is accountability. This isn't targeting. This is transparency. This isn't anti-police. This is pro people," Myrie said.

The bill to repeal 50-a passed along party lines in the senate, 40-22. All Republicans voted against it. In the Assembly, it was approved by a margin of 101-43, also along party lines.

After the repeal passed, the New York City police unions responded with a joint statement claiming that releasing disciplinary records could leave their officers vulnerable to facing "unavoidable and irreparable harm to reputation and livelihood."

"We, as professionals, are under assault," Pat Lynch, the president of the Police Benevolent Association, said during a press conference the day after the bill passed.

For Myrie and the others who pushed to pass the repeal, this was a historic moment. "50 years from now, some other kid from Brooklyn will look back and hopefully say, 'we used to have a system that didn't hold bad actors accountable, now we have something better,'" he said.

Speaking in 2021 — about a year after the repeal — he started to talk about when the vote happened, "I remember when the bill passed..." Then, Myrie grew emotional. He paused to collect himself. It took him a moment. The truth is, at this point he hadn't had a lot of time to think about this. After they passed the repeal, it was back to business as usual — dealing with Covid-19, an upcoming election. He says he didn't have a real chance to "stop and reflect."

He remembered after the bill passed he walked over to Sen. Bailey, his fellow senator who pushed the repeal and got it on the floor for vote. Myrie thanked him.

"I gave him a hug, thanked him for his leadership, for what it meant," he said.

Two days after the repeal vote, Gov. Cuomo signed the bill. Along with the repeal of 50-a, the governor signed into law a number of police reform bills that had been pushed in the state over the years. Another piece of legislation made the state attorney general's special unit for prosecuting police killings permanent. Another bill called the "Eric Garner Anti-Chokehold Act" made the use of an illegal chokehold by police a felony. That law created a new crime in the state called "aggravated strangulation" and carried a maximum sentence of 15 years.

"This is not just about Mr. Floyd's murder," Cuomo said before signing the new laws. "It's about being here before, many, many times before. It is about a long list that has been all across this country that always makes the same point: injustice against minorities in America by the criminal justice system."

Immediately following the repeal of 50-a, journalists and advocacy organizations began to file Freedom of Information Law requests with New York City to get their hands on NYPD disciplinary records. One such request was made by the NYCLU, seeking decades of disciplinary case information from the city's NYPD oversight body, the Civilian Complaint Review Board.

A few days after Cuomo signed the bill, de Blasio spoke out about the change to the law and said that next month the city planned to release a "massive" database of NYPD disciplinary records.

The mayor also said that he instructed the NYPD to publish its own disciplinary files online. He said the plan was for the police department to "do something historic" and publish "all records for every active member available in one place," including any "formal actions" that came out of disciplinary proceedings.

"Transparency is not something to fear, but something to embrace because that's where trust and faith will deepen, when people see that all this information is out in the open, just as it would be for any of us as citizens," the mayor said.

A New York City civil rights attorney involved in the 50-a repeal effort texted me that week with their reaction: "Winning is nice. The lawsuits come next."

They were right. About a month after the repeal, the police unions filed lawsuits in state and federal court to block the city's release of disciplinary data. They claimed in the lawsuit that the planned "data dump" of police records would "absolutely destroy the reputation and privacy — and imperil the safety" of many police officers.

They argued that the change to the law might lead to the release of "unsubstantiated" complaints that haven't been proven, which would violate their members' collective bargaining agreement, as well as due process under the Constitution, and "unfairly stigmatized" the city's 60,000 law enforcement officers and firefighters.

The fight to keep these law enforcement personnel records a secret was on. The unions hired veteran New York City public relations man Hank Sheinkopf as their spokesman. A high school dropout turned political super consultant, Sheinkopf had a PhD in political science, not to mention experience working on around 700 campaigns for a wide range of clients — including for Bill Clinton during his presidential reelection, former New York City mayor and billionaire Michael Bloomberg, police departments in over 20 states, and Local 237 in New York City, the largest local Teamsters union in the world.

A long-time defender of organized labor, when the unions reached out to him to handle their PR over their 50-a legal fight, Sheinkopf was more than happy to take the job. On the issue of the employee personnel records and disclosure, Sheinkopf said, "I thought it could have been settled through collective bargaining."

The union coalition dubbed themselves We Are All New York in their publicity campaign to get the word out about their legal fight against the release of disciplinary records. "We are defending privacy, integrity and the unsullied reputations of thousands of hard-working public safety employees," Sheinkopf told the media after the lawsuits were filed.

Initially, the unions won a small victory when a judge ordered a temporary stay to block the release of any records while the unions' case was heard. So whatever plan that the de Blasio administration concocted to release NYPD misconduct data would have to wait. The court battle also put a hold the NYCLU's plans to publish data that it received from the CCRB.

At the same time however, more NYPD disciplinary data started to make its way out of the shadows and into the sunlight. About two weeks after the unions filed their lawsuits against the city, *ProPublica* published a database of records it obtained from the CCRB. The database contained a list of about 4,000 active NYPD officers that had at least one allegation against them substantiated by the CCRB. Thus, it revealed that about 1-in-9 of the roughly 36,000 active cops on the force had a confirmed record of misconduct.

The unions' victory in court to suppress the release of NYPD misconduct data in the summer of 2020 was short lived. In August, the Second Circuit Court of Appeals held a hearing over the NYCLU's desire to publish its database of CCRB records it obtained via a public records request. The civil liberties group argued that the federal court order preventing them from publishing violated their First Amendment rights. The unions on the other hand accused the CCRB of engaging in an "unlawful scheme" by turning over the records to the NYCLU.

"Where is the concern?" Judge Rosemary Pooler asked the unions' attorneys in court. "You imply that there's something really malevolent of CCRB responding to this perfectly legitimate request for public information."

The Second Circuit ruled that the NYCLU could go ahead and publish and on August 20, 2020 the civil liberties organization put the records online. It was a truly massive trove of information. The database initially contained more than 300,000 disciplinary cases for 89,000 current and former NYPD officers. (A few months later, the NYCLU pared the database back to about 280,000 records after deduping the data.)

The data showed that nearly 20,000 officers had five or more civilian complaints of misconduct. According to the NYCLU, 8,699 of those complaints resulted in an officer facing punishment from the department. Twelve officers were terminated and dismissed after receiving one of these complaints.

Further analysis by the NYCLU revealed that White cops had been accused of misconduct far more often than cops of color. According to the data, White officers were accused in 61% of CCRB cases, Blacks in 14% and Latinos in 23%.

The next day, Manhattan federal court Judge Katherine Failla held a conference call with the media and the parties in the case brought by the unions to block the de Blasio administration from publishing its own database of NYPD misconduct records. On the call, Judge Failla read her opinion, in which she said the decision by the legislature to repeal 50-a was "not made haphazardly" and had been done "to aid underserved elements of New York's population." She denied the unions' motion and ruled the de Blasio administration could publish the disciplinary records online.

The judge said the unions had failed to demonstrate that releasing the records would cause reputational or physical harm to the officers and their families. She noted that the unions "could not provide a single example" of a time when the release of misconduct records created a threat to public safety.

"There are numerous states with more robust" access to law enforcement disciplinary records, the judge noted, "I don't see any safety issues in those states."

She also cited the release of NYPD records more than two years earlier through the BuzzFeed database and pointed out that she had seen no danger or threats arise from it.

The unions managed to tie the case up in court with its appeal for another few months. In February 2021, the Second Circuit made its decision to uphold Judge Failla's decision. In their ruling, the three-judge panel echoed the judge from the lower court, noting that many other states have made misconduct records at least partially public "without any evidence of a resulting increase of danger to police officers."

The panel said that the unions' arguments were "without merit." On their argument that the release of records would violate their contracts, the judges said that state law superseded their agreements. "The NYPD cannot bargain away its disclosure obligations," the ruling said.

Hank Sheinkopf said that the court decision was "not a great shock" to his clients.

"Everyone wished it went in another direction," he added.

The next month, the city put up its records from the CCRB of complaints for more than 83,000 current and former officers dating back to 2000.

In March 2021, the NYPD published its own database of officer personnel information online, a highly anticipated event. What the NYCLU and the city had put online thus far was limited to disciplinary information that an outside agency — in this case, the CCRB — had in its possession for the small percentage of police misconduct cases that it worked on.

Conversely, the department's database would contain the NYPD's own internal investigations. And it would be the first time since a few years earlier when the secret disciplinary files were published by

BuzzFeed that the public would have access to the NYPD's own records.

The NYPD's database published in spring 2021 included information for about 35,000 active police officers, the department said. In announcing their online portal, the NYPD's head of discipline Matthew Portillo told the media the searchable database contained a "baseball card" style profile of the officers. The publicly accessible records included information on each officer's awards and promotions, as well as limited disciplinary information. Portillo said the initial rollout would have information dating back to 2018, and eventually include records going back to 2009.

The disciplinary records initially put online by the NYPD were limited to decisions reached after a department trial. Cases that ended in "negotiated plea agreements" were not included. Some criminal justice advocates were disgusted by the limitations of what the NYPD put out itself. NYCLU director Donna Lieberman called it a "slap in the face." The PBA responded by calling the critics "the anti-cop lobby" that would never be satisfied.

"The anti-cop lobby got exactly what they wanted: a searchable database with more info about NYC police officers than is available for any other public employee," the Police Benevolent Association tweeted. "But they're still not happy. Why? Because "transparency & accountability" were never the goal."

From the people protesting in the streets after Eric Garner was killed in the summer of 2014, to the families of victims of police violence in New York; from the advocates and activists who fought for years to have 50-a repealed, to the people who demanded that police secrecy be addressed in the summer of 2020— the message was clear: New Yorkers wanted more accountability and transparency from the NYPD.

The NYPD received that message and responded that they would make up their own rules for how to do that.

The police department continued to periodically update their online portal with officer disciplinary records. As of January 2022, the NYPD said online that its databases included "charges and specifications and corresponding penalties resulting from a plea of guilty, plea of nolo contendere, or a finding of guilty after trial" for the years 2010 through 2021. The department also noted that they "will continue to work towards increasing transparency by expanding the information displayed on this site."

But two years after the initial rollout, many internal misconduct records were still missing from their database.

For NYPD cop Raymond Marrero, one of the officers featured in the original BuzzFeed investigation into the NYPD's secret disciplinary files, you'll find some details in the NYPD database about the internal charges and penalties he faced for beating a handcuffed person in the head with a police baton. But under Marrero's name there is something missing.

A year after that beating, Marrero held down a person in custody while another officer stepped on the person's head. He was charged with unnecessary use of force, failing to make a record of the incident in his activity log, and failing to notify Internal Affairs of the incident. He was also charged with making misleading statements for denying during his Internal Affairs interview that anybody used force against the person in custody.

When the Commission to Combat Police Corruption wrote about these incidents, they concluded that Marrero should have been fired because all of this misconduct — including the earlier baton beating — happened within four years of him joining the force. But Marrero kept his job.

As for the NYPD's online disciplinary database, it fails to mention that Marrero faced charges and was found guilty after he held down a person while they were stomped on. The database also doesn't list the charge he faced for misleading investigators. The database does note however that Marrero was promoted to sergeant in 2020.

In fact, a 2022 comparison of the Buzzfeed database to the NYPD's online disciplinary files shows that at least 40 NYPD cops like Marrero who committed documented dishonest acts have no record of their misconduct on the police department's website. Each of these cops was found guilty of charges including: making false or misleading statements to investigators, lying in court, or providing untruthful information on official police documents.

For example, in 2011, Bronx NYPD officer Lisa Marsh was penalized for acting with other officers to "defraud" the department by helping to cover up a crime. In October 2010, Jose Ayala was brutally beaten by a paint store manager after a fight over a parking spot in the Bronx. The man who beat up Ayala called a friend who worked at the NYPD's local 48th precinct and asked them to make the case go away. Marsh and several other officers helped sweep it under the rug. But it turned out that one of the officers involved in the conspiracy was part of an ongoing wiretap investigation and the plot was revealed.

Three other officers were criminally charged for the cover-up of the crime. Marsh was spared criminal charges but was suspended by the department for 30 days, docked 30 vacation days, and given a year of dismissal probation. However, if you search for her online profile, under disciplinary history it says: "This officer does not have any applicable entries."

Or, for example, in 2011, Officer Angela Polancobrito was charged with beating an individual with an asp — an expandable police baton that NYPD officers frequently carry on patrol. When she was interviewed by the Civilian Complaint Review Board about the incident she failed to report all the facts and identify herself on video, according to internal NYPD documents. The department placed Polancobrito on dismissal probation, suspended her for 32 days, and docked her 20 vacation days. However, if you search the NYPD's own database there is no record of this incident.

In 2011, Bronx DA Robert Johnson exposed a massive ticket fixing scandal at the NYPD. It cost the city millions in revenue, according to Johnson. Sixteen officers were criminally charged in the conspiracy. Scores of other officers were disciplined by the department for their involvement in squashing the tickets of friends and family. For the most part, those officers didn't lose their jobs, but they received a serious penalty of a year of probation and a 30 or 45 day suspension or loss of vacation time.

The data that was leaked to BuzzFeed covered penalties from 2011 to

2015, so there were at least a hundred misconduct entries in the files for ticket fixers. A database comparison to the NYPD's online portal shows that at least 42 NYPD officers who faced discipline for ticket fixing did not have a record of the misconduct in their online NYPD profile.

In total, I was able to identify 102 active officers with documented histories of serious misconduct missing from their online NYPD profiles in 2022. Along with the missing records of officer dishonesty, the NYPD database also failed to include the disciplinary history for other disturbing incidents. For example, in 2011, Officer Roberson Tunis was charged with repeated touching, making inappropriate comments, and "propositioning" another member of the force. He was found guilty of the charges, placed on dismissal probation, suspended for 30 days and docked another 30 days of vacation time. But under Tunis's disciplinary history in the NYPD's database it says: "This officer does not have any applicable entries."

In 2014, Officer Genti Bektashaj was found guilty of wrongfully using force against a person in custody. Bektashaj lifted the person up by handcuffs and twisted their arms. He also kicked and punched the person, according to the official NYPD documents. Bektashaj lost 10 vacation days as a penalty. Less than a month after the disciplinary case was closed, he was promoted to sergeant. Seven years later in 2021, he was promoted again to lieutenant. Under his disciplinary history on the department website it said: "This officer does not have any applicable entries."

In 2012, Officer Jarrett Dill was penalized for repeatedly calling and texting an individual in violation of a court order of protection. There are only sparse details available in the NYPD's disciplinary report, which was part of the leak to BuzzFeed, but the information does note that he threatened to kill the person. It also mentions that the offense happened while Dill was on dismissal probation.

The NYPD reserves the right to fire any officer who commits any infraction, no matter how minor, while on dismissal probation. But Dill wasn't fired over this violent threat. Instead, he was given another year of probation and suspended for 32 days.

Like the other officers discussed above, there was no mention of this misconduct in Dill's online profile in the NYPD database. When you search for Dill's name however, it does list other discipline he has faced — a penalty of probation and suspension for a 2016 incident where he struck a motorcyclist while driving drunk.

Assemblymember Dan O'Donnell said 50-a had to go because there was "40 years of bad case law out there."

"In order to get rid of the case law entirely, it had to be repealed," he said.

But on how satisfied he is with the NYPD's transparency efforts since 50-a repeal, he said, "I'm not."

On how he felt about the NYPD's transparency efforts since the repeal of 50-a, Zellnor Myrie said, "I think they have continued to obfuscate, to make excuses," he said.

He said that he appreciated that there have been "some efforts" at being more transparent by the police department. But he has his "suspicions" that the NYPD is "still trying to shield as much as they can."

Myrie and Assemblywoman Diana Richardson sued the city and the police department after the 2020 protests. But two years later, he still hadn't learned the identity of any of the cops that brutalized him on May 29, 2020.

"I still have no idea who pepper sprayed me," he said.

15

THE FIGHT FOR JUSTICE AFTER THE GEORGE FLOYD PROTESTS

On June 5, 2020, NYPD Commissioner Dermot Shea came out and said that the police department "had a plan" for the Mott Haven protest that the department "executed nearly flawlessly."

Shea was the third police commissioner to take charge of the NYPD under Mayor de Blasio, following Bill Bratton and James O'Neill.

The son of immigrants, Shea grew up in a small apartment with his family in Woodside, Queens. He and his brother both joined the NYPD as police officers in 1991.

Shea rose through the ranks at the department. Before being named Commissioner, he was Chief of the Department and the highly capable steward of Bill Bratton's signature data-driven crime fighting creation, CompStat. A gushing profile of Shea by *The Daily News* from 2017 talked about how he obsessed over the crime numbers, sleeping at the office on a cot the night before the weekly Compstat meeting. That way, he could stay up until the wee hours of night analyzing the numbers he planned to grill his commanders about the next morning.

On June 5, Shea directed his outrage at the protesters in the Bronx. He denigrated the Mott Haven demonstration, saying that it wasn't about protest rather, it was about "tearing down society." He claimed a gun and gasoline were recovered from individuals who intended to use them as weapons at the protest. This wasn't accurate however, and a few days later the department cleaned up the facts of Shea's statements. The gun, for instance, was recovered a mile from the protest from an individual with gang ties. As for the gasoline, there was none. But before these clarifications were put out by the NYPD's press shop, Mayor de Blasio went on WNYC's The Brian Lehrer Show and parroted Shea's earlier comments.

In the aftermath of the 2020 protests, the state Attorney General (AG) and the city's Department of Investigation (DOI) launched two investigations into NYPD conduct. The details of these probes would provide much more insight into how top police officials perceived what happened during the tumultuous eight days of demonstrations.

Shea told the AG's office that the police exercised "extreme discretion" during what he called "violent" protests citywide. He said incidents of police misconduct were "isolated." When AG Letitia James brought up the incident where NYPD officers drove into a group of protesters in Brooklyn, Shea defended the cops who he said "were set upon and attacked and got out of [the] situation with no injuries." He also said that the officers who were driving the cars did not violate the department's Use of Force policy.

A strong defense by Shea of his officers in the face of scrutiny by the AG, the state's top law enforcement official, should have been expected. Still, some of his answers during his interview with James were baffling because they didn't seem to fully comport with the NYPD's own policies and practices. For example, when he was asked about the kettling of protesters — like what occurred in Mott Haven — Shea suggested he'd never heard of the term.

"I was never familiar with it until about two weeks ago and I've heard it more in two weeks than I've ever heard it. I believe I know what they're referring to — it's corralling, if you will, protesters. But it's not something that to my knowledge exists in our policies," Shea said.

While the word "kettling" may not appear in the NYPD's Patrol Guide there is evidence that the police department trains its officers in this tactic. The NYPD Strategic Response Group (SRG), for example, teaches its officers to do what they call "encirclement," which according to the unit's field guide refers to a formation to be "utilized when there is a need to take a group of people into custody."

Similarly, when Shea was asked about the arrests of legal observers during the protests, he said, "Legal observers, I'm not sure what you're referring to there."

"Having a shirt or a hat that says Legal Observer, does not mean that person is an attorney ... that they're actually performing any legal function," Shea said.

If he was truly confused by what James was referring to when she asked about legal observers, then Shea need not look any further than his department's own Patrol Guide for answers. The Patrol Guide outlined the "Demonstration Observer Program" and recognized the rights of people to observe, record, and document police activity at protests. It stated that officers are supposed to be courteous and cooperate with observers.

"Observers shall be permitted to remain in any area, or observe any police activity, subject only to restrictions necessitated by personal safety factors, as determined by the incident commander," the Patrol Guide said.

James's office said during their investigation that they found that during the 2020 protests the NYPD beat people with blunt instruments at least 50 times, unlawfully pepper-sprayed them in at least 30 instances, and pushed or struck protesters at least 75 times. They said that the SRG used their bikes as "weapons" against the demonstrators. The attorney general concluded that the police "blatantly violated the rights of New Yorkers."

"It is impossible to deny that many New Yorkers have lost faith in law enforcement," James told the media on the day she released her report.

When Shea met with the DOI, he told them that the police did a "phenomenal job." He initially conceded during his interview that at times the police department was "flying blind" during the protests — a contrast to the message he put out the day after Mott Haven when he said the police executed its plan "flawlessly." However, asked later in the interview if he thought the NYPD was "sufficiently prepared" for the demonstrations, the commissioner replied, "I do."

During its investigation, the DOI also interviewed Chief of Department Terence Monahan. In the months that followed the wave of protests over George Floyd's murder, Monahan emerged as a key figure in the NYPD's response. During the week of demonstrations, he made headlines when he took a knee and locked hands with protesters. He told them that not a single cop here thinks that what happened to George Floyd was "justified."

Like Shea, Monahan also said he wasn't previously familiar with the term kettling. "First time I heard kettling was when I read it in the paper," he told DOI.

"The word 'kettling' has been used by the media, it's never been used by the police," Monahan later told me. Asked if he wished he did anything differently in Mott Haven, he said, "that night, no."

In December 2020, DOI issued a 111-page report on its investigation into the NYPD's response to the George Floyd protests. The investigators found that the police department's use of force and crowd control tactics "contributed to the heightened tension" of the times. They said the department's response to the protests lacked a "clearly defined strategy" and the "fact that the target of the protests was policing itself" did not appear to be factored into the NYPD's strategy "in any meaningful way."

The report criticized the police's use of "encirclement (commonly called "kettling"), mass arrests, baton and pepper spray use" as a "failure" by the police to strike a balance between public safety, officer safety and the rights of protesters to express their First Amendment-protected views. On the curfew, DOI said the NYPD's application was "inconsistent" and raised concerns about "selective enforcement."

DOI concluded that the police kettled and mass arrested the protesters at Mott Haven without evidence that violence was imminent, as some at the department had suggested. They said that the Mott Haven episode was an example where "limited intelligence was used to justify a disproportionate response." Furthermore, DOI concluded the police trapped the protesters "prior to the curfew" and prevented them from leaving before playing the order to disperse message on a loud-speaker.

"Even if protesters received and heard the message ... it was impossible for most protesters to leave before the curfew because by that point officers ... had already employed formations that surrounded a substantial number of the protesters prior to the curfew and blocked their ability to move," the report said.

Among the 20 recommendations that DOI made in its report was that the department stop sending the SRG to protests. They recommended that the department create a new 'Protest Response Unit,' that does not report to the SRG. They said the SRG should stick to handling "counterterrorism, riots, and other serious threats."

However, the NYPD continued to use the SRG to police protests after the fact. And as of 2022, a description of the unit on the department website still listed "crowd control" as one of the group's missions. It stated that the SRG "has proven to be a critical asset during events like parades, protests ... demonstrations, or other significant incidents."

On what NYPD officials said about the department's performance during the 2020 protests, the DOI investigators wrote that while they acknowledged some "shortcomings" the officials interviewed "did not otherwise identify any flaws" in the NYPD planning or performance.

"When DOI asked NYPD officials whether, in retrospect, the Department could have done anything differently and made any further changes to improve its response to the protests, with few exceptions, officials offered none," the report said.

The morning DOI announced its findings, Mayor de Blasio issued an apology video. "I wish I had done better," the mayor said, adding "our police department has to do better." Asked later on that day to clarify what actions specifically he was apologizing for, de Blasio didn't provide any further details but said that the DOI report "makes clear that we should have had a better strategy."

"We really missed an opportunity given the tremendous frustration that people had after the murder of George Floyd, to try to exhibit a more understanding," de Blasio said.

Both de Blasio and Shea initially vowed in the summer of 2020 that any officer who committed wrongdoing during the George Floyd protests would be held accountable through discipline. But in the months that followed, the department disciplinary process for alleged misconduct at the rallies proved to have very limited impact.

In his interview with the attorney general, where Shea said that the misconduct by NYPD officers at the protests was "isolated," he told the AG that only ten officers had been disciplined. That summer, reports surfaced of just two suspensions of officers seen harming people at protests. One of those officers, Vincent D'Andraia, the cop caught on camera throwing a woman to the ground, was also criminally charged. New York City later paid the woman $387,000 to settle her lawsuit against the city. D'Andraia was ordered to pay $3,000 of his own money as a condition of the settlement.

The vast amount of cell phone and other video of the clashes between the NYPD and protesters didn't necessarily translate to more accountability for the police. In the immediate aftermath of the protests, *The New York Times* put together a compilation of police brutality that showed 64 cops attacking and beating demonstrators. De Blasio responded that any officer caught on camera committing a violent act would be disciplined. But New York City-based local online media outlet *The City* later found out that of the dozens of cops captured in these videos, just five faced discipline while the rest were cleared by the department of any wrongdoing.

The moment officers grabbed legal observer Krystin Hernandez and slammed them to the ground was captured on video by a nearby protester. The clip of their violent detainment was among the many videos that went viral on social media that week. It was also included in the *New York Times* video compilation. But *The City* later learned that the officers who detained Hernandez were "exonerated" by the NYPD and never disciplined.

Separately, the CCRB launched investigations into the hundreds of complaints they received from those harmed at the protests. The agency said it received over 750 complaints of police misconduct stemming from the protests. Those complaints resulted in 321 cases involving over 2,000 misconduct allegations against over 500 officers that fell within CCRB's jurisdiction.

During its investigation, the CCRB said it faced "unprecedented challenges" because of a "lack of proper protocol" by officers during the protests. This included officers covering their names and shields, wearing protective equipment that belonged to someone else, improperly using body worn cameras, and improperly completing paperwork, the agency said.

Two years into its investigation into the protest complaints, the CCRB said it was only able to substantiate misconduct in just 27% of the 321 cases that fell under its jurisdiction.

"Out of the 321 cases, the CCRB conducted full investigations for 223 cases and substantiated misconduct in 87 cases," said CCRB Interim-Chair Arva Rice at the agency's monthly board meeting in May 2022. "The CCRB has recommended misconduct against 143 members of service, 88 of whom have been recommended the highest level of discipline."

But of those 143 officers that the CCRB recommended discipline for, as of May 2022, just 18 officers — or about 12% — were actually punished by the department.

In early 2021, it became clear that at least one high ranking official would face no repercussions: Chief of the Department Terence Monahan. In February 2021, Monahan announced he was retiring from the force after 39 years. The NYPD's highest ranking patrol cop wasn't planning on leaving the public sector, however. Mayor de Blasio tapped him for the role of his senior Covid advisor. Monahan's new gig came with an annual salary of more than $240k, which he would collect on top of his six-figure police pension.

Regarding Monahan's actions at the 2020 protests, the mayor said that he would still be interviewed by the CCRB for their investigations. However, since he was no longer officially with the police department, any potential disciplinary charges over Monahan's conduct was a moot issue.

At the press conference announcing Monahan's new role, de Blasio called him a "passionate" NYPD leader who "loves this city" and "loves making sure people are safe." The mayor was asked by a reporter what message it sends to the NYPD rank-and-file that its highest ranking officer can retire, get a new job, and won't face any potential consequences over what happened during the 2020 protests. "I think the message this sends is that we're moving the recovery forward and the city needs to move forward," de Blasio responded.

The police crackdown in the summer of 2020 mirrored the NYPD's actions during the 2004 Republican National Convention (RNC). Among the scores of misconduct allegations by protesters against the NYPD during the RNC were the unlawful detainment of hundreds at a dirty, dark, damp pier on the banks of the Hudson River. A decade later, the city ended up paying out more than $18 million to settle civil rights lawsuits with protesters who claimed they were brutalized.

Monahan was in the middle of the NYPD's RNC protest response as well. On August 31, 2004, a group of protesters marching down Fulton Street in Manhattan were told by an NYPD inspector they could keep going if they stayed on the sidewalk. "Have a safe march," the inspector told the group, according to an internal CCRB memo.

Moments later, Monahan, a deputy chief at the time, ordered them to stop. He was without a bullhorn, so he yelled out to the group that they were blocking the sidewalk and would be arrested if they did not disperse. But the group had nowhere to go. They were trapped between a fence and a row of cops that had kettled them. Less than a minute later, Monahan ordered the entire group arrested.

In a 2006 letter to NYPD Commissioner Ray Kelly, the CCRB's leadership wrote that the Fulton Street marchers "who wanted to comply" with Monahan's order to disperse had "limited means" to leave the area because they were trapped between a fence and the police.

"They were blocked by a wrought iron fence on their left, a line of police officers on bicycles on their right, and other marchers in front of and behind them," the letter said. "The only realistic departure route for those who wished to leave — and the footage suggests that many marchers did not want to be arrested — would have been through the line of officers, some of whom did not hear the chief's dispersal order and therefore prevented civilians from passing."

Just as was the case following the RNC protests, the city and the police department found themselves facing multiple lawsuits over alleged NYPD misconduct in 2020. In the fall of 2020, advocates from the NYCLU and the Legal Aid Society, as well as the state's attorney general, filed lawsuits.

Civil rights attorneys Gideon Oliver, Elena Cohen and Remy Green were all being contacted by people who had been victims of police brutality at the George Floyd protests. Oliver knew Cohen and Green — who met at a dog fashion show years earlier then later decided to form a law firm — through the National Lawyers Guild. Oliver had experience representing protesters harmed by the police dating back to the RNC. Cohen and Green had been representing protesters who were arrested since the "Occupy Wall Street" demonstrations in 2011. The trio of attorneys all worked together on a lawsuit on behalf of Black Lives Matters protesters who won a $750,000 settlement after they were targeted by NYPD with Long Range Acoustic Devices (LRAD) — also known as a sound cannon — during a demonstration following Eric Garner's death in 2014.

They decided to join forces again to represent many of the people who were reaching out after the George Floyd protests. The group's clients included brutalized legal observers like Krystin Hernandez and protesters like Brett Bates and Dan Edelstein who suffered injuries and were arrested in Mott Haven.

With the lawsuits flooding in, a Manhattan federal judge decided to consolidate the cases in January 2021 for the purposes of hopefully streamlining what was sure to be an arduous discovery process. The judge put the case on an accelerated timeline — colloquially referred to as a "rocket docket" — and said that she wanted it to reach a resolution in about a year's time. For a litigation this complex — hundreds of alleged victims, dozens of officers accused of violating civil rights — this was a staggeringly ambitious timeline.

The city moved to have the lawsuits dismissed. Attorneys for the Law Department cited reforms by the NYPD — like a new disciplinary matrix that laid out proposed penalties for different types of misconduct — as reasons to throw out the case. But the judge didn't buy the argument that these policy changes were enough for the city and the police to atone for what the 2020 protesters were claiming. In the summer of 2021, she ruled that the case would continue.

It was a big win for the plaintiffs, but in order to keep fighting their cases they needed the city to start turning over the evidence. Their attorneys made a 50-page request for information like police body worn camera footage and internal investigation documents. They also wanted to interview dozens of cops. But months into the litigation, the defense attorneys for the city had provided only a small portion of the records to the other side. The protesters' attorneys pleaded with the judge, who threatened to sanction the city if they continued to miss deadlines. But the delays continued.

"The city's recalcitrance has paid off so far," Gideon Oliver said about a year into the litigation.

The city's tactic is "delay, delay, delay, obfuscate, refuse to give information," Elena Cohen said, adding that this was "an incredibly effective strategy."

"They know if they just delay, promise, don't produce, maybe you're going to forget about stuff," she said. "It's a very frustrating process."

Cohen called this the "standard way" that the city approaches cases involving police misconduct. She said that when she talks to other attorneys from other places around the country, they are "shocked" that New York attorneys "have to spend so many hours" on these types of cases.

The idea of a rocket docket for the 2020 protest litigation was not really panning out. The deadline for discovery set by the judge was the last day of the year, December 31, 2021. But the city continued to miss deadlines. By early 2022, the judge had sanctioned Law Department lawyer Dara Weiss, the senior attorney on the litigation who had worked at the Law Department for 18 years, five times for failing to comply with the court's direction.

No other episode better epitomized how fraught the situation with the protest litigation had become than what happened in the spring of 2022, nearly two years after the actual demonstrations in New York City.

And at the center of the incident was infamous police union boss Ed Mullins.

Civil rights attorney Rob Rickner was one of the more than dozen attorneys representing people suing the city and the police. Rickner, a member of the National Lawyers Guild like Cohen, Green and Oliver, recalled how he and other guild members started discussing prior to the protests in the spring of 2020 what to expect in terms of a police crackdown. "We knew what was coming," he said. "It was like, 'Here we go again.'"

When the lawsuits started getting filed after the police brutality in the summer, Rickner was brought in by some colleagues to represent a number of clients, including the Sierra sisters, Amali and Samira, two Black Dominican women and life-long Bronx residents who were at the protest in Mott Haven.

During the Mott Haven protest, the Sierra sisters were caught in the kettle when the police moved in on the demonstrators. Amali was thrown to the ground by police while she was simply putting a water bottle into her backpack. Samira pleaded with the police to stop, telling the officers that her sister had multiple sclerosis. One of the officers responded: "Don't come to a riot when you have MS, how about that!" Both women were arrested with the other protesters and spent the night locked up in Queens.

Rickner and his colleagues wanted to illustrate to the court their claim that the NYPD targeted areas like Mott Haven with brutal crackdowns because they were poor and mostly minority neighborhoods. So during the discovery period they requested that the city and NYPD turn over all documents and communication connected to a video that they learned was shared on email amongst police officers the summer before the protests. The video was loaded with racist commentary about lower income city dwellers. The email was sent by none other than Ed Mullins.

In August 2019, the *New York Post* reported that Mullins sent an email to union members with a link to a video and a message: "Pay close attention to every word. You will hear what goes through the mind of real policemen every single day on the job. This is the best video I've ever seen telling the public the absolute truth."

The 15-minute video depicts a police shooting in Los Angeles while an overtly racist narrator delivers remarks like, "Cops will continue to wade into that fray and Blacks will continue to attack and ambush us forever."

The narrator — identified by *Gothamist* as Willie Shields, a radio host and conspiracy theorist — says while reading from a letter from a police officer: "One of the most astonishing aspects of police work in an urban environment is that almost literally no one has a job."

"Section 8 scam artists and welfare queens have mastered the art of gaming the taxpayer. Bounce from baby mama to baby mama, impregnate as many women as possible." Shields adds.

The *New York Post* reported that after Mullins shared the video one of recipients emailed him back and asked, "Did you listen to this thing?" Mullins then wrote a follow-up email apologizing for sharing the video. "There is no one to blame but me for the video that was distributed," Mullins wrote. "For those members who may have been offended by the video, I sincerely apologize."

Rickner and his colleagues believed that the disparaging attitude towards poor minorities that Mullins conveyed with his email reflected what you saw on the street with how the NYPD policed these lower income neighborhoods like Mott Haven in New York City. During the discovery period in the litigation, the attorneys requested all the records that the NYPD had on file related to the email and the embattled union leaders. It was their theory that after Mullins sent this message to over 1,000 other officers, his decision to share the racist video must have traveled up the chain of command.

"It obviously got passed around a lot afterwards. The idea that nobody said anything anywhere is ridiculous," Rickner said. "We wanted that piece of the puzzle."

The judge ruled that the city had to turn over what it had on Mullins to the protest plaintiffs. But Weiss and her team at the Law Department failed to comply with this order for months. Rickner pressed the judge to sanction the city over its resistance to provide the

Mullins files. Eventually, the city sent the plaintiffs some of Mullins' disciplinary history, but what they turned over didn't include anything related to the 2019 email.

Rickner claimed to the judge that the files that the city turned over were incomplete and the court ordered Weiss and her team to meet with him and the other plaintiffs' attorneys to discuss. Then, after months of this arguing over the Mullins file, an absolute bombshell landed. In the spring of 2022, Weiss was fired from the Law Department.

After the judge ordered that Weiss meet with the plaintiffs' attorneys to discuss their claims that there were missing Mullins documents, the Law Department again failed to respond and set up a meeting. When Rickner complained to the judge that Weiss hadn't responded to his emails about this meeting, she accused him of making a false statement in court. To back this up, Weiss sent Rickner and his colleagues a PDF of an alleged email from her to prove that she did respond to Rickner and others. However, Rickner and the other attorneys noticed irregularities in the PDF, including that some of the email addresses were misspelled.

Rickner pressed Weiss to forward the actual emails but she resisted. He then informed Weiss that he hired a digital forensic expert who investigated and concluded that the email in the PDF wasn't real. At that point, Weiss wrote back to Rickner: "While attempting to send the email to you as an attachment, I came to realize that the email was never actually sent, which explains why no counsel never received it."

A couple days later, Patricia Miller, the head of the Law Department's Special Federal Litigation Division informed the court it had become clear to them that Weiss made "misrepresentations" involving these communications and her employment has been terminated. After she was fired, Weiss told the *New York Times*, "Under great pressure I made an unintentional mistake."

The following week, the city declared on the court record that the NYPD never conducted a probe of Mullins for the racist email. Genevieve Nelson, another senior attorney from the Law Department's Special Federal Litigation Division, wrote to the court telling the judge that a police department attorney "reiterated that NYPD did not conduct an investigation into the circulation of a 2019 video."

Even two years after the 2020 protests, it was evident that it would be a long time before many of the lawsuits would reach their conclusions. Still, by then the actions of the NYPD in the summer of 2020 had already cost NYC taxpayers millions.

When he was in the cell on the night of June 4, 2020 somebody made a remark to Brett Bates that he'll "get some money" for what the NYPD did to him. Getting compensated for his injuries wasn't on Bates' mind at the time. But after he was charged with unlawful assembly he thought he should get a lawyer to help him deal with that.

A friend told Bates to call Gideon Oliver. When he talked to Oliver about what happened they agreed that Bates had grounds to pursue a lawsuit. But Bates was uneasy about it.

"It obviously feels very odd," he said. "Like there's a conflict or something seedy about going to protest and coming out looking for money."

But after talking with Oliver, he was convinced it was "morally acceptable." Bates began working with Oliver, Cohen and Green, and within six months, they got the unlawful assembly charge thrown out. It would take longer to deal with the civil claim, however.

Bates met with the city comptroller's office over his claim. He first had to sit through a 50-h hearing, in which the comptroller would decide whether or not Bates had a legitimate claim. Bates was asked who he had attended the protest with and whether he was a member of any organizations. But for the most part the interview was "pretty low-key," he said.

Dan Edelstein also put in a claim with the comptroller's officer. He said that when he sat for his interview with the comptroller the city's lawyer was a "real asshole." He said the attorney was trying to "put words in my mouth" and asked him questions about what he had been chanting and who started the pushing. In the end, the comptroller's office offered him $60,000 to settle out of court and he accepted. It was more than enough to cover his medical bills — which, at around

$6,000, for the CAT scan on his broken hand, physical therapy, etc. were not insignificant.

In his interview, Bates told the investigators that he was scared to go to protests and rallies after what happened to him in the Bronx. The annual PRIDE parade took place in New York City during the same month of the Mott Haven protest. Bates is gay and normally PRIDE is a "big deal" for him. But he decided to skip it that year.

"I had no interest in mixing it up with the NYPD," he said.

While the city continued to litigate numerous lawsuits, more and more brutality claims were being settled out of court with the comptroller. After the police violence in Mott Haven on June 4, 2020, the Bronx Defenders brought a claim on behalf of a group of 23 people who dubbed themselves the "Mott Haven Collective." In their claim, they made a demand to the comptroller that the city should "fairly compensate people" and they shouldn't have to file lawsuits.

"It should be that the city does right by those people, does right, right away," Bronx Defenders' attorney Jennifer Rolnick Borchetta said.

Within a year of what happened in Mott Haven, Borchetta said the group of 23 received offers from the city comptroller to settle cases ranging from $30,000 – 90,000, totalling over a million dollars. Remy Green also said that within about a year of the protests that their team had already settled claims with the comptroller for clients that cost the city around $1 million.

While the offers they got were good, Borchetta said "this process treated our clients like processed meat." The victims of abuse at the protest were subjected to lengthy interviews and had to turn over "intimate details" about their lives in order to even get a settlement offer, she said. In contrast, Borchetta said, the NYPD officers don't "even come into this process."

"The NYPD officer who beat somebody bloody doesn't have to talk, turn over video, provide nothing," she said. While she understands the comptroller's obligation to ensure that the people who come forward have real claims, Borchetta said the extensive questioning and documentation requirements "cause more harm."

"It's not necessary," she said.

In total, the city settled 183 claims from 2020 protesters out of court, according to data obtained from the comptroller's office. These settlements ranged from $3,000 to $185,000. All together, these out-of-court settlements cost the city's taxpayers $5,209,620.

Bates' lawyers told him that if he went forward with a lawsuit they thought he could possibly get a lot more money, especially if they went to trial and it was up to a Bronx jury, which would likely be comprised of people who have witnessed police brutality first hand. But they also told him it might be five years or a very long time before that happened. Bates wanted to put all this behind him and to get closure in his life. The comptroller's office offered him $65,000. He took the money.

He still doesn't know the identity of the cop that hit him on the head. He briefly spoke to the CCRB but decided not to go forward with a complaint.

"I got hit from behind. I'm not even sure who I would be trying to hold accountable," he said.

Bates believed that even if he were able to identify the cop, it wouldn't have been worth it to go through a "prolonged process" with the CCRB. He didn't have much confidence in the police disciplinary system or its ability to hand down serious consequences for violent cops like the one who attacked him.

"Frankly, I feel this guy would have gotten a slap on the wrist, then some cop's wife would've made him lasagna and told him 'it's so terrible what they do to cops,'" he said.

16

THE ELECTION OF MAYOR ERIC ADAMS: A NEW ADMINISTRATION MOVES AWAY FROM POLICE ACCOUNTABILITY

During the campaign in 2021 to succeed Bill de Blasio as mayor, Eric Adams, a former NYPD captain who spent 22 years on the force before entering politics, positioned himself as the most *tough on crime* candidate in a crowded Democratic field. In his eyes, he was the perfect person to lead the city's public safety efforts because of his experience as an NYPD insider; and he vowed to have the cops' backs as their mayor. At the same time, Adams pledged that he would be intolerant of abusive cops who he said would have no place in the police department under his administration.

Adams entered the mayoral race in late 2020 with New York City still in the thick of the Covid-19 pandemic. At the time, the city was also set to conclude the year with grim spikes in shootings and murders. New York City ended 2020 with 468 murders — a 47% spike compared to 319 the year before 2019. The police also tallied 1,531 shooting incidents in 2020, up 97% from 2019 (776). These levels of violent crime numbers had not been seen in New York in fifteen years. However, the numbers were nowhere near what occurred in the city during the peaks in the 1990s.

Because Democrats outnumbered Republicans nearly 7-to-1 in New York City, the results of the summer 2021 Democratic primary were overwhelmingly likely to decide the next mayor. And in the months leading up to that pivotal primary vote, polls revealed that crime was a key issue with voters. A Spectrum News NY1/Ipsos poll in the spring showed that for 51% of Democratic voters in New York City, the Covid-19 pandemic was the main issue but "crime or violence" was second — 39% called it the main problem. When asked what the next mayor's priorities should be, 32% of voters said crime and safety, which ranked third behind stopping the spread of Covid-19 and reopening business.

On the campaign trail, Adams argued for increasing support and resources for the city's law enforcement to lower crime. He defended the police department's use of stop and frisk, which he called a "great tool" if used the right way. He also decried the notion of defunding the police that several of his fellow candidates supported. In 2020, in the wake of George Floyd's death, de Blasio and the City Council claimed to shift $1 billion from the NYPD budget amid an outcry from advocates and police reform activists calling for a cut to the police funding. In reality, the police budget cuts amounted to less than half of what de Blasio claimed. And in subsequent budgets, items that the lawmakers claimed they were scaling back — like for example the hundreds of millions spent on police overtime each year — were increased for the NYPD.

During his campaign, Adams told *Bloomberg News* he had always been against defunding the police. "I have been fighting for police reform and safer streets for decades — and I have never been in a neighborhood meeting in a high-crime community of color where someone has asked for fewer police," Adams said. "That is why I have been against the defund movement from the start."

In what some activists and progressive New Yorkers saw as his most controversial public safety idea, Adams also vowed to revitalize the NYPD's anti-crime unit, a controversial group of plainclothes officers within the department. Initially known at the NYPD as the 'Street Crimes Unit,' these plainclothes cops were responsible for a disproportionately high number of police killings in the city. This included the 1999 killing of Amadou Diallo, who was shot by four police officers who fired at him 41 times while he was on his apartment stoop.

After Diallo's killing, a report commissioned by the state's attorney general Eliot Spitzer revealed that the unit unfairly targeted the city's Black and Hispanic residents. In 2002, Commissioner Ray Kelly announced that the NYPD was disbanding the Street Crimes Unit. But the officers from those teams were just assigned to other plainclothes anti-crime units and the problems persisted. Between 2000 and 2018, the anti-crime cops were responsible for about a third of the police killings by the department, despite accounting for just 6% of the force. The former officer who killed Eric Garner in 2014, Daniel Pantaleo, was a plainclothes member of the anti-crime unit.

In the wake of the George Floyd protests in the city, in June 2020, NYPD Commissioner Dermot Shea announced that the police department was disbanding its anti-crime units. Shea said that the roughly 600 plainclothes officers from 77 precincts around the city would be reassigned. The commissioner called the move a "seismic shift." He declared that it was time for the police department to "move away" from the "brute force" tactics of the past.

The following year, Adams promised to bring back a reformed version of the anti-crime unit if elected. "We should not throw out the baby with the bathwater. Having a good Anti-Crime team will continue to take guns off the streets," Adams said in an interview with WNYC. "We can do it right, we'll get it right, and we'll make sure our city is safe." But in making good on this promise, Adams would also reveal that in terms of tolerating abusive cops within his NYPD ranks, Adams was willing to bend.

In the summer of 2021, Adams emerged as the victor in the Democratic primary and went on to be elected mayor that November. He became just the second Black mayor in the city's history after David Dinkins decades earlier.

In the early days after he took office, Adams spoke of his commitment to hold officers accountable. On his first day on the job, Adams paid a visit to the NYPD's 103rd precinct in Queens, the precinct that policed the neighborhood where he grew up. Over the years, Adams talked frequently about how he grew up as a poor Black boy in Queens who had his share of run-ins with the police. At age 15, Adams and his brother were arrested and brought to the 103rd precinct where they were beaten by the cops, he said. Later on, Adams said he was recruited to join the NYPD and try to change its culture from the inside. In 2015, he told Liz Strong, an oral historian at Columbia University, that he saw joining the police department as "an opportunity to go in and just aggravate people."

Addressing the group of Queens officers gathered inside the station house on New Year's Day in 2022, Adams told the cops, "We have the finest among us and sometimes unfortunately we have a small number of the worst among us."

"I'm going to have your backs," he told them. "But if you are abusive to my community, I'm going to make sure you don't serve in my department and you don't hurt your fellow officers."

As his first police commissioner, Mayor Adams appointed Keechant Sewell, making her the first female NYPD commissioner in the history of the department. Adams announced Sewell's appointment at an event outside the Queensbridge Houses in Long Island City, Queens where she grew up. He told the press that he conducted a "nationwide search" for his police commissioner and believed Sewell was "the right woman to lead New York's Finest at this critical moment in our city's history." During the ceremony, Adams brought up his own history with the NYPD and once again reaffirmed his commitment to police accountability.

"As someone who wore a bulletproof vest for 22 years protecting the children and families of this city, today is a very meaningful day." he said, adding that he personally has "been a clear and consistent voice for accountability throughout my law enforcement career."

"Because I know that when an officer violates their oath to protect and serve, it undermines the nobility of public protection," Adams added.

Not unlike his predecessor de Blasio — who made good early in his first term on a campaign promise when he dropped the city's appeal in the class action lawsuit over the NYPD's use of stop and frisk — Adams also fulfilled a promise he made to voters — he reestablished the police department's anti-crime unit. In March 2022, Adams and Sewell introduced their new iteration of the unit, rebranding it the "Neighborhood Safety Teams." The mayor and commissioner told the public that these officers would be deployed throughout the city to areas experiencing the highest levels of shootings and other violent crimes. The new unit would have the same primary mandate as before: get illegal guns off the street. Adams and Sewell said that the officers would no longer work in plainclothes; instead, they would wear uniforms and equip themselves with body cameras. And the city officials ensured the public that this new anti-gun unit would not continue the abuses of the past.

On who would be eligible to join the new unit, Adams said they planned on picking the "right officers."

"You must have the right training, the right mindset, the right disposition and be, as I say all the time, emotionally intelligent enough that you are getting ready to engage someone in the street," Adams said at a March 2022 press conference. "So we are going to make sure the 400-plus people in the pipeline to go into our new unit, that they are the best fit for the unit."

After the Neighborhood Safety Teams launched in the spring of 2022, the city denied public records requests from journalists to learn which officers had been appointed to the teams. The NYPD claimed that revealing the rosters "could endanger the life or safety" of those officers. Furthermore, the department said that releasing the names "would allow for an individual or group to modify their conduct to evade or undermine the NYPD's capabilities." It appeared that the police department and Adams administration was determined to keep the members of its new anti-gun operation a secret. But one journalist found a loophole.

In the spring of 2022, a reporter for NYFocus.com, Chris Gelardi, published a list of NYPD officers who had undergone the NYPD's new Neighborhood Safety Teams training program. Gelardi wrote that he obtained the list of officers from citizen watchdogs who were monitoring the NYPD's online portal, which tracks what training each officer receives. The NYPD responded to the report by saying that just because the officers underwent the training didn't necessarily mean that they'd be assigned to the Neighborhood Safety Team. However, as Gelardi noted in his article, the number of officers who received the training matched up nearly exactly with the number of officers that the NYPD said were assigned to the teams. As of May 2022, "164 patrol officers and 43 higher-ranked officers were listed as having taken both courses, while the NYPD said that 163 patrol officers and 45 "supervisors" had been assigned to the teams as of the same date," Gelardi wrote.

When he dug into who these officers were, Gelardi found that many of the officers who had undergone the training for the new anti-gun unit had been accused of abusing the public in the past. "13 percent of the officers who have taken both [Neighborhood Safety Team] courses have at least five complaints, and eight of the officers have at least 10," he wrote.

This analysis focused on each officer's history of complaints to the department's outside watchdogs at the CCRB. However, a closer look at the officers on the list of trainees showed that several of these cops also had a documented history of being found guilty and subsequently disciplined by the department for serious misconduct.

Since he started on the force in 1997, Lieutenant Mervin Bennett had faced 19 complaints from civilians containing 34 allegations over his career. According to the CCRB, none of those complaints were sustained. However, Bennett faced serious department discipline on two occasions in consecutive years, according to NYPD records.

In 2017, Bennett was ordered to undergo counseling and docked 30 vacation days after he made multiple telephone calls and sent multiple text messages and gifts to a former girlfriend after she asked him to stop. The following year, Bennett was disciplined again for failing to comply with a "lawful order to cease contact with a person known to the department."

A few years earlier in 2013, Lieutenant Bennett, who was one of the most senior cops to undergo training for Adams's new "elite" unit during its initial roll-out period, also had his name come up at the trial in the *Floyd* stop and frisk case.

One of the secret tapes that was recorded by an officer who testified about the NYPD's alleged quota system for making stops contained audio of Bennett condoning the unconstitutional stop and frisk practice deployed by the NYPD in the Bronx. In one of the tapes played at trial — which was secretly recorded by Officer Adhyl Polanco — Bennett can be heard seething over officers who don't make the '20-and-1' quota (20 stops, 1 arrests per month) that several of the officers who testified at the *Floyd* trial complained was being foisted upon them.

"If you want to be a zero, I'll treat you like a zero," said Bennett, a patrol sergeant at the time who supervised Polanco.

"So we're going to start correcting and treating those who want to fight the cause and fight the power — that's no problem. No problem. Your names, each one of your names are important ... Trust me, your name is important," Bennett added.

Bennett was captured on tape telling the Bronx officers to "do your 8 hours and 35 minutes a day and go home, and just do your job."

"You could be disgruntled, fine," he said. "Welcome to the NYPD. That's part of the nature of the job."

Another of the most highly ranked officers who underwent Neighborhood Safety Team training, Lieutenant Ramiro Ruiz, faced at least 15 civilian complaints stemming from 33 allegations. Unlike Bennett, several of the alleged incidents of misconduct contained in these complaints were sustained by the CCRB, including an allegation that Ruiz hit someone with a nightstick. According to NYFocus.com, the CCRB also confirmed Ruiz was the arresting officer among a group of plainclothes cops who allegedly choked a man and tried to delete video from his phone when he began recording them during a traffic stop. Ruiz was also included on the Manhattan DA's adverse credibility list — a group of cops whose credibility has been questioned by judges in court. Because of this history of dishonesty in court, prosecutors were advised to think twice about calling officers like Ruiz to testify in their cases.

Just like Bennett, according to the NYPD's own records Lieutenant Ruiz also had a documented history of abuse and dishonesty on his record. Ruiz's internal disciplinary history showed that in one case he was found guilty by the NYPD of failing to provide additional information and impeding investigators at a scene where a firearm was discharged. In another case, the department found that Ruiz improperly used physical force against someone, failed to arrest a person who struck an officer, then made misleading statements and impeded the department's investigation by failing to identify a fellow officer involved in the incident.

Another officer who underwent the training in 2022 for the new anti-gun unit, Jean Alejandro, was disciplined less than five year earlier for striking a person in the face after failing to provide the person medical attention. NYPD records showed that Alejandro faced a department trial over the incident. A man who Alejandro arrested for jumping a subway turnstile alleged that the officer ignored his multiple pleas from a holding cell to be taken to a hospital to receive his diabetes medication. The man claimed that Alejandro took him out of the holding cell and then flipped a camera facing the cell in the opposite direction. Alejandro got in the man's face and said, "Say it one more time." Then, the officer punched him under the left eye. The CCRB presented interviews with the victim and another witness who was locked up in the station that night and an NYPD judge found Alejandro guilty of the charges. NYPD Commissioner James O'Neill docked the officer 25 vacation days and put him on a year of dismissal probation.

Other documented misconduct that the trainees for the new anti-gun unit had been found guilty of included illegal stops and frisks, unlawful arrests and illegal strip searches. Some of the other officers identified in the group also had a history of dishonest behavior while policing. For example, one of the officers arrested someone and signed a criminal complaint claiming that he observed the person blocking pedestrian traffic when that was not true. Another officer was found guilty of wrongfully warning another member of the force of the imminent execution of a search warrant at a location that they were known to frequent.

In April 2022, Adams took the stage at Brooklyn's Kings Theater to mark his first 100 days in office. The event was supposed to serve in part as a substitute for the mayor's January inauguration celebration that was canceled due to rising cases of Covid-19 at the time.

As Frank Sinatra's "New York, New York" blared from the auditorium speakers, Adams walked out on stage. He carried with him a framed photo of his late mother, Dorothy Mae Adams-Streeter. The photo captured Adams' mother, who died the previous spring, posing for a portrait at her 75th birthday party and depicted her image in a brandy snifter. It was the same picture that he carried with him as he entered his polling place to cast his ballot in the election, then again the night of January 1, 2022 when he was sworn into office. Before he began his address, Adams propped the picture of his mom on a chair next to the lectern at center stage.

"I feel sorry for people who live in a small town and don't live in New York," Adams said to open his address.

Adams, smiling ear to ear, exuded some of his familiar braggadocio and swagger during the speech, at one point comparing himself to former US president Franklin Delano Roosevelt. "FDR, like ELA (Eric Leroy Adams) understood that people needed an honest and reckoning of the problems and bold plans to solve them. That is what I intend to deliver for my fellow New Yorkers."

Despite his cheerfulness, Adams's first hundred days had proven his administration had a long way to go to fulfill the promises of his campaign. The new mayor, who staked his candidacy on being New Yorkers' best option to reverse the trend of rising violent crime had seen those numbers go the other way. According to statistics from the NYPD, overall crime across the city was up more than 36% percent and shootings were up about 16% compared to the year before.

As for his Mayor Adams's new anti-gun unit, a report by the *New York Post* found that in its first couple of weeks of operation, the Neighborhood Safety Team was mostly pulling over suspects in cars for minor infractions including tinted windows, drug possession and bogus license plates. As for guns, the *Post* revealed the unit had only recovered three in as many weeks. A few months later, the NYPD put out data claiming that in its first two months on the street, the Neighborhood Safety Teams had made 448 arrests. But as for firearm charges — the teams' stated goal — just 86 people that they arrested— less than 20%— were charged with criminal possession of a gun. Most of the charges continued to be for other low-level offenses, the data showed.

Still, the always confident Adams told the crowd gathered at Kings Theater that the city and the NYPD could get policing in the city right, once again suggesting that holding police accountable was a priority, too.

"And so when you hear people say, "We don't need our police." Let me tell you right here and right now, I will support my police and we will make our city a safe city. And there's a covenant and commitment I'm giving to you," Adams continued. "We will give the police the tools they deserve and they require, but my men and women that wear that black and blue uniform, we will not be abusive to the public that we swore to serve and protect. That is our obligation. That's the partnership."

17

HOW AN ERA OF FIGHTING ENDED IN DISAPPOINTMENT FOR THE FAMILIES OF LOVED ONES KILLED BY THE NYPD

C onstance Malcolm is no longer fighting the city and the NYPD in court over the death of her son. Her legal cases are settled. Still, nearly a decade after Ramarley Graham was killed, the NYPD continued to suppress information about one of the officers involved in his death who remains on the force.

The NYPD put Officer John McLoughlin on dismissal probation and docked him 45 vacation days as a penalty for breaking department rules when he kicked in Graham's apartment door. In response to a FOIL request in 2021 for McLoughlin's disciplinary history, the NYPD provided me with some details indicating that the officer was disciplined for these actions. However, the department neglected to provide details about the penalties he faced. McLoughlin's online profile on the NYPD personnel website omits this information, too. According to the NYPD database, his only disciplinary history is for a 2016 illegal stop and frisk where he also refused to provide his name and shield number.

After Malcolm's personal battles with the NYPD and the city ended, she stayed active with the groups that supported her over the years, like Communities United for Police Reform. Joo-Hyun Kang, the former

CPR director, even recruited her to work with other families who suffered the tragedy of police violence.

"Constance was one of our media trainers," Kang said. "I've been telling her for years, teasing her about it, asking her 'what Saturday are you off work?'"

"She was amazing," Kang added.

When speaking about the NYPD in 2021, Malcolm frequently segues to defunding the police to free up resources for better mental health services and schools in parts of the city like the Wakefield neighborhood of the Bronx where they used to live. She thinks this would be a better way for the city to spend its money, instead of on more cops.

For years, Malcolm and her other son Chinnor didn't talk about what happened to Ramarley. But during the Covid-19 pandemic, when the two were spending more time together at home, she said they spoke about the police more frequently and the details of February 2, 2012, sometimes filtered into the conversations.

In the summer of 2021, Chinnor, now a teenager, started speaking out himself at rallies and demonstrations. At one rally, Chinnor talked about processing his brother's death. "The first year, I got angry a lot, I had trouble in school," he said to the crowd, "It took me a while, I got stronger, I started marching with my mom."

With an engaged crowd encouraging him, Chinnor ended his brief speech by calling for the NYPD budget to be cut by a billion dollars and for more money to be spent on "counselors for after school."

In conversation with her son, Malcolm told Chinnor that if he comes in contact with the police to listen to the officer, but keep his eyes on the badge and make a mental note of the number, just in case he needs it later. She was never totally sure what Chinnor was thinking about this advice, but she believed it was important that she try to teach him to be respectful.

"I try to talk to him. Tell him I'm not blaming the whole police force," for what happened to Ramarley, she said. "I don't know what he's feeling. I can tell him that all police aren't bad. But I don't know what he's feeling."

In the back of her mind, she said, she couldn't help but think to herself, "You don't have to do anything to get killed by the police."

For some of the families who fought for years to get justice for their loved ones killed by the NYPD, the de Blasio administration ended with bitter disappointment.

In June 2020, Gwen Carr filed a petition calling for a judicial inquiry into her son Eric Garner's killing. Rarely used in New York City, a judicial inquiry allows the public to probe what city officials knew about an event and whether they neglected to do their duty. The petitioners, which included Carr, Garner's sister, Ellisha Flagg Garner, and several activists from the police reform movement, said in the petition that "city taxpayers have been denied access to fundamental information concerning Mr. Garner's death."

The city fought Carr and the others to prevent the Garner inquiry from going forward. If it proceeded, it could force the mayor as well as former top NYPD brass such as James O'Neill to testify. After more than a year of fighting in court, a New York Supreme Court judge ruled in the petitioners' favor and a public hearing was scheduled to take place in October 2021. But the judge also ruled that Mayor de Blasio and O'Neill would not be compelled to testify. It was a crushing blow to the family and advocates who had hoped to learn more about the involvement of senior city officials during the Garner death investigation.

During the eight days of the hearing, some of the NYPD officers involved in Garner's arrest took the stand, but their testimony didn't reveal much more than had come to light at former officer Daniel Pantaleo's disciplinary trial. Officer Justin D'Amico, Pantaleo's partner that day, was asked about why he tried to charge Garner with a felony cigarette tax evasion charge in the hours after his death. D'Amico said that "due to the circumstances I wasn't thinking clearly."

"I may have rushed the paperwork a little bit," he said. He called it a "total mistake." Just hours after Garner's death, D'Amico listed a felony charge against him on an online arrest form. For that to be true, he would have needed evidence that Garner illegally sold at least 10,000 cigarettes. D'Amico never faced any department discipline over the error.

Lieutenant Chris Bannon was asked during the inquiry about the text message he sent to a sergeant at the scene saying "no big deal" after learning that Garner might be "DOA." Bannon said that he sent the text because he was concerned about his fellow officers and wanted to "bring their mindset back to center," echoing his testimony during Pantaleo's 2019 trial. In the years since Garner's death, Bannon also never faced any department discipline.

But at least one high-ranking NYPD official was called to give his account of what happened after Garner was killed for the first time publicly.

Joseph Reznick, a 48-year NYPD veteran who was made the head of NYPD's Internal Affairs Bureau the year Garner was killed, confirmed that IAB sent a recommendation to internally charge Pantaleo the year after Garner's death. But as to why the NYPD didn't move forward at that time with the case, Reznick suggested asking people with more authority than him at the department.

After Reznick's testimony, Carr and the other petitioners tried to get the judge to reconsider her earlier ruling and order de Blasio and other city officials to testify. The night before they sent the judge the motion, two new affidavits were filed that they hoped would help their case.

Maya Wiley, the former CCRB chair who initially investigated the Pantaleo case, said that in her experience "in high profile matters" like the Pantaleo investigation the Mayor, First Deputy Mayor, Corporation Counsel, and their respective staff "are briefed throughout the process."

Queens Borough President Donovan Richards, a former city councilman at the time of Garner's death, wrote in an affidavit that at the time the mayor, the police commissioner, and other high ranking officers declined to share information about the investigation into Garner's death with him while he was serving as the chair of the city's Public Safety Committee.

"However, they indicated knowledge of and input into the disciplinary process, but were not at liberty to disclose information about an open investigation," Richards said in the affidavit.

The petitioners tried to use this new information to sway the judge. But in the end she denied the new motion calling for de Blasio and other officials to testify.

"To me, there's nothing new that came out of the testimony and nothing new in the information that would lead me to believe that their testimony would be appropriate under the circumstances," the judge said.

In the spring of 2022, the court held its final hearing in the judicial inquiry. After the preceding, Gwen Carr said in a statement: "I have been fighting for years to get the NYPD to fire the officers who helped kill my son and helped cover it up."

"We fought for this once-in-a-century judicial inquiry and it exposed some of the misconduct by city officials and the NYPD, but officers who did wrong like Justin D'Amico and Lt. Christopher Bannon are still getting paid by the city which is very frustrating," Carr said.

While issues clearly persist with the NYPD's disclosure of disciplinary matters even following 50-a's repeal in 2020, not all internal cases and their details have stayed under wraps.

After his series of social media attacks in 2020, SBA President Ed Mullins was internally charged with violating department policies for the explosive tweets that he posted from the official union account.

Mullins faced two separate internal disciplinary trials over his social media posts. The CCRB brought a case against him over the tweets targeting former city health commissioner Dr. Oxiris Barbot and Councilman Ritchie Torres. In a separate matter, the NYPD charged him over his tweet doxing Mayor de Blasio's daughter by posting her personal information contained in an arrest report.

Before the trials, Mullins tried to get the charges thrown out. He claimed that he had immunity from department discipline because of his SBA status. He said that a city executive order that releases officers in union positions from day-to-day police duties so they can focus on union business also prevented him from being disciplined. He also argued that as the head of the SBA his tweets are protected by the First Amendment when he speaks on a matter of public concern.

Mullins claimed that disciplining him for his tweets intended to have a "chilling effect on his willingness to speak out and advocate for the union." Furthermore, he suggested that because his social media post about de Blasio's daughter was actually a retweet of a photo of the arrest report published by a *Daily Mail* journalist that the information he shared was no longer private.

The NYPD judge was having none of this. He said that the executive order "provides no absolute refuge" from internal misconduct charges. On the First Amendment questions that Mullins' raised, the judge said the argument about a chilling effect had "no credence." The judge also concluded that Mullins "republishing of an arrest report" of the mayor's daughter was not a matter of "public concern for First Amendment purposes."

In the fall of 2021, Mullins went on trial over the tweet targeting Chiara de Blasio. At trial, Mullins testified that the purpose of his tweet was to draw attention to what he believed was the mayor and the city holding back police resources during the protests. The judge said that while he credited Mullins testimony, in that he admitted to posting the tweets, his arguments were "unpersuasive." He recommended that Mullins be disciplined for violating the NYPD Patrol Guide's regulations on "prohibited conduct."

The judge wrote that Mullins, while "in his role as president of the [SBA], had the right to advocate for his members, the means he used to do so exceeded the bounds of legitimate debate."

"He weaponized personal information obtained in the regular course of providing police services," the judge said.

The judge said that Mullins' act of publishing the mayor's daughter's personal information "degraded his purported advocacy to the level of blood sport, where any means of achieving the SBA's goals became permissible." He recommended that Mullins lose 30 vacation days. The police commissioner agreed and signed off on the penalty.

Four days after his first trial ended, Mullins was back in front of the NYPD tribunal for his second disciplinary trial. This second case was being prosecuted by the CCRB over his tweets attacking the former health commissioner and a city councilman. The CCRB wanted the department to fire Mullins over the charged misconduct in their case.

Mullins claimed at trial that he was not trying to target their gender or sexual orientation when he called Dr. Barbot a "bitch" and Councilman Ritchie Torres a "first class whore." He insisted that he did not do anything improper by speaking out on behalf of his members, who he said were being put "in harm's way" by Barbot and Torres. Barbot had clashed with the NYPD over a request for 250,000 masks during the Covid-19 pandemic, telling a department official "I don't give two rats' asses about your cops." Torres, Mullins claimed, was incorrectly suggesting that a rise in gun violence in the city was the police's fault when he called for an investigation into a possible police work slowdown in 2020. Mullins said it would have been "irresponsible" for him not to say anything.

The department judge who heard the case said that in these instances Mullins' "attempt at zealous advocacy" for the police does not "excuse the derogatory and demeaning words he used." Rather, the judge said, Mullins "brought discredit" to his fellow officers with his slurs.

The judge noted that Mulins was not being disciplined because he voiced his concerns, rather it is "the slurs he chose in his criticism that constitute misconduct." In the case, the judge found him guilty of two counts of "offensive language" and the department docked him 40 vacation days — 20 for each tweet. The decision disappointed the CCRB who wanted Mullins fired.

In the two cases, Mullins lost a grand total of 70 vacation days, which cost him about $32,000 in salary.

In October 2021, the same month that he was put on trial by the department, the FBI raided Mullins' union office and home on Long Island as part of an investigation over the alleged theft of union funds. Later that day, he resigned his position as SBA president. Following his departure, the SBA archived their Twitter account and launched a new one. The next month, Mullins retired from the NYPD.

A few months later, in February 2022, Mullins was charged in federal court with defrauding the union. Federal prosecutors said that Mullins stole hundreds of thousands of dollars from official union funds by filing phony and inflated expense reports. The feds claimed that the money was spent on lavish meals, clothing, jewelry, appliances and even a relative's tuition. For example, one expense report showed that Mullins changed a $45.92 credit card charge from a wine bar in New Jersey to $845.92, prosecutors said in the charging documents. Another report showed that Mullins bumped up a steakhouse bill from $609.89 to $909.89, the court filing said. The prosecutors said that Mullins then submitted the expenses to the union treasurer — who was also ousted from his position after Mullins was charged — who signed off on them even though he rarely submitted receipts.

The de Blasio era ended in New York with several other high-profile NYPD disciplinary cases failing to be resolved.

In 2020, Hawa Bah filed a complaint with the CCRB against Det. Edwin Mateo, the NYPD officer that a jury found liable in the death of her son, Mohamed Bah. The detective countered with a lawsuit claiming that it was too late for Bah to file the complaint with the watchdog group against him. A year later, in the summer of 2021, a judge ruled against Mateo and allowed the CCRB's investigation to proceed. But after that, months passed and the NYPD still had not moved forward with a disciplinary hearing for Mateo.

Almost a decade after Mohamed Bah was killed in 2012, Hawa Bah said she remained determined to see Mateo fired. "Since Mohamed die, up to today, I never rest," she said in 2021.

But later that year, Bah hit yet another roadblock in her pursuit of justice for her son: Edwin Mateo retired from the force in October.

The following year, in May 2022, Bah met with the CCRB about the Mateo case. She said that they told her that investigators were prepared to recommend to the board that they charge him with excessive force over the deadly shooting of her son. But Mateo retired before the board could vote on the charge. After learning that the case against Mateo was over, Bah put out a statement saying she was "outraged" that he "escaped accountability" but not surprised.

"At least my tireless fight for justice means Mateo is no longer a police officer and cannot kill another mother's child," she said.

Victoria Davis, the sister of Delrawn Small, said she looks back on the criminal trial of Wayne Isaacs, the NYPD officer who was acquitted of killing her brother, and she "feels two ways" about how the case was prosecuted.

Davis said that the prosecutors from the state's attorney general's office treated the family well and were open with them. She said that while the case was going on, they were always available and she appreciated them "walking us through things."

For example, one day she went to their office, and Jose Nieves, one of the trial prosecutors, pulled her aside. They went into a room. He wanted to show her some pictures of Small's body that might appear at trial. Nieves needed Davis to see these pictures before the trial. He couldn't risk her reacting to them for the first time in the courtroom. "I let it out in that room," she said, adding that was the "type of humanity" from the AG's office that she appreciated.

Still, she wonders why they didn't try to humanize Delrawn more in court. Davis said that even though her brother's life had not gone smoothly, he was doing better at the time of his death. He was working a steady job as a janitor in Manhattan. He was also an aspiring actor. Before his death, he appeared in one film, "Another Zero In The System," which streamed on NetFlix. His coworkers even asked the family if they could keep his work shoes after he was killed.

Davis said that after her brother died, she couldn't believe how many people showed up in support. She thought, "wow, there's an underground of people who care about other people." She didn't know about these groups before, but she knew she wanted to get involved and pay it forward.

She began to travel to Albany to lobby for legislative efforts, including the repeal of 50-a. She liked lobbying and didn't even mind speaking to people who probably wouldn't sponsor the legislation she was pushing for them to pass. "I'm highly social," Davis said, describing herself as being similar to Elmyra from the cartoon Looney Tunes. "I'm like, '*Hi! Humans!*'" she said, laughing.

But Davis said she struggled sometimes being a sibling in the movement. "I'm with the moms all the time," she said. "That was difficult. I'd be like, why is this all on me?"

Small's brother Victor Dempsey never thought he would become an organizer either. When everything was going on after his brother's killing, he was just doing what needed to be done for his family. He would speak out. Tell people to pack the courtroom. He got the attention of the Legal Aid Society. They were forming an organizing department. They reached out and asked him to join. "I thought it was a great fit for me," he said.

Davis said that the year before Small died, she remembers calling him on his 36th birthday. When he told her how old he was, she said to him that didn't sound right — he had to be at least 40.

Davis told him, "But you're an *adult* adult. You were an adult when we were little."

Delrawn laughed. He didn't laugh much. He always had a soft grin, but he was serious much of the time. On this particular phone call, however, her brother laughed hard.

She said that phone conversation was the first time she realized that her brother, who is only four years older than Davis, wasn't a "real adult" when he was acting as a parent for younger siblings. Maybe she hadn't thought about it before because, as Davis said, Delrawn never complained about having to be a "parent as a little kid."

"All this time, he has taken on this burden," Victoria thought. "Wow, that's sad."

In early 2021, the CCRB substantiated second-degree assault charges against Wayne Isaacs more than four years after the killing of Small on July 4, 2016. Isaacs faced a possible firing from the force if he was found guilty. Dempsey said that they had "some great traction" initially about moving the case towards a resolution. But then things started to stall.

Isaacs sued to stop the disciplinary proceedings from going forward. But in early 2022, a judge denied his attempt to block the CCRB's case. It was a win for the family but it still meant that they had to wait for the NYPD to move forward with disciplinary proceedings for Isaacs. A few months later, Isaacs and his police union attorneys made another attempt to stop his disciplinary from going forward. They wrote to the new police commissioner, Keechant Sewell, and asked her to use her authority to remove the case from the CCRB and prevent it from moving forward. Sewell denied Isaacs' request to block the case.

Over a year after they learned that the officer who killed their brother would face internal charges, Dempsey and Davis were still waiting for a department trial to be set.

"I'm not really sure what the tactic is," Davis said about delays. "Maybe they think she'll get tired, sit down somewhere and leave him alone."

Dempsey said he doesn't let the delays with the NYPD and the city over Isaacs' case get him "nervous" anymore. "I'm not trying to put myself in that space," he said.

"I'm sure we'll get a hearing," he said.

He paused, then added, "Eventually."

AUTHOR'S NOTES

This book was reported entirely during the Covid-19 pandemic. I'm forever grateful to the people who took the time to speak with me while also dealing with the immense challenges of a global public health crisis. Furthermore, some of the subjects I spoke to decided to tell their stories despite having endured the trauma of police violence themselves or against a loved one, family member or friend for, in some cases, over a decade. I'm profoundly thankful for and in awe of their courage to do so.

I spoke to dozens of people while reporting this book and reviewed thousands of pages from court records, police documents, disciplinary records, media reports and several books. All quotes unless noted in the notes section are from interviews I conducted with the person who the commentary is attributed to.

For the NYPD officers mentioned in this book I sought to interview them and/or get them to comment on the details contained in the book multiple times through multiple channels. I reached out multiple times for their comments through the office of the New York Police Department's Deputy Commissioner of Public Information (DCPI), their respective police unions, and the union and private attorneys who represented the officers mentioned in the book during various criminal and civil legal proceedings and internal NYPD disciplinary cases.

As the book mentions, I conducted my own comparison of the disciplinary records contained in two databases — the one published by BuzzFeed in 2018 and the online portal created by the NYPD after the repeal of 50-a in 2021. I focused this research on disciplinary cases of officers who were found guilty of serious offenses like making false and misleading official statements, wrongful use of force, defrauding the police department and others. I shared the missing information with NYPD's DCPI multiple times over the course of my reporting and they failed to get back to me.

There are several people mentioned in this story that did not respond to my multiple requests for an interview, including former New York City mayor Bill de Blasio. I made many various efforts to speak to Mr. de Blasio for this book. I reached out to his press secretary multiple times during his final year in office in 2021. I also contacted several close contacts of his from the New York City political world who were unable to put me in touch with the former mayor. And, in addition to trying to contact the former mayor himself via phone and email, I also sent several letters to his Brooklyn homes to provide details of the book.

The "defund the police" movement in New York City only gets a brief mention in this book. *Defund* is a topic worthy of its own book. It felt out of place to devote a large chunk of the text of a book focused on police accountability and transparency to this complex issue. However, during the course of completing this book I reported on the 2020 claims by Bill de Blasio and former City Council speaker Corey Johnson that they shifted $1 billion from the NYPD budget for fiscal year 2021. As I note in the book, the budget math proves that this claim was untrue. Over the course of my reporting, I spoke to several sources about *defund* and New York City, including some former City Council members involved in those budget negotiations in 2020, and independent budget auditors from the Citizens Budget Commission and Independent Budget Office.

Some of the narrative of this story is derived from documents obtained through my own public records request from the City of New York and NYPD. In general, I have a mostly unsuccessful personal history of getting the NYPD to provide documents through the FOIL process. However, in the case of the Miguel Richards files, I was able to get the police department to provide a trove of records. In March 2021, I filed a FOIL request for the entire file from the NYPD Force Investigation Division's (FID) investigation into Richards' death. For eight months, the police department ignored my request. Then, on December 31, 2021, and after multiple appeals of my FOIL request, the NYPD sent me thousands of records, which included all the body camera footage, scores of audio files of interviews from officers on the scene, and hundreds of pages from FID. It was through these records that I was able to create the narrative for Chapter 10 of this book, which is devoted to the killing of Miguel Richards.

Finally, after Mayor Eric Adams took office in January 2022 I also reached out to his staff multiple times for an interview but they did not respond. In addition, I shared with his office the disciplinary records for the 102 officers I identified were missing from the NYPD online portal, and noted that the police department failed to respond to multiple requests to comment on why this misconduct information had been omitted from its online database. The Adams administration also did not respond.

Thanks for reading.

Mike

NOTES: CHAPTER 1

- **In his hand that day:** NYPD press conference, December 2014
  - **"Watch what I'm gonna do":** ibid.
- **NYPD officers Wenjian Liu and Rafael Ramos:** media reports from New York Post, New York Daily News, December 2014
  - **"shooter's stance":** NYPD press conference, December 2014
- **The two ambushed officers:** media reports from New York Post, New York Daily News, New York Times, December 2014
- **Bill Bratton:** memoir by Bill Bratton & Peter Knbler, "The Profession," (Penguin Press, 2021)
- **"in evolution":** Bill de Blasio interview with the New York Times, December 2014
- **For more than a decade, New York City was engaged in a court battle over the police department's use of stop and frisk:** reporting from court records in *Floyd v. New York City* lawsuit; interview with Darius Charney, senior staff attorney at the Center for Constitutional Rights
- **"I have my own army in the NYPD, which is the seventh biggest army in the world":** Michael Bloomberg speech at MIT, November 2011
- **"of profound progress":** Transcript: Mayor Bill de Blasio

Announces Agreement in Landmark Stop-And-Frisk Case January 30, 2014 Brownsville Recreation Center, Brooklyn, NY

- **"sound cannon"**: media report from NY Post, December 2014
- **"Ugly"**: media reports on Bill de Blasio press conference, December 2014
- **"unacceptable departure"**: ibid.
- **"allegedly"**: ibid.
- **He did use the occasion to talk about his 17-year-old Black son Dante**: Transcript: Mayor de Blasio Holds Media Availability at Mt. Sinai United Christian Church on Staten Island December 3, 2014
- **Lynch responded**: media reports on PBA President Patrick Lynch, December 2014
- **Mullins**: NY Mag, 'Sgt. Mullins Goes to War,' 2020
- **The PBA circulated a form**: media reports on PBA, December 2014
- **When de Blasio took office every labor union in the city ... was working under expired contracts**: media reports, December 2014
- **Lynch and his union had declared an impasse**: *Politico*, "With negotiations at impasse, PBA appoints big-name arbitrator," April 2018
- **"There's going to be a feeling, sort of a calming dynamic as people settle into a new approach"**: *New York Times*, "In Police Rift, Mayor de Blasio's Missteps Included Thinking It Would Pass," January 2015
- **About 75 NYPD officers responded to the shooting scene in Bed-Stuy**: media report from The New York Daily News, December 2014
- **"they want some"**: media report from the *New York Post*, December 2014
- **"everybody get down!"**: media report from the New York Post, December 2014
- **"I was afraid for myself and my baby."**: ibid.
- **"Oh, shit."**: ibid.
- **"Yo, that is crazy"**: Facebook video from bystander, December 2014
- **"What's going on?"**: ibid.

- "Two cops just got shot in the head": ibid.
- Information quickly surfaced about Brinsley: media reports from The New York Daily News; KHQ.com; NBCNews.com; The New York Times, December 2014
- *"Never Had A Hot Gun On Your Waist And Blood On Your Shoe":* Instagram post from Ishmael Brinsley, user account: Dontrunup, December 2014
- When the Baltimore County police discovered the posts, they alerted the NYPD: media report from NBC News, December 2014
- 'Gunman executes 2 NYPD cops in Garner 'revenge': media report from New York Post, December 2014
- "No warning, no provocation, they were quite simply assassinated, targeted for their uniform": ibid.
- Rumors began to swirl about Brinsley and his motive for shooting Liu and Ramos: ibid.
- *New York Times* poked holes in this narrative that Brinsley was a part of some conspiracy to wage a revenge war against the police: *New York Times,* 'Many Identities of New York Officers' Killer in a Life of Wrong Turns,' January 2015
- Bratton wrote in his memoir that after hearing rumors that the officers might turn their backs on the mayor: memoir by Bill Bratton & Peter Knbler, "The Profession," (Penguin Press, 2021)
- "You are full of shit!": ibid.
- "These guys will do whatever you tell them to do! Now this is about you fuckers, instead of the two dead cops downstairs": ibid.
- "despicable act": Transcript: Mayor de Blasio, Commissioner Bratton Deliver Remarks at Woodhull Hospital, Take Q&A December 2014
- "When a police officer is murdered ... an attack on everything we hold dear.": ibid.
- "blood on many hands"
- "There's blood on many hands tonight ... That blood on the hands starts on the steps of City Hall, in the office of the mayor.": media reports on PBA press conference, December 2014
- "Police officers and police families are a different breed --

thank God for them": Remarks by Vice President Biden at a Service for NYPD Officer Rafael Ramos, December 2014

- "the best father I could ask for": media reports on Rafael Ramos funeral, December 2014
- "Everyone says they hate cops but they are the people that they call for help.": Facebook post by Jaden Ramos, December 2014
- "Divisive politics polarized the city and country — maybe that sounds familiar.": media reports on Bill Bratton funeral eulogy, December 2014
- "taken from us on the day he was meant to graduate.": Mayor de Blasio Delivers Remarks at the Funeral Service of Police Officer Rafael Ramos, December 2014
- "blasting Spanish gospel music from his car.": ibid.
- "you epitomize the family of New York.": ibid.
- "peacemaker": ibid.
- While leaving the church, De Blasio and Lynch nodded to each other. *The Guardian*, 'De Blasio and police at odds as thousands mourn NYPD officer Ramos,' December 2014
- "Hero": media reports from New York Post and New York Daily News on Wenjian Liu funeral service, January 2015
- "Soulmate": ibid.
- "We are very proud of you, we love you forever.": ibid.
- "A much larger part of this city, of this country, a much larger part than you think, is proud of you": Wenjian Liu funeral remarks by Bill Bratton, January 2014
- "A hero's funeral is about grieving, not grievance": media reports on Bill Bratton, January 2015
- "young man who came here from China at the age of 12 in search of the American dream.": Transcript: Mayor de Blasio Delivers Remarks at Funeral Service of Detective Wenjian Liu, January 2014
- "Let us rededicate ourselves to those great New York traditions of mutual understanding and living in harmony": ibid.
- "has no respect for us ... why should we have respect for him?" *Associated Press*, 'NYPD officers again turn backs on mayor at cop's funeral,' January 2015

- "a cop hater since before he got elected mayor": *New York Times*, 'Another Silent Protest of Mayor de Blasio as Officer Liu Is Laid to Rest,' January 2015
- "They feel that City Hall has turned their back on them ... not inside the church": media reports on PBA President Patrick Lynch, January 2015
- "Slowdown": *New York Daily News*, 'Arrests for low-level crimes increase as NYPD slowdown gradually ends,' January 2015
- "comprehensive review": Transcript: Mayor de Blasio and Commissioner Bratton Announce 2014 Saw Fewest Murders in Recorded City History; Lowest Murders, Robberies, Buglaries in 10 Years, January 2015

NOTES: CHAPTER 2

- "The people hated the British for doing that ... saw the proposed police force as another occupying army.": Bruce Chadwick, *'Law & Disorder, The Chaotic Birth of the NYPD,'* (St. Martin's Press, 2017)
- On September 16, 1992, the PBA mobilized 10,000 cops to City Hall: New York Times, *'Officers Rally And Dinkins Is Their Target,' September 1992*
- "Now you got a nigger inside City Hall. How do you like that? A nigger mayor." report from *Newsday* columnist Jimmy Breslin, September 1992
- "Take the hall!": ibid.
- "This nigger says she's a member of the City Council.": New York Times, *'Officers Rally And Dinkins Is Their Target,' September 1992*
- Another Black member of the City Council, Mary Pinkett: ibid.
- Virginia Santana ... was blocked on the bridge while driving her child to the hospital for chemotherapy treatment.: ibid.
- "The emotional level did get a little out of control ... the community do not listen.": ibid.
- "Hooliganism": ibid.
- "I see New York as a gorgeous mosaic ... coming through Ellis

Island, or Kennedy Airport, or on Greyhound buses bound for the Port Authority": David N. Dinkins, 'A Mayor's Life,' (Public Affairs, 2013)
- "In that spirit, I offer this fundamental pledge: I intend to be the mayor of all the people of New York.": ibid.
- Proposals for versions of a civilian review board in New York City date back to the 1930s: ibid.
- On July 16, 1964, 15-year-old James Powell: Michael W. Flamm, 'In The Heat Of The Summer,' (University of Pennsylvania Press, 2017)
- "Dirty niggers, I'll wash you clean.": ibid.
- "Hit him!": ibid.
- "I'm a police officer, come out and drop it!": ibid.
- The following year, Lindsay was elected mayor: John Lindsay, 'The Ungovernable City,' (Basic Books, 2001)
- When Dinkins took office, crime had been on an unmitigated climb for the last 15 years: David N. Dinkins, 'A Mayor's Life,' (Public Affairs, 2013)
- On an August evening in 1991, 7-year-old cousins Gavin and Angela Cato were playing with a bike: media reports from The New York Daily News and New York Times, August 1991
- A 16-year-old in the group pulled out a knife and stabbed him four times: ibid.
- Thirty-eight people and 150 police officers were hurt: ibid.
- Bill de Blasio ... was stationed at City Hall fielding calls from Jews in the neighborhood about the violence: ibid.
- "pogrom": David N. Dinkins, 'A Mayor's Life,' (Public Affairs, 2013)
- "There is nothing worse than being falsely accused.": David Dinkins interview with Gothamist.com, 2016
- "the most extensive racial unrest in New York City in over 20 years.": Richard Girgenti, 'A Report To The Governor On The Disturbance In Crown Heights,' September 1993
- "under control": ibid.
- "failed to fulfill his ultimate responsibility ... preserve the public peace.: ibid.
- "persuasive": ibid.

- "in a dramatic and sustained manner, and was conveyed well before": ibid.
- "If the Mayor was told ... systemic problems in City Hall's flow of information and decision-making would be revealed.": ibid.
- "The report concludes that I should have rejected the Police Department's assurances ... I accept that criticism.": David N. Dinkins, *'A Mayor's Life,'* (Public Affairs, 2013)
- He lost out to Rudy Giuliani by just two points.: ibid.
- In 2009 ... introduced legislation to expand the power of the Civilian Complaint Review Board: Observer, *'De Blasio and Company Seek Changes to Civilian Complaint Review Board,'* August 2009
- "will help restore public confidence": ibid.
- "rededicate ourselves to getting it right.": ibid.
- "Ticket-fixing": media reports on NYPD "ticket fixing" scandal, May 2011
- "need the facts and we need them sooner rather than later": ibid.
- "I think it's time that they come out and say ... This is what we're looking at": ibid.
- "provocations under cover of darkness" Observer, *'De Blasio Calls Mayor's OWS Decision "Needlessly Provocative and Legally Questionable,"'* November 2011
- "only escalate tensions in a situation that calls for mediation and dialogue": ibid.
- "Time is of the essence ... expedite his investigation into the incident": Observer, *'Bill de Blasio Asks Bronx D.A. To Expedite Ramarley Graham Shooting Investigation,'* February 2012

NOTES: CHAPTER 3

- **On a February afternoon in 2008, 28-year-old David Floyd:** trial testimony from David Floyd, *Floyd, et. al v. City of New York* 2013
  - ***Terry v. Ohio:*** U.S. Supreme Court *Terry v. Ohio*, 392 U.S. 1, 1968
  - **"burglary tools":** trial testimony of NYPD witnesses, *Floyd, et. al v. City of New York* 2013
  - **"I felt like I was being told I should never leave my home":** trial testimony from David Floyd, *Floyd, et. al v. City of New York* 2013
  - **Later that year, the New York State Attorney General issued a report that found that the Street Crimes Unit:** New York State Office of the Attorney General, 'New York City Police Department's "Stop & Frisk" Practices: A Report to the People of the State of New York From the Office of the Attorney General,' 1999
  - **the *Daniels* settlement:** court documents from Daniels, et. al v. City of New York, 1999
  - **In 2011, the NYPD stopped a total of 685,724 people**
  - **Professor Jeffrey Fagan:** trial testimony from Professor Jeffrey Fagan, *Floyd, et. al v. City of New York* 2013
  - **Adhyl Polanco:** recording transcript and trial testimony from NYPD Officer Adhyl Polanco, *Floyd, et. al v. City of New York* 2013

- **Adrian Schoolcraft:** recording transcript and trial testimony from NYPD Officer Adrian Schoolcraft, *Floyd, et. al v. City of New York* 2013
- **Pedro Serrano:** recording transcript and trial testimony from NYPD Officer Pedro Serrano, *Floyd, et. al v. City of New York* 2013
- **Chris McCormack:** ibid.
- **"almost like you're purposely not doing your job at all":** ibid.
- **"Red Rage":** ProPublica, *'Over a Dozen Black and Latino Men Accused a Cop of Humiliating, Invasive Strip Searches. The NYPD Kept Promoting Him,'* 2020
- **"the right people, the right time, the right location.":** recording transcript and trial testimony from NYPD Officer Pedro Serrano, *Floyd, et. al v. City of New York* 2013
- **"And who are the right people":** ibid.
- **"Depends where you are":** ibid.
- **"Mott Haven. Full of black and Hispanics... What am I supposed to do? Stop every black and Hispanic?":** ibid.
- **"this is about stopping the right people, the right place, the right location":** ibid.
- **"Again take Mott Haven ... robberies and grand larcenies.":** ibid.
- **"And who are those people robbing?":** ibid.
- **"The problem was, what, male blacks ... I said this at roll call.":** ibid.
- **"Absolutely never.":** trial testimony from NYPD Officer Christopher McCormack, *Floyd, et. al v. City of New York,* 2013
- **"policy of indirect racial profiling":** Judge Shira Scheindlin, Floyd liability opinion, *Floyd, et. al v. City of New York,* 2013 (https://ccrjustice.org/sites/default/files/assets/Floyd-Liability-Opinion-8-12-13.pdf)
- **"blacks and Hispanics who would not have been stopped if they were white.":** ibid.
- **"nearly 90 percent ... without the officer finding any basis for a summons or arrest":** ibid.
- **"not ordering an end to the practice of stop-and-frisk":** ibid.
- **"a fair trial":** *New York Times*, Judge Rejects New York's Stop-and-Frisk Policy, 2013

- "not understand how policing works": ibid.
- "I think, particularly for young men of color ... they are not part of this society in the same way": Bill de Blasio interview on *Morning Joe*, MSNBC, 2013
- "Dante": New Yorkers for de Blasio Television Ad: "Dante," 2013 (https://www.youtube.com/watch?v=GgvXniTz7D8)
- "the ad ... killed us.": The Daily Beast, *'Dante de Blasio's Killer Ad May Have Won NYC Primary for His Dad,'* 2013
- "Can't go back": Campaign ad by Joe Lhota For Mayor, Inc., 2013
- "Bill de Blasio's recklessly dangerous agenda on crime will take us back to this.": ibid.
- "fear tactics": media reports from the *New York Daily News* and *New York Post,* 2013
- Fact-checkers had a field day with Lhota's ad: The Nation, *'Lhota's Mistake-Filled Attack Ad Depicts de Blasio as Soft on Crime,'* 2013
- "front-row seat": media reports from the *New York Daily News,* 2013
- "right hand": ibid.
- "I remember vividly being on the receiving end of a deep, deep concern, particularly from members of the Jewish community": ibid.
- "I came away with very strong views ... from day one. No question": ibid.
- "unmitigated failure ... stayed with Bill de Blasio.": media reports from the *New York Daily News* and *New York Post,* 2013
- "ran afoul": ruling by the Court of Appeals for the Second Circuit, *Floyd, et. al. v. City of New York,* 2013
- "no findings of misconduct, actual bias or actual partiality": New York Times, *'Federal Panel Softens Tone on Judge It Removed From Stop-and-Frisk Case,'* 2013
- Finally, We're Winning The War Against Crime. Here's Why. Time Magazine, *'William Bratton, New York City's Top Cop,'* 1996
- "America's Top Cop": William Bratton, *'The Turnaround: How America's Top Cop Reversed the Crime Epidemic'* (Random House, 1998)
- "broken windows": The Atlantic, *'Broken Windows,'* 1982

- "The concern about equity is more serious ... that the police do not become the agents of neighborhood bigotry": ibid.
- "We can offer no wholly satisfactory answer to this important question": ibid.
- **George Mason University:** George Mason University, Center for Evidence-Based Crime Policy, *'Broken Windows Policing'*
- "I still to this day do not know if improving order will or will not reduce crime": New York Times, *'SCIENTIST AT WORK -- Felton Earls; On Crime As Science (A Neighbor At a Time),'* (2004)
- "People have not understood that this was a speculation": ibid.
- "These conditions didn't just happen": William J. Bratton, George L. Kelling, The Manhattan Institute, *'The Assault On 'Broken Windows' Policing,'* 2014
- "homicide rates also have decreased sharply in cities ... such as San Diego.": Richard Rosenfield, Sage Publications, *'Crime Decline in Context,'* 2002
- "entirely distinct": William J. Bratton, George L. Kelling, The Manhattan Institute, *'The Assault On 'Broken Windows' Policing,'* 2014
- "is based on reasonable suspicion that a crime has occurred, is occurring, or is about to occur": ibid.
- "is not a tactical response based on reasonable suspicion of possible criminality": ibid.
- "is a more broadly based policy mandating that police will address disorderly illegal behavior": ibid.
- **The rates of arrests and charges for minor offenses soared:** media reports from the *New York Daily News* and *New York Post,* 2014
- "Broken windows works, and it will remain the cornerstone of the New York City Police Department.": New York Times, *'Street Stops Still a 'Basic Tool,' Bratton Says,'* 2014
- "We will be focusing on ensuring that aggressive begging and squeegee pests": ibid.
- "still the right approach.": media reports from the *New York Daily News, New York Post* and *Gothamist*

NOTES: CHAPTER 4

- "the perpetrator's condition did not seem serious ... he was having difficulty breathing": New York Daily News, *'Internal NYPD report on incident with Staten Island dad Eric Garner does not mention chokehold, states he was not 'in great distress,"* 2014
  - "maintaining control ... did not appear to be in great distress.": ibid.
  - according to an internal NYPD report: ibid.
  - "As defined in the department's Patrol Guide ... this would appear to have been a chokehold": Transcript: Mayor de Blasio Holds Media Availability With Police Commissioner Bratton On The Death Of Eric Garner, 2014
  - Civilian Complaint Review Board ... released a report: Civilian Complaint Review Board, *'A Mutated Rule,'* 2014
  - OIG looked at ten illegal chokehold cases: OIG-NYPD, *'Observations on Accountability and Transparency in Ten NYPD Chokehold Cases,'* 2015
  - "that chokeholds are in fact prohibited by the NYPD": Transcript: Mayor de Blasio Holds Media Availability With Police Commissioner Bratton On The Death Of Eric Garner, 2014
  - "final determination": ibid.

- "too early to jump to conclusions": ibid.
- "I'm tired of this! It stops today!": Ramsey Orta video of Eric Garner arrest, 2014
- Lieutenant Chris Bannon was driving by Staten Island's Tompkinsville Park: media reports and NYPD trial judge's opinion, New York City Police Department disciplinary case number 2018-19274
- "To who? To who?": Ramsey Orta video of Eric Garner arrest, 2014
- "I did nothing." ibid.
- Bloomberg slapped a tax: New York Times, 'Bloomberg's Plan Would Make Stores Conceal Cigarettes,' 2013
- "I was just standing here minding my own business": Ramsey Orta video of Eric Garner arrest, 2014
- Garner was telling the truth: New York Times, 'Beyond the Chokehold: The Path to Eric Garner's Death,' 2015
- "don't touch me": Ramsey Orta video of Eric Garner arrest, 2014
- "I can't breathe": ibid.
- "Let up, you got him already": New York Times, 'Beyond the Chokehold: The Path to Eric Garner's Death,' 2015
- "Sir? We're EMS. We're here to help you...Get in the stretcher" Taisha Allen video of Eric Garner arrest, 2014
- "he's breathing.": ibid.
- "Danny and Justin went to collar Eric Garner ... Might be DOA.": media reports and NYPD trial judge's opinion, New York City Police Department disciplinary case number 2018-19274
- "For the smokes?" ibid.
- "Yeah they observed him selling ... He's most likely DOA." ibid.
- "Not a big deal. We were affecting a lawful arrest": ibid.
- "Don't forget on Saturday it's our family reunion in Prospect Park": Gwen Carr, 'This Stops Today,' (Rowman & Littlefield, 2018)
- "I didn't forget. What do you need me to bring?": ibid.
- "Just bring soda and water. We got the rest.": ibid.
- "OK, bye, Ma. I love you.": ibid.
- "Love you too.": ibid.
- Carr had suffered loss in her life before: ibid.

- "immediate area had been the subject of numerous community complaints ... as well as 646 nine-eleven calls for service within the immediate area of that very small park": Transcript: Mayor de Blasio Holds Media Availability With Police Commissioner Bratton On The Death Of Eric Garner, 2014
- "Broken Windows, Broken Lives": New York Times Editorial Board, *'Broken Windows, Broken Lives,'* 2014
- "acknowledge the heavy price paid for heavy enforcement": ibid.
- "Broken windows and its variants ... have pointlessly burdened thousands of young people...": ibid.
- "that wasn't right": Gwen Carr, *'This Stops Today,'* (Rowman & Littlefield, 2018)
- "As a mayor, when something horrible happens in your city, you change your plans and show up": ibid.
- "incessant and draining and intense": Wall Street Journal, 'Q&A With Mayor Bill de Blasio in Italy,' 2014
- "steady drop in crime ... should be an expectation that the intrusion of police into citizens' lives should also diminish.": Transcript: Mayor de Blasio Swears in Police Commissioner William J. Bratton, Hosts Media Availability at 1 Police Plaza, January 2014
- "low-level offenses": Transcript: Mayor de Blasio Holds Media Availability with Police Commissioner Bratton, 2014
- "breaking a law is breaking a law, and it has to be addressed in one form or another.": ibid.
- "a roundtable on police-community relations": Transcript: Mayor de Blasio Hosts Roundtable on Police-Community Relations, 2014
- "no justification ... subjected to a chokehold and the result is he is no longer with us." ibid.
- "Fight back, community ... We're redeemers of this city.": media reports on Eric Garner's funeral, 2014
- "When Bratton was under Giuliani ... knew him as 'friend.'": New York Daily News, *'Rev. Al Sharpton says with Bill Bratton as top cop, there's reason for hope,'* 2013

- "have had shared interests in keeping our streets safe.": ibid.
- "It's important to remember ... at the end of the day we are all in the same bed": ibid.
- "practice what Mandela preached: freedom for all, respect for all, compassion for all.": media reports on Bill Bratton's visit to ev. Al Sharpton's National Action Network office, 2013
- "Those were the prophetic words that were uttered by Eric Garner on July 17 just before he was put into a chokehold.": Transcript: Mayor de Blasio Hosts Roundtable on Police-Community Relations, 2014
- "Let me be very direct": ibid.
- "captured the hope of the city ... seemed sensitive ... caught in between two serious problems.": ibid.
- "gone over the line.": ibid.
- "But now...we have to go from that hope to actuality ... transformational ... not just another politician.": ibid.
- "If Dante wasn't your son, he'd be a candidate for a chokehold": ibid.
- "You don't need training if a man saying 11 times I can't breathe, and you still hold him in a grip": ibid.
- "I heard the commissioner say race wasn't involved ... tell the community to wait on the results?": ibid.
- "I personally don't think that race was a factor ... I don't think the issue of race entered into this at all.": The Observer, 'Bratton on Eric Garner Death: 'I Personally Don't Think That Race Was a Factor,' 2014 (https://observer.com/2014/07/bratton-on-eric-garner-death-i-personally-dont-think-that-race-was-a-factor/)
- "The best way to make police stop using illegal chokeholds is to perp walk one of them that did.": Transcript: Mayor de Blasio Hosts Roundtable on Police-Community Relations, 2014
- "disagreed in some respects": ibid.
- "essential catalyst": ibid.
- "deficient": ibid.
- "the good that came out of it, not just the negative.": ibid.
- "the man who put an end to stop and frisk": ibid.

- "deeply troubled": ibid.
- "It pains us to this hour": ibid.
- "It would be a great disservice and injustice to not find change and reform out of this moment": ibid.
- "create a mutual respect": ibid.
- "We have to do both...one without the other is a disservice to the communities we all serve": ibid.
- "protect Al Sharpton's right to have his opinion, but his opinion should not be elevated.": television interview on NY1 by PBA President Patrick Lynch, 2014
- "I'll shake hands with the devil if necessary to keep this city calm, safe, and secure": media reports from *New York Daily News*, *NY Post*, and *Gothamist*, 2014
- "compression of neck (choke hold) ... Garner's asthma, obesity, and hypersensitive cardiovascular disease were "contributing conditions.": media reports from *New York Times*, *New York Daily News*, *NY Post*, and *Gothamist*, 2014
- "no reasonable cause": media reports from *Staten Island Advance*, *New York Daily News*, and *NY Post*, 2014
- That effort failed: media reports from *Staten Island Advance*, *New York Daily News*, 2015
- "I said they put him in a chokehold ... you can't say they put him in a chokehold.": New York Times, *'Beyond the Chokehold: The Path to Eric Garner's Death,'* 2015
- "a mature, mature police officer who's motivated by serving the community": PBA President Patrick Lynch press conference, 2014
- "He literally, literally, is an Eagle Scout": ibid.
- "Textbook": ibid.
- "We feel badly that there was a loss of life ... Garner made a choice that day to resist arrest.": ibid.
- "take special care": Transcript: Mayor de Blasio Holds Media Availability at Mt. Sinai United Christian Church on Staten Island December 3, 2014
- "under the bus": media reports on comments from PBA President Patrick Lynch, 2014

- "We have a team here that's focused and ready to get things done": Transcript: Mayor de Blasio Hosts Roundtable on Police-Community Relations, 2014
- "understands the important role of oversight": ibid.
- "Burden": ibid.
- "a well-known reformer and change agent": ibid.
- "to help us make ... fair to both community members and police officers.": ibid.
- "unprecedented and huge step for progress.": ibid.
- "aggressively settled outstanding lawsuits": ibid.
- "The change has been happening. The change will continue to deepen. And it will be felt in every neighborhood of this city": ibid.
- "Who's The Boss!": *New York Post* front page, August 1, 2014

NOTES: CHAPTER 5

- **"ice box."**: media reports *New York Post* and *New York Times*, 2017
  - **Narcotics-lite**: New York Times, *'After Suspect's Killing, Kelly Orders Review of Drug Units,'* 2012
  - **The 30-year-old ex-Marine**: New York Magazine, *'The Bullet, the Cop, the Boy,'* 2017
  - **"you ready?"**: testimony from Richard Haste and John McLoughlin at Haste NYPD disciplinary trial, 2017
  - **"Show me your hands!"**: ibid.
  - **Patricia Hartley**: court documents from *Estate of Ramarley Graham v. The City of New York* (1:13-cv-02015), Southern District of New York, 2013
  - **"Fuck you ... Suck my dick."**: New York Magazine, *'The Bullet, the Cop, the Boy,'* 2017
  - **"Why did you shoot him ... Get the fuck away before I have to shoot you too."** court documents from *Estate of Ramarley Graham v. The City of New York* (1:13-cv-02015), Southern District of New York, 2013
  - **Haste admitted that he yelled at the grandmother ... said he didn't threaten to shoot her**: New York Magazine, *'The Bullet, the Cop, the Boy,'* 2017
  - **"the homicide"**: interview with Constance Malcolm, 2021

- "They killed Marley!": ibid.
- "You gonna kill me like you killed my son?": ibid.
- Patricia Hartley claimed the police kept her at the precinct for seven hours that day: court documents from *Estate of Ramarley Graham v. The City of New York* (1:13-cv-02015), Southern District of New York, 2013
- "Part of the healing process ... derives from a fair, speedy and transparent investigation": media reports on comments by Public Advocate Bill de Blasio by *The Observer* and *New York Times*, 2012
- "That work should begin immediately": ibid.
- **Jateik Reed:** interview with attorney Gideon Oliver and media reports from the *New York Daily News*.
- "expedite his investigation ... Time is of the essence": media reports on comments by Public Advocate Bill de Blasio by *The Observer* and *New York Times*, 2012
- **Graham struggled with the officer:** media reports from the *New York Daily News* and *New York Post*.
- "We're still evaluating the actions here": ibid.
- "We see an unarmed person being shot. That always concerns us": ibid.
- "This was a tragic case ... in the best interest of the city.": ibid.
- "should not be allowed to sully the badge that so many other good cops wear with honor": media reports from the *Associated Press* and *New York Post*.
- **Richie Perez:** interview with Joo-Hyun Kang and 'The Richie Perez Papers,' archives of the Puerto Rican Diaspora Centro de Estudios Puertorriqueños, Hunter College

NOTES: CHAPTER 6

• The Legal Aid Society is the largest public defender organization in the country: Legal Aid Society "About us" section on website

  • Freedom of Information Law request: court documents from *Luongo v. CCRB Records Officers and Daniel Pantaleo*

  • "Body Snatchers": New York Daily News, *'Repeated charges of illegal searches, violence, racial profiling, racial slurs and intimidation against Lt. Daniel Sbarra and his team have cost the city more than $1.5 million in settlements,'* 2013

  • By 2013, Sbarra himself had been the subject of 30 civilian complaints in 15 years: ibid.

  • a staggering 58 times: ibid.

  • Sbarra was personally named in at least 15 lawsuits: ibid.

  • those suits cost the city almost $500,000 to settle: ibid.

  • "Nigger": ibid

  • In one of Conti-Cook's cases ... lawsuit was settled for $50,000: ibid.

  • the police department docked him 20 vacation days: ibid.

  • 230,000 cases per year: Slate, *'The Bad Cop Database,'* 2015

  • On Christmas Eve, the CCRB responded to Conti-Cook's

request for Pantaleo's files: court documents from *Luongo v. CCRB Records Officers and Daniel Pantaleo*

• **"personnel records ... not subject to inspection or review":** 50-a bill text and jacket; Bill No. 7635, Bill Jacket 1973, ch. 413 ¶ 6

• **"fishing expeditions":** ibid.

• **"The Patrolmen's Benevolent Association of the New York City Transit Police ... and have abused and misused these files.":** ibid.

• **During the Summer of 1967, violence and riots broke out in 150 cities across the country:** Michael W. Flamm, *'In The Heat of the Summer'* (UPENN Press, 2017)

• **The National Advisory Commission on Civil Disorders:** KERNER COMMISSION REPORT ON THE CAUSES, EVENTS, AND AFTERMATHS OF THE CIVIL DISORDERS OF 1967

• **"Our nation is moving toward two societies, one black, one white, separate and unequal.":** ibid.

• **In 1961, the court held that any evidence obtained by unconstitutional search and seizure is inadmissible in court:** *Mapp v. Ohio*, U.S. Supreme Court, 1961

• **A couple of years later in 1964, the court ruled that statements made by a suspect after they requested and had been denied an attorney were also not admissible at trial:** *Escobedo v. Illinois*, U.S. Supreme Court, 1964

• **In 1966 — in one of the most well-known Supreme Court rulings ... commonly known as the *Miranda* rights, after the name of the case:** *Miranda v. Arizona*, U.S. Supreme Court, 1966

• **"*us vs. them*" mentality:** Katherine J. Bies, *'LET THE SUNSHINE IN: ILLUMINATING THE POWERFUL ROLE POLICE UNIONS PLAY IN SHIELDING OFFICER MISCONDUCT,'* (Stanford Law & Policy Review, Vol. 28)

• **Going back more than ten years earlier, in 1950:** Vincent J. Cannato, *'The Ungovernable City,'* (Basic Books, 2001)

• **In 1965, John Lindsay promised during his campaign for mayor he would create a "mixed" review board of police and citizens:** ibid.

• **After he was elected, the following year in 1966, Mayor Lindsay attempted to reform the CCRB:** ibid.

- By 1966, the PBA had grown its ranks to 20,000 members: ibid.
- The PBA staged a rally to protest the mayor's restructuring of the CCRB: ibid.
- The PBA set out to get a referendum to repeal Lindsay's CCRB placed on the New York City ballot: ibid.
- "The addict, the criminal, the hoodlum — only the policeman stands between you and him.": ibid.
- "This is the aftermath of a riot in a city that had a civilian review board": ibid
- Philadelphia established the first civilian review board ... the police commissioner in Philly during the riots: ibid.
- "The Civilian Review Board must be stopped...Her life...your life...may depend on it.": ibid.
- "slimiest kind of racism.": ibid.
- "The only thing it didn't show was a gang of Negroes about to attack her. It was a vulgar, obscene advertisement if I've ever seen one.": ibid.
- The referendum passed by almost a two to one margin, 63 to 37 percent: ibid.
- "wielded crucial authority over legislation substantially affecting the police ranks" became a "focus": ibid.
- "Accustomed to lobbyers, the representatives and senators welcomed the PBA as a source of campaign funds, support, and good times": Anthony V. Bouza, *'Police Unions - Paper Tigers or Roaring Lions?'* (From Police Leadership in America, P 241-280, 1985, William a Geller, ed. - See NCJ-98325)
- During a five year period, from 2015 to 2020, the union shelled out more than $1.4 million: The City, *'Police Union Poised to Tap War Chest to Shield Cop Discipline Records,'* 2020
- From January 2015 through May 2020: ibid.
- In 1974 ... the state enacted its first Freedom of Information Law (FOIL): NY State Legislature, PUBLIC OFFICERS LAW, ARTICLE 6 SECTIONS 84-90 FREEDOM OF INFORMATION LAW
- Governor Malcolm Wilson vetoed it: Albany Times-Union, *'Court rulings shroud records,'* (2016)

- Hugh Carey, vetoed it again: ibid.
- the state's budget office said the bill created unnecessary court procedures: 50-a bill text and jacket; Bill No. 7635, Bill Jacket 1973, ch. 413 ¶ 6
- "All the participants in the criminal justice system should ... with the trust of maintaining the public's right to justice.": ibid.
- "analogous to a village placing a glass dome over Town Hall ... fears the custodian will forget to put up the screens in May.": ibid.
- "These abuses can be stopped and the civil rights of police officers upheld by enactment of this bill": ibid.
- In 1999, a group of off-duty cops from Schenectady, New York: court documents from *Daily Gazette v. Schenectady*, 1999
- *The Daily Gazette:* ibid.
- "was to stop private attorneys from using subpoenas ...if the law is being misused, then obviously an amendment might be in order.": Albany Times-Union, *'Court rulings shroud records,'* (2016)
- Legal Aid decided to take the matter further and sue the CCRB and the city for Pantaleo's records in early 2015: court documents from *Luongo v. CCRB Records Officers and Daniel Pantaleo*
- In a sworn statement, Pantaleo said he'd already received a death threat from a person in Michigan on Facebook, leading to 24-7 police protection: ibid.
- "any adverse reactions expressed ... the Staten Island Grand Jury's subsequent decision not to indict him." ibid.
- "we've never seen [the CCRB] work in a consistent manner.": Transcript: Mayor de Blasio appoints Commissioner of The Department of Buildings, Chair of Civilian Complaint Review Board, Chair and Vice Chair of Mayor's Advisory Committee on the Judiciary, 2014
- a settlement paid out to about 100,000 people: New York Times, *'City Reaches $33 Million Settlement Over Strip Searches,'* 2010
- the city agreed to pay him $1.9 million: L.A. Times, *'Wrongly Convicted Man Wins $1.9-Million Judgment, but Normal Life May Elude Him,'* 1989
- *Guilty Until Proven Innocent:* IMDB, Guilty Until Proven Innocent, 1999

• **New York City's Board of Estimates, an opaque, 200-year-old government body:** Gotham Gazette, *'26 Years Since the Board of Estimate's Demise,'* 2015

• **The justices ruled in his favor 9-0:** ibid.

• **Statistics about the agency at this time revealed its ineffectiveness:** OIG-NYPD, *'Observations on Accountability and Transparency in Ten NYPD Chokehold Cases,'* 2015

• **In the CCRB's 2014 year-end report:** CCRB Annual Report 2014 January-December

• **"During the CCRB's internal review of past practices ... pertaining to the complaint histories of specific police officers":** ibid.

• **"even though this information is confidential and protected from public disclosure.":** ibid.

• **"The person responsible for these breaches is no longer an employee of the CCRB":** ibid.

• **"he felt that the judge's opinion was right ... with our appeal.":** Public Board Meeting of the Civilian Complaint Review Board, September 2015

• **"And I strongly disagree with him":** ibid.

• **Pantaleo denied that he had used a prohibited chokehold during the Garner altercation:** interview with Richard Emery, media reports and NYPD trial judge's opinion, case 2018-19274

• **"Colluded"** media reports from *Gothamist* and the *New York Daily News,* 2014

• **"Frivolous":** ibid.

• **In early 2016, two of the city's unions ... called for Emery's removal:** media reports from the *New York Post* and *New York Daily News,* 2014

• **Before becoming agency chair, the city's Conflict of Interest Board cleared Emery:** ibid.

• **"I'm not going to deprive the public and people ... because some union is squealing like a stuck pig":** New York Daily News, *'CCRB chairman says police unions are 'squealing like a stuck pig' for calling for his removal,'* 2016

• **"takes every opportunity to trample on the rights of and retal-**

iate against those who complain about his misogynistic views": New York Daily News, *'Civilian Complaint Review Board Chairman Richard Emery steps down a day after he was sued over misogynistic comments,'* 2016

- **Malik dropped her suit a month later:** ibid.
- **the city settled with Tracy Catapano-Fox for $275,000:** ibid.
- **In early April, the *New York Daily News* reported that Pantaleo was accused ... more than two years before Garner's death:** New York Daily News, *'Daniel Pantaleo — cop who dodged charges in Eric Garner's death — disciplined by NYPD for bogus stop-and-frisk,'* 2016
- **"Bulge":** ibid.
- **"unauthorized frisk without legal authority.":** ibid.
- **As for how the *Daily News* learned about the incident, it turned out the reporters had seen the information posted on a clipboard:** interview with Cynthia Conti-Cook and media report from *The New Yorker*
- **Conti-Cook and Legal Aid upped the ante in their pursuit of NYPD disciplinary history:** court documents from *Luongo v. CCRB Records Officers and Daniel Pantaleo*
- **"a lapse in oversight on our part"** New York Daily News, *'Bratton defends NYPD's move to stop sharing cops' disciplinary records,'* (2016)
- **"brought to our attention, we corrected it"** ibid.
- **"So all the focus, all the ire, all the concern, basically go a couple hundred miles north ... rather than continuing to harangue the New York City Police Department":** ibid.
- **"In terms of the specific disciplinary pieces that state law precludes that disclosure, so we obviously have to honor state law":** Transcript: Mayor de Blasio Announces Major Increase in the Number of Tenants in Housing Court Who Have Legal Representation, 2016
- **a 2011 lawsuit from the New York Civil Liberties Union:** court documents from *Matter of New York Civ. Liberties Union v New York City Police Dept.*

NOTES: CHAPTER 7

• "He's stabbing me! Shoot him!": media reports and court documents from *Bah v. City of N.Y.* (13-cv-6690), 2013

• According to the NYPD ... piercing two of their vests with the blade, police said: media reports from the New York Post and New York Daily News, 2012

• The confrontation between the ESU team and Bah lasted about 15 seconds: court documents from *Bah v. City of N.Y.* (13-cv-6690), 2013

• When they tried to subdue Bah ... Mateo extended his hand and fired five bullets at Bah during the confrontation: ibid.

• The officers shot a total of ten bullets ... The final shot to his head killed him: ibid.

• This was essentially the story that the NYPD put out on that night: New York Daily News, *'Man shot and killed by police in upper Manhattan was wielding 13-inch knife: NYPD,'* 2012

• He said that Bah was not stabbing him when he called out to his fellow officers to shoot him: Washington Post, *'Did New York police lie about the death of Mohamed Bah?,'* 2015

• Det. Mateo was about to eat with another ESU officer ... hold back a suspect: trial transcript and court documents from *Bah v. City of N.Y.* (13-cv-6690), 2013

- The ranking officer on the scene ... spoke with Hawa Bah: court documents from *Bah v. City of N.Y.* (13-cv-6690), 2013
- "a male black opened the door, that he had a knife in his hands, and then the door was closed": ibid.
- Before they went in, the ESU unit popped out the door's peephole ... Bah didn't respond: ibid.
- "Go": ibid.
- "two seconds": ibid.
- "all the pops going off at the same time": ibid.
- An internal investigation by the NYPD found the shooting justified: New York Post, *'Cops who shot man dead cleared of wrongdoing,'* 2013
- A little over a year later, in November 2013, a grand jury declined to indict the officers on criminal charges: ibid.
- As for officer discipline ... his penalty was a letter asking him to review department policy: ibid.
- Hawa Bah sued the NYPD and city for $70 million: media reports and court documents from *Bah v. City of N.Y.* (13-cv-6690)
- According to recent data from the city ... the data shows that the city spent over a billion dollars settling suits against the police: Pro Publica, *'New York City Paid an NBA Star Millions After an NYPD Officer Broke His Leg. The Officer Paid Little Price.'* 2021
- Joanna Schwartz: JOANNA C. SCHWARTZ, 'Police Indemnification' NEW YORK UNIVERSITY LAW REVIEW ISSUE Volume 89, Number 3 JUNE 2014
- NYPD officers tackled NBA player Thabo Sefolosha outside a Manhattan club: Pro Publica, *'New York City Paid an NBA Star Millions After an NYPD Officer Broke His Leg. The Officer Paid Little Price.'* 2021
- *NYC gives machete-wielding thug $5K for menacing cops:* New York Post, *'NYC gives machete-wielding thug $5K for menacing cops,'* 2015
- "Outrageous": New York Post, *'Bratton 'outraged' NYC gave machete man $5K for menacing cops,'* 2015
- "make him go away": ibid.
- "Our cops work very hard trying to keep this city safe, and if

they're not going to be backed up by the city law office, we need to do something about that": ibid.
- "We should stand and fight in these lawsuits. These are frivolous lawsuits. They're just an attempt to scam the city for money" Transcript: Mayor de Blasio Holds Impromptu Press Gaggle, 2015
- "not fair": ibid.
- "[It's] some ambulance-chasing lawyers trying to make a lot of money": ibid.
- "Frivolous": ibid.
- "broken policy": ibid.
- "it's worth it to end the madness": ibid.
- "coddle these ambulance-chasing lawyers anymore": New York Times, *'New York City Takes Steps to Better Fight Suits Against Police,'* 2015
- The year before he was elected ... in the 1989 rape of a female jogger in Central Park: New York Times, *'In Final Weeks, a Push to Put Bloomberg's Stamp on Major Legal Cases,'* 2013
- "It's long past time to heal these wounds...As a city, we have a moral obligation to right this injustice.": ibid.
- the city settled the case and paid the men ... about $1 million for each year they collectively spent in jail: New York Times, *'Settlement Is Approved in Central Park Jogger Case, but New York Deflects Blame,'* 2014
- That year, de Blasio made good on his promise to bolster the legal resources of the city to defend the NYPD: New York Times, *'New York City Takes Steps to Better Fight Suits Against Police,'* 2015
- "nuisance value": ibid.
- "Today, the taunt on the street is, 'Go ahead and arrest me because I'm going to file my lawsuit, and the city's going to give me money'": ibid.
- "simply not true.": ibid.
- Edward Byrne: media reports from the *New York Times* and *Staten Island Advance,* 2012
- Larry Byrne led a campaign against their release: ibid.
- $200 million: Pro Publica, *'New York City Paid an NBA Star Millions After an NYPD Officer Broke His Leg. The Officer Paid Little Price.'* 2021

- **Kenneth Chamberlain, Sr.:** New York Times, *'Police Killing of Mentally Ill Black Man Is, 5 Years Later, Headed to Trial,'* 2016
- "I don't need you! I didn't call you!": ibid.
- "Nigger": ibid.
- Police claimed Chamberlain was holding a knife, and it was an act of self-defense: ibid.
- No officers were criminally charged over Chamberlain's death: ibid.
- a lawsuit by Chamberlain's family was still ongoing: ibid.
- "Mr. Bah wasn't stabbing you while you were on the ground, was he?" media reports and court documents from *Bah v. City of N.Y.* (13-cv-6690), 2013
- "No": ibid.
- "When you said, 'He's stabbing me. Shoot him,' did you see Mr. Bah stabbing anybody?": ibid.
- "No.": ibid.
- *Washington Post:* Washington Post, *'Did New York police lie about the death of Mohamed Bah?,'* 2015
- "never vouchered": New York Daily News, *'NYPD destroyed evidence in 2012 Harlem shooting that killed Mohamed Bah, lawsuit says,'* 2016
- The city claimed both the knife and Mateo's shirt were contaminated during the storm and unavailable: ibid.
- "the strongest sanctions possible": ibid.
- "outlandish and inflammatory": ibid.
- "They're getting away with murder. The intentional shooting of an individual and then covering it up — that's murder.": ibid.

NOTES: CHAPTER 8

• Delrawn Small spent July 3, 2016, at a pre-Fourth of July party with family and friends in the East New York neighborhood of Brooklyn: media reports from *New York Daily News*, *NY Post* and *DNA Info*, 2016
   • a Nissan Altima cut them off: media reports of trial testimony from Zaquanna Albert
   • Zaniah, who had her head on the baby's car seat in the back: media reports of trial testimony from Zaniah Albert
   • Wayne Isaacs: media reports and trial testimony from Zaquanna Albert
   • exchanged a look: ibid.
   • "Don't get out": ibid.
   • "The kids are in the car.": ibid.
   • "What the fuck is wrong with you? You cut us off. You could've killed my family": media reports of trial testimony from Wayne Isaacs
   • he could tell he was laser-focused on him: ibid.
   • When Small got to his vehicle, he reared back with his fist and punched Issacs in the face through the driver's side window: ibid.
   • Albert saw a spark: media reports of trial testimony from Zaquanna Albert
   • Small stumbled back and ... and fell facedown between two

parked cars: New York Post/YouTube 'Video surfaces of an off-duty NYC cop shooting a man during a road-rage incident,' 2016

• **One bullet hit Small in the stomach, another grazed his head, and a third hit him in the chest and pierced his aorta:** New Republic, *'How Videos of Police Brutality Traumatize African Americans and Undermine the Search for Justice,'* 2019

• **EMS pronounced him dead at the scene:** ibid.

• **After he shot Small ... he just turned and walked back towards the Altima, still idling on the street with the hazard lights on:** New York Post/YouTube 'Video surfaces of an off-duty NYC cop shooting a man during a road-rage incident,' 2016

• **"I'm a police officer, and I was attacked."** media reports and recording of Wayne Isaacs 911 call

• **"It's an emergency.":** ibid.

• **"Oh my god!":** ibid.

• **repeatedly punched:** New York Post, *'Road-rage incident leads off-duty cop to fatally shoot man,'* 2016

• **"discharged his firearm during the assault.":** ibid.

• **"kept hitting me":** New York Daily News, *'NYPD cop Wayne Isaacs 'had no legal justification' for firing his weapon in the murder of Delrawn Small, prosecutor says,'* 2016

• **"much, much too early":** New York Post, *'Road-rage incident leads off-duty cop to fatally shoot man,'* 2016

• **"traffic dispute":** ibid.

• **"We are comfortable, based on preliminary investigation, that it was an apparent road-rage incident that precipitated the events":** ibid.

• **Alton Sterling:** media reports from Associated Press, NBC News, NY Times, and others, 2016

• **Philando Castile:** ibid.

• **She live-streamed the aftermath of the incident on Facebook:** ibid.

• **Dallas:** ibid.

• **he killed five officers and wounded seven more along with two civilians:** ibid.

- **"punching the shit"**: New York Post, *'Motorist appears to punch off-duty cop before fatal shooting,'* 2016
- **"big haymakers"**: ibid.
- **arrested 19 times**: ibid.
- **a new video of the incident**: New York Post, *'Video surfaces of NYPD cop's road-rage shooting,'* 2016
- **"waited just one second"**: ibid.
- **"barely has time to look the cop in the eye or even utter a word before Isaacs opens fire, causing him to stagger back"**: ibid.
- **"So, when you think about that, the lives of everyday New Yorkers are freer ... And people have every reason to feel safer"**: Transcript: Mayor Bill de Blasio, Police Commissioner William Bratton Hold Media Availability To Discuss Latest Crime Statistics, 2016
- **"When you say Black lives matter, that's inherently racist"**: ibid.
- **"Black lives matter. White lives matter. Asian lives matter. Hispanic lives matter. That's anti-American, and it's racist"**: interview with Rudy Giuliani, CBS's "Face the Nation," 2016
- **"The reason the morale of the police department of the City of New York is so low is one reason and one reason alone: David Dinkins!"**: New York Magazine, *'The Forgotten City Hall Riot,'* 2021
- **"The mayor doesn't know why the morale of the police department is so low ... he blames it on me. He blames it on you. Bullshit!"**: ibid.
- **"trial by combat"**: media reports from Associated Press, CNN, New York Times, and others, 2021
- **Giuliani's legal representatives**: Forbes, *'Giuliani Claims His Call For 'Trial By Combat' On Jan. 6 Shouldn't Have Been Taken Literally As Legal Woes Mount,'* 2021
- **"When there are 60 shootings in Chicago over the Fourth of July and 14 murders, and Black Lives Matter is nonexistent ... and then there's one police murder of very questionable circumstances and we hear from Black Lives Matter, we wonder: Do Black lives matter, or only the very few Black lives that are killed by White policemen?"**: interview with Rudy Giuliani, CBS's "Face the Nation," 2016

• **Bratton and Giuliani clashed:** New York Times, *'THE BRATTON RESIGNATION: THE OVERVIEW;BRATTON QUITS POLICE POST; NEW YORK GAINS OVER CRIME FED A RIVALRY WITH GIULIANI,'* 1996

• **"When I see marches....only on the issue of shootings by police...I say there's a different kind of bigotry because, like all prejudices, it is based on stereotypes and labels":** Transcript: Mayor Bill de Blasio, Police Commissioner William Bratton Hold Media Availability To Discuss Latest Crime Statistics, 2016

• **"We need to see police not as racists and bigots and murderers ... Unfortunately, some are. And we'll find them, and we'll deal with them":** ibid.

• **Bill Bratton announced he was leaving his position as NYPD commissioner:** New York Times, *'Police Commissioner Bratton Won't Stay on the Job Past 2017,'* 2016

• **the NYPD's Inspector General (IG) issued a blistering report:** OIG-NYPD, *'An Analysis of Quality-of-Life Summonses, Quality-of-Life Misdemeanor Arrests, and Felony Crime in New York City, 2010-2015'*

• **"It is not an expert study":** WNYC, *'Bratton and NYPD Bigs Trash Inspector General Report,'* 2016

• **"It is deeply flawed. It is of no value at all":** ibid.

• **"I'm not sure of the quality of the researchers at the OIG ... The city spends a lot of money on staffing that. I think we have made it quite clear if you want to delve into these types of areas, you're going to need experts, not amateurs.":** ibid.

• **"Broken Windows is Not Broken":** William J. Bratton, *'Broken Windows Is Not Broken: The NYPD Response to the Inspector General's Report on Quality-of-Life Enforcement,'* 2016

• **"betrays a complete ignorance":** ibid.

• **"Questionable":** ibid.

• **"faulty statistical reasoning":** ibid.

• **"is not strong enough to make valid causal conclusions regarding the relationship between the practices of the police and crime outcomes":** ibid.

- "recommendation that the NYPD should rely on a 'more data-driven approach ... is certainly a very good one.'": ibid.
- "There are police reformers from outside the profession ... more or less legislating a new order. It is not." New York Times, *'William J. Bratton: How to Reform Policing From Within,'* 2016
- "Such oversight usually has only marginal impact ... What changes police culture is leadership from within.": ibid.
- "very disturbing" New York Daily News, *'De Blasio calls video of Delrawn Small's fatal shooting by an off-duty cop in road-rage dispute 'disturbing,'* 2016
- "hard to make out exactly what happened.": ibid.
- "We have to hear from the attorney general what his investigation reveals": ibid.
- "major step forward." New York Times, *Cuomo to Appoint Special Prosecutor for Killings by Police,* 2016
- "A criminal justice system doesn't work without trust": ibid.
- The attorney general at the time, Eric Schneiderman, had pushed the governor to give him this power after the local DA failed to indict the officer who killed Eric Garner in 2014.: ibid.
- "create an independent prosecutor who does not have that kind of connection with the organized police departments.": ibid.
- "gravely flawed ... I am more than able to thoroughly and fairly investigate any fatality of an unarmed civilian by a police officer." Observer, *'Brooklyn D.A. Rages Against Special Prosecutor Proposal for Eric Garner-Like Cases,'* 2016
- Carr and Malcolm authored an op-ed that ran in *The Daily News:* New York Daily News, *'Cuomo's Unkept Justice Promise,'* 2016
- "I'll hug you when I get justice for my son.": Huffington Post, *'Cuomo Appointed A Special Prosecutor For New York Killings Involving Police,'* 2016
- In New York state, a person has the right to use deadly physical force if they reasonably believe that the assailant is using or about to use lethal force against them or commit a violent crime, such as rape or robbery: New York State SECTION 35.15, Justification; use of phys-

ical force in defense of a person, Penal (PEN) CHAPTER 40, PART 1, TITLE C, ARTICLE 35

- **In September 2016, the New York attorney general charged Isaacs with second-degree murder and manslaughter:** media reports from *New York Daily News*, *New York Times* and *New York Post*

- **He spent six nights in jail under protective custody at Rikers Island before posting bail:** New York Daily News, *'Cop facing 25 to life for killing unarmed Brooklyn man out on bail after less than a week at Rikers,'* 2016

NOTES: CHAPTER 9

- **state criminal charges against Haste fell apart:** New York Times, *'Grand Jury Decides Not to Charge Officer Who Fatally Shot Unarmed Youth in Bronx,'* 2013
  - **federal prosecutors decided against criminally charging Haste:** press release: *U.S. Attorney's Office Closes Investigation Into The Death Of Ramarley Graham,* 2016
  - **Preet Bharara:** ibid.
  - **"The mayor has not spoken with any of the involved parties so as to avoid prejudicing the process ... move forward":** The Observer, *'Ramarley Graham's Mother Wants Answers From the City on Unarmed Son's Death,'* 2016
  - **his salary grew by $30,000 to more than $94,000 from the regular raises he enjoyed:** New York Times, *'The Police Killed My Unarmed Son in 2012. I'm Still Waiting for Justice,'* 2017
  - **NYPD's internal Firearms Discharge Review Board found the shooting justified:** New York Times, *'Cop who killed Ramarley Graham in 2012 faces NYPD justice as victim's friends and family look on,'* 2017
  - **Instead, they opted to charge him with a violation of department procedures:** ibid.

- "barricaded suspect": media reports and documents from New York City Police disciplinary proceedings 2012-7616
- "poor tactical judgment": ibid.
- "The rules are simple ... Isolate and contain.": ibid.
- "Ramarley Graham was a son, a brother, and a friend ... The tragic death of Ramarley Graham could have and should have been avoided": ibid.
- "Scapegoat": ibid.
- "Hero": ibid.
- "Second-guessing": ibid.
- "Show me your hands — that's all Ramarley Graham had to do": ibid.
- "within department guidelines": ibid.
- "one hundred percent ... there was a man with a gun": ibid.
- "No": ibid.
- "We were in hot pursuit of an armed suspect. I thought we could handle it": ibid.
- "Sarge, I saw him reach": ibid.
- "show me your hands": ibid.
- "I thought I was about to be shot ... I expected to be dead.": ibid.
- a bag of marijuana was found floating in the toilet: Associated Press, *'I thought I was about to be shot,' white NYC officer says,'* 2017
- "Liar!": ibid.
- "I know what I did was justified in that I protected my life and my team, based on the information we had at hand ... I'm not pleased with the result.": media reports and documents from New York City Police disciplinary proceedings 2012-7616
- "He doesn't have any remorse ... Every day he comes to court, he have that stupid grin on his damn face.": Associated Press, *'I thought I was about to be shot,' white NYC officer says,'* 2017
- "repeated, flagrant, and avoidable." media reports and Final Order of Dismissal from New York City Police disciplinary proceedings 2012-7616
- "A reasonable officer in that position would have proceeded very differently": ibid.

- Haste learned about Maldonado's decision on Friday, March 24, 2107: New York Daily News, *'NYPD cop who killed unarmed teen Ramarley Graham quits before he's fired; victim's outraged mom slams Mayor de Blasio,'* 2017
- "chose to go out on my terms": CBS News, *'Ex-NYPD Officer Richard Haste Says He 'Chose To Go Out On My Terms','* 2017
- McLoughlin and Morris were also disciplined after making plea deals with the department: New York Daily News, *'Two Bronx cops finally punished for their roles in 2012 fatal shooting of teen Ramarley Graham,'* 2017
- "the right decision": media reports from New York Post, Gothamist, CNN and others.
- "Nothing can take away the profound pain left after his loss... But I hope the conclusion of this difficult process brings some measure of justice to those who loved him": ibid.
- "should be ashamed of themselves ... This is just another example that the de Blasio administration doesn't care about justice and accountability": Gothamist, *'Cop Who Killed Ramarley Graham Quits After NYPD Trial Says He Should Be Fired,'* 2017
- A 2013 audit of 38 city agencies reviewed their responsiveness to FOIL: Public Advocate Bill de Blasio, *"Transparency Report Card,"* 2013
- "is inviting waste and corruption by blocking information that belongs to the public": ibid.
- At a press conference to announce the request, somebody held a sign with Mayor de Blasio's initial statement from after Graham's death which read: The Observer, *'Ramarley Graham's Mother Wants Answers From the City on Unarmed Son's Death,'* 2016
- The records showed that in an official police report filed the night Graham was killed, officers wrote that he struggled with Haste for his gun: FOIL files 'Constance Malcolm,' % CPR & Justice Committee
- "Perp": ibid.
- "Struggled": ibid.
- November 2017 it finally went to trial: media reports and court documents from *Bah v. The City of New York* (SDNY, 1:13-cv-06690)

- An NYPD sergeant who fired his Taser testified: ibid.
- autopsy: ibid.
- Lieutenant Michael Licitra: ibid.
- "So you did say at some point when you were on the ground say 'shoot him, he's stabbing me,' right?": ibid.
- "That's correct": ibid.
- "And at that point, Mr. Bah wasn't stabbing you, was he?": ibid.
- "He was advancing at me.": ibid.
- "Was he stabbing you, sir, at that moment when you were on the ground...I can't recall,": ibid.
- "Can you just explain to the jury, on September 25, 2012, why did you shoot your weapon?": ibid.
- "On the evening of September 25, 2012 ... I was in a fight for my life.": ibid.
- "So just what was it that you saw or observed that caused you to employ your firearm?": ibid.
- "I observed Mr. Bah coming at me, and he was stabbing me. He was stabbing my vest, my lower torso area.": ibid.
- Det. Mateo fired five shots inside Bah's apartment: ibid.
- Baden: bio page: https://www.drmichaelbaden.com/bio
- Baden said the bullet entered Bah's head behind his ear ...from two feet away or less. media reports and court documents from *Bah v. The City of New York* (SDNY, 1:13-cv-06690)
- In Baden's opinion: ibid.
- The jury ruled in Hawa Bah's favor. They awarded her $2.2 million in damages to be paid by the city: Associated Press, *'NY jury awards $2.2 million in police shooting of immigrant,'* 2017
- Liable: media reports and court documents from *Bah v. The City of New York* (SDNY, 1:13-cv-06690)
- They filed a motion asking the judge to overturn the jury's verdict on a judgment of the law: ibid.
- "no evidence that disputes Mr. Bah posed a threat of death or serious injury at the time Mateo fired" : New York Post, *'City wants judge to toss $2.2M verdict awarded to family for fatal police shooting,'* 2018

- They requested that the jury's verdict — and the $2.2 million payout — be thrown out and a new trial ordered: ibid.
- "Isn't a jury entitled to say, 'I don't believe this guy? I don't believe this guy because he has contradicted himself?'": ibid.
- "reasonably believed, even if mistakenly, that Mr. Bah was in urgent need of medical assistance when Mr. Bah became silent inside the apartment." court documents: *Bah v. The City of New York et al*, No. 1: 2013cv06690 - Document 175 (S.D.N.Y. 2017)
- "Before he authorized entry ... Hindsight would have taught a different lesson if Bah had seriously injured himself during further delay." : ibid.
- "objectively reasonable": ibid.
- "any similar case that could clearly establish the law": ibid.
- "did not have a reasonable belief": ibid.
- a clearly established right": ibid.
- "the final shot to the head that killed Bah ...multiple times by the officers": ibid.
- He overturned the judgment against Licitra. But the judge let the jury's judgment against Mateo stand. Mateo kept his job: ibid.
- notice of appeal: media reports and court documents from *Bah v. The City of New York* (SDNY, 1:13-cv-06690)
- the city agreed to pay his mother $1.9 million: New York Daily News, *'NYC agrees to pay $1.9 million for NYPD killing of Mohamed Bah,'* 2019
- "Given the many levels of oversight that already exists ... the sake of public perception, and that does not serve the ends of justice.": Washington Post, *'New York will have a special prosecutor look into some deaths at the hands of police,'* 2015
- By the start of Isaacs' trial, the unit had investigated eleven other cases. Six were closed, while five others remained open. The team also declined to investigate more than 80 other cases: Biennial Report of the Office of the Attorney General's Special Investigations & Prosecutions Unit, 2017
- The state of New York requires regular people to use a parallel level of force when faced with a threat: New York Penal Law

ARTICLE 35 Defense of Justification, Penal (PEN) CHAPTER 40, PART 1, TITLE C

- The twelve-person jury that would decide Isaacs' fate in Brooklyn criminal court was made up of five Whites, five Blacks, one Hispanic and one Asian: New York Daily News, *'NYPD cop Wayne Isaacs found not guilty in killing of Delrawn Small as family calls it 'murder, in cold blood,'* 2017

- The judge told one spectator wearing a shirt with a large "Black Lives Matter" to turn his clothing inside out during the trial: Yahoo News, *'Police Uniforms in the Courtroom: Unconstitutional Intimidation?,'* 2017

- **PBA Group:** ibid.

- **5 million a year:** Pro Publica, *'A Police Union Contract Puts Taxpayers on the Hook to Defend Officers When the City Won't,'* 2021

- **Amadou Diallo:** New York Times, *'Similar Tasks, Different Methods, for 2 Lawyers for Police Officers,'* 1999

- **Abner Louima:** ibid.

- **"brutal and deliberate act.":** media reports from The New York Daily News, New York Post, Gothamist, 2017

- **"pulled out his gun, pulled the trigger three times, and killed Delrawn Small in the blink of an eye.":** ibid.

- **"Then he strolled over to his body, took a look, and walked away":** ibid.

- **"Coldly":** ibid.

- **"to allege he was attacked, punched, as Delrawn Small laid on the concrete in his own blood.":** ibid.

- **"There was absolutely no time for anything ... Even if you believe Delrawn Small may have thrown a punch at this defendant":** ibid.

- **"acted professionally":** ibid.

- **"as he was trained to.":** ibid.

- **"Police officers are trained to shoot in three-shot bursts and then assess the situation, and that's exactly what he did":** ibid.

- **"big guy":** ibid.

- **"You could tell he was upset with me":** ibid.

- "That never happened": ibid.
- "what was going on or what was going to happen": ibid.
- "He came and said, 'I'm gonna fucking kill you,'... I turned my body to the left...he struck me right away": ibid.
- "stop the threat.": ibid.
- "At that point, I thought I was going to lose my life ... That's the only reason I had to stop the threat of me losing my life.": ibid.
- The prosecution questioned Isaacs' testimony that his window was already rolled down while he was driving: Mic.com *'Prosecutor: NYPD Officer Wayne Isaacs rolled down his car window with intent to kill Delrawn Small,'* 2017
- "The window is up": ibid.
- "less than forthright with you about that window being down.": ibid.
- "He lowered his window for one reason, to kill...that's murder": ibid.
- "that the defendant was not justified" in his use of force: ibid.
- In an anonymous interview with the *New York Times* after the trial: New York Times, *'Jurors, Seeing a Punch, Found an Officer Justified in a Fatal Shooting,'* 2017
- "His head kind of goes all the way down": ibid.
- "Then you see his shoulder come up very clearly, and strike forward.": ibid.
- The jury acquitted Isaacs of the charges: New York Daily News, *'NYPD cop Wayne Isaacs found not guilty in killing of Delrawn Small as family calls it 'murder, in cold blood,'* 2017
- supporters of the officer clapped: ibid.
- "He got off!": ibid.
- A red-eyed Isaacs turned and hugged his wife and embraced his attorney: ibid.
- "Only you know what exactly happened out there ... let's try to hope that we have no further incidents like this in the future.": New York Times, *'Police Officer Found Not Guilty in Off-Duty Shooting of Unarmed Man,'* 2017
- "I guess that's the only thing I can hope for": ibid.

- The other examples included a St. Louis police officer who shot and killed Anthony Smith in 2011 and was acquitted in September 2017: Mic.com, *'16 recent police brutality cases that show how often officers aren't held accountable,'* 2017
- A Tulsa police officer killed Terrence Crutcher in 2016, and a jury acquitted him in June 2017: ibid.
- A University of Cincinnati cop who killed Samuel DuBose had two mistrials, the most recent in June 2017: ibid.
- A Minneapolis police officer who shot and killed Syville Smith in 2016 was also acquitted in June 2017: CNN.com, *'Milwaukee ex-cop who fatally shot Sylville Smith found not guilty,'* 2017
- The officer testified that he feared that Castile was grabbing for a gun when he reached for his glove compartment during the traffic stop: New York Times, *'Minnesota Officer Acquitted in Killing of Philando Castile,'* 2017
- Castile's girlfriend maintained that he was trying to pull out his identification to give to the officer: ibid.
- In June 2017, the Minnesota cop who killed Castile just two days after Small died was acquitted: ibid.
- "Goes to show the system is not for Black people," he said. "I don't care how we look at it": New York Times, *'Police Officer Found Not Guilty in Off-Duty Shooting of Unarmed Man,'* 2017
- A year after the trial, the NYPD quietly closed its internal investigation and said that Isaacs did not violate its use of force guidelines: New York Daily News, *'Brooklyn cop who killed man in 2016 road rage incident will face internal NYPD discipline trial,'* 2021
- He was restored to full duty: ibid.

NOTES: CHAPTER 10

• Originally from Jamaica, Richards moved into the apartment a few months earlier. Back home, he was studying information technology at a community college and an exchange program brought him to New York to finish his degree: New York Times Student Journalism Institute, 'A 'wellness' check killed Miguel Richards. His family still questions why.,' 2021

• The NYPD Patrol Guide outlines the department's procedures for dealing with mentally ill or emotionally disturbed people: NYPD Patrol Guide, Procedure No. 221-13, 'MENTALLY ILL OR EMOTIONALLY DISTURBED PERSONS'

• The department's policy says the "primary duty of all members of the service is to preserve human life.": ibid.

• "is dangerous to himself or others": ibid.

• "a last resort to protect the life of the uniformed member of the service assigned or any other person present.": ibid.

• "armed or violent": ibid.

• "without the specific direction of a supervisor unless there is an immediate threat of physical harm to the EDP or others present.": ibid.

- "If an EDP is not immediately dangerous, the person should be contained until assistance arrives": ibid.
- In 2017, the NYPD launched an initiative to outfit its officers with body cameras while on patrol: NYPD Body-Worn Camera Program, 'What you need to know,' NYC.gov
- Richards was the first person fatally shot by the NYPD whose death was captured on body cam: New York Times, 'Police Consider Releasing Body Camera Footage in Fatal Bronx Shooting,' 2017
- "very real and substantial risk of harassment, reprisals, and threats to their safety": New York Times, 'Police Release Body Camera Footage of Shooting Death in Bronx,' 2017
- "is committed to being as transparent as possible": WNYC, 'NYPD Releases Footage of Fatal Shooting Caught on Bodycam,' 2017
- "In the vast majority of these cases, we believe that body-worn camera video will confirm the tremendous restraint exhibited by our officers": ibid.
- The NYPD put out a 16-minute video, which was a compilation of footage from the officers at the scene: New York Police Department YouTube Channel, 'NYPD Bodycam Footage of Police Shooting' September 2017
- New York Lawyers for the Public Interest: media reports and court documents from NYLPI V. NYPD
- Richards was also the tenth person killed during a mental health episode by the NYPD since Mohamed Bah in 2012: Community Access, 'CCIT-NYC: IN REMEMBRANCE'
- "It was apparent, or should have been apparent ... was experiencing a mental health crisis and/or was emotionally disturbed": court documents from The Estate of Miguel Antonio Richards v. The City Of New York, et al, No. 1:2018cv11287, SDNY
- The lawsuit claimed that the NYPD officers violated department policy for how to handle an EDP.: ibid.
- The attorneys cited other police killings: ibid.
- Bill de Blasio announced he was creating a task force on Behavioral Health and Criminal Justice: press release: De Blasio Administration Launches $130 Million Plan to Reduce Crime, Reduce

Number of People with Behavioral and Mental Health Issues Behind Bars, 2014

• "how the criminal justice and health systems ... those needlessly cycling through the system.": ibid.

• In December 2014, the group announced an action plan, which included a plan to provide 40 hours of crisis intervention team (CIT) training to NYPD officers: ibid.

• Memphis: Univ. of Memphis CIT Center, *'Memphis Model'*

• In January 2017, a report by the city's Office of the Inspector General (OIG) found: OIG-NYPD, DOI'S OFFICE OF THE INSPECTOR GENERAL FOR THE NEW YORK CITY POLICE DEPARTMENT RELEASES A REPORT AND ANALYSES ON THE NYPD'S CRISIS INTERVENTION TEAM INITIATIVE, 2017

• "CIT-trained officers are consistently assigned to calls involving people in mental distress.": ibid.

• "no dedicated personnel": ibid.

• "NYPD's current policies for responding to people in mental crisis focus on containment, placing individuals into custody, and tactics for dealing with potential violence from a person in crisis": ibid.

• *ProPublica* report: ProPublica, *'It Wasn't the First Time the NYPD Killed Someone in Crisis. For Kawaski Trawick, It Only Took 112 Seconds.,'* 2020

• A *Washington Post* analysis: Washington Post, *'Fatal Force'* database

• A study in 2015 by the Treatment Advocacy Center: Treatment Advocacy Center, *'People with Untreated Mental Illness 16 Times More Likely to Be Killed By Law Enforcement,'* 2015

• CAHOOTS: White Bird Clinic, 'CAHOOTS CRISIS ASSISTANCE HELPING OUT ON THE STREETS'

• Across the US, similar non-police emergency response programs were being established in cities like Denver, Oakland, Olympia, Washington, New Haven, Connecticut and San Francisco: media reports and court documents from *Baerga, et. al. v. City of New York, et al.*

- **Behavioral Health Emergency Assistance Response Division (B-Heard) program:** Mayor's Office of Community Health, *'Re-imagining New York City's mental health emergency response,'* 2021
- **data from the initial pilot:** court documents from *Baerga, et. al. v. City of New York, et al.*
- **class action lawsuit:** ibid.
- **"systemic failure to provide safe, appropriate, and immediate responses to New Yorkers experiencing mental health crises" violated the Fourth and Fourteenth Amendment rights of New Yorkers, as well as the American Civil Disabilities Act:** ibid.
- **"Despite the myriad civil rights violations ... continued to use armed police officers as first responders to mental health crises":** ibid.
- **The FID was created in 2015 by former NYPD commissioner Bill Bratton after Eric Garner was killed:** Staten Island Advance, *'EXCLUSIVE: NYPD poised to create special unit to investigate officer-involved shootings, sources say,'* 2015
- **The new division was given a significant purview of investigatory responsibilities at the NYPD:** NY1, *'Inside the NYPD Unit That Studies Use of Police Force,'* 2019

NOTES: CHAPTER 11

- In the summer of 2016 ...Daniel Pantaleo had a history of misconduct while working at the NYPD: New York Daily News, 'Daniel Pantaleo — cop who dodged charges in Eric Garner's death — disciplined by NYPD for bogus stop-and-frisk,' 2016
  - In 2011, the police stopped a record 685,724, a 14% increase from the year before: Online data records from the NYPD Stop, Question, and Frisk database: https://www1.nyc.gov/site/nypd/stats/reports-analysis/stopfrisk.page
  - In the FOIL, she indicated that for years the NYPD posted the information she was after on the clipboards they hung inside the stationhouses and headquarters: court documents from *Luongo v. Records Access Officer*
  - In August 2016, the NYPD denied her FOIL request: media reports, interview with Cynthia Conti-Cook and court documents from *Luongo v. Records Access Officer*
  - The department officials thanked Conti-Cook for the heads-up about the process with the clipboards: ibid.
  - The NYPD said it had made a mistake putting that information out publicly. Upon review, they realized those releases violated civil rights law 50-a, the department said: ibid.

- **Mayor de Blasio backed the decision:** media reports from New York Daily News, New York Post and Gothamist, 2016
- **In October 2016, the mayor quietly proposed an amendment to 50-a. In a press release posted to the mayor's website on a Friday afternoon:** press release from Mayor de Blasio, *'Mayor de Blasio Outlines Core Principles of Legislation to Make the Disciplinary Records of Law Enforcement and Other Uniformed Personnel Subject to Disclosure,'* 2016
- **In December, Legal Aid filed a lawsuit over the FOIL denial for the NYPD's disciplinary records dating back to 2011:** New York Daily News, *'EXCLUSIVE: Legal Aid Society sues NYPD for concealing cop discipline records from public,'* 2016
- **ThinkProgress:** ThinkProgress, *'EXCLUSIVE DOCUMENTS: The disturbing secret history of the NYPD officer who killed Eric Garner,'* 2017
- **Using about ten years of CCRB data, ThinkProgress found that only 1,750 current officers — less than 5% of the total force — had received eight or more complaints:** ibid.
- **The report said that an unidentified CCRB employee leaked the files to ThinkProgress:** ibid.
- **Leaker:** New York Times, *'Employee Accused of Records Leak in Eric Garner Case Resigns,'* 2017
- **"regrettable but not a surprise":** New York Daily News, *'Lawsuit seeking disciplinary records of cop who put Eric Garner in fatal chokehold tossed,'* 2017
- **The courts also blocked the release of all the NYPD disciplinary records dating back to 2011 that Legal Aid sought:** ibid.
- **In total, the cache contained over 2,000 secret records for more than 1,800 officers from the years 2011 to 2015:** BuzzFeed News, *'Here's What We Learned From Thousands Of Secret NYPD Disciplinary Files,'* 2018
- **dismissal probation:** NYPD Patrol Guide, Section: Disciplinary Matters Procedure No: 318-09, 'DISMISSAL PROBATION GUIDELINES'
- **delay those dismissals for one year:** ibid.
- **CCPC:** index for Commission to Combat Police Corruption, about section

- **Brooklyn's 75th precinct:** media reports and Mayor Rudolph Giuliani, Executive Order No. 18., 1995
- **Officers from the precinct were making up to $8,000 a week:** media reports from Associated Press, New York Times, Washington Post and others, 1993
- **Mayor Dinkins appointed Judge Milton Mollen:** New York Times, *'Dinkins Names Police Corruption Panel and Urges Civilian Police Review,'* 1992
- **"willfully blind":** Milton Mollen, City of New York, *'Commission to Investigate Allegations of Police Corruption and the Anti-Corruption Procedures of the Police Department Commission Report,'* 1994
- **"We find as shocking the incompetence and the inadequacies of the department to police itself":** New York Times, *'NEW YORK'S POLICE ALLOW CORRUPTION, MOLLEN PANEL SAYS,'* 1994
- **Mollen said the body should have subpoena power to legally compel the NYPD to produce documents.:** ibid.
- **The City Council agreed and started to move to create such an agency:** ibid.
- **Rudy Giuliani:** New York Times, *'MAYOR VETOES BILL CREATING A PANEL TO MONITOR POLICE,'* 1994
- **Each year, the CCPC issues a report:** Commission to Combat Police Corruption, annual reports on NYC.gov, 1994-2019
- **For example, in one of the reports ... while taking him out of a police car at a Bronx station house:** ibid.
- **The use of force against the man:** ibid.
- **In their report, the commission wrote that the officer should have been fired:** ibid.
- **In March 2018, BuzzFeed's first big story on the files hit:** Buzz-Feed, *'Secret NYPD Files: Officers Can Lie And Brutally Beat People — And Still Keep Their Jobs,'* 2018
- **Q&A:** BuzzFeed, *'Responding To BuzzFeed News NYPD Investigation, Top Officials Call For Change,'* 2018
- **"bad law":** ibid.
- **"has to become more transparent"** ibid.

- "There are many things we do well at the NYPD ... that's not something that we do very well at all": ibid.
- online database: BuzzFeed, *'Here Are The Secret Records On Thousands Of New York Police Misconduct Cases,'* 2018
- 250 NYPD employees: BuzzFeed, *'Here's What We Learned From Thousands Of Secret NYPD Disciplinary Files,'* 2018
- 100 NYPD employees: ibid.
- the police unions publicly attacked BuzzFeed: letter from Patrolmen's Benevolent Association, Office of the President, *RE: Buzz-Feed News Disclosure of Stolen Police Personnel Records,* 2018
- "likely have been stolen or misappropriated from the NYPD": ibid.
- "stolen Confidential files": ibid.
- "In the interest of our members' safety ... but not limited to, seeking an injunction in court": ibid.
- "Testilying": New York Times, *"Testilying' by Police: A Stubborn Problem,'* 2018
- fake witnesses to close grand larceny cases: New York Daily News, *'NYPD detective stripped of gun, shield for allegedly making up bogus witnesses to bury grand larceny cases,'* 2018
- 20 vacation days: ibid.
- forced to retire: ibid.
- three-person independent commission: BuzzFeed, *'The NYPD Announces An Independent Panel Will Review Its Disciplinary Program,'* 2018
- Mary Jo White: ibid.
- Robert Capers: ibid.
- Barbara Jones: ibid.
- O'Neill: ibid.
- "This new panel will undoubtedly increase the pressure on the NYPD": ibid.
- "tooth and nail": Mary Jo White, et al, *'The Report of the Independent Panel on the Disciplinary System of the New York City Police Department,'* 2019
- "robust and fair": ibid.

- "a fundamental and pervasive lack of transparency" ibid.
- "The public confidence in the department to hold its own accountable depends on its openness and candor": ibid.
- **Recommendations:** ibid.
- **Commission to Combat Police Corruption:** ibid.
- "upgrade and integrate its disciplinary record-keeping and case management systems": ibid.
- "external expert to periodically audit the disciplinary system": ibid.
- "ensure that it is producing fair, unbiased, and consistent outcomes" ibid.
- "strongly support": ibid.
- "The current law keeps the public in the dark ... and reduces accountability": ibid.
- "strong recommendations" BuzzFeed, *'NYPD Discipline Needs More Transparency, A Panel Of Experts Said,'* 2019
- "wholesale change": ibid.
- **Laquan McDonald:** media reports from *Associated Press, NBC News, New York Times* and *Washington Post* and others.
- **Chicago Police Department:** ibid.
- **That video, released in November 2015:** ibid.
- **Van Dyke had an extensive history of documented citizen complaints — 20 in total:** Invisible Institute, Citizens Police Data Project (CPDP)
- **University of Chicago:** ibid.
- **In the aftermath of the Laquan McDonald killing:** media reports from the Chicago Tribune, Associated Press, NBC News, New York Times and others.
- **50 years:** media reports from the Chicago Tribune, Chicago Sun-Times, New York Times and others.
- **Rahm Emanuel:** ibid.
- **May 2019:** media reports from Associated Press, New York Daily News and New York Post.

NOTES: CHAPTER 12

- **Daniel Pantaleo on trial for his job:** media reports from *Associated Press*, *New York Daily News* and *New York Post* and others, 2019.
- **New York state:** New York Civil Service Law § 75(4).
- **The prosecution had to prove by a preponderance of the evidence that he committed at least one criminal offense:** ibid.
- **Pantaleo committed assault in the third degree, a misdemeanor, and intent to strangle, a felony:** media reports and court documents from New York City Police Department disciplinary case number 2018-19274
- **"We have completed our investigation":** New York Daily News, *'NYPD investigation of Eric Garner death is complete, but Bratton won't take action until fed probe wraps up,'* 2016
- **"effectively stopped our investigation until they complete their investigation":** ibid.
- **The DOJ had its own statute of limitations to contend:** ibid.
- **"I know the Garner family and they have gone through so much...the NYPD is going to go ahead with its disciplinary process":** Mayor Bill de Blasio at Democratic presidential candidate debate, July 2019

- "I don't know if the Justice Department is ever going to act …. I'm astounded": ibid.
- "It's not my place to pass judgment" ibid.
- The PBA claimed: New York Daily News, 'PBA lawyers say tipster in Eric Garner case got it wrong,' 2019
- "Jada Wilson": ibid.
- "Anti-police": Wall Street Journal, 'New York Police Union Amps Up Its Criticism of Watchdog Board,' 2017
- State court: court documents from Pantaleo v. CCRB, Article 78, 2019
- "These are just tears from heaven": media reports from NPR.org and NBC News, 2019
- "Eric is crying from heaven … fight for justice for him." ibid.
- His daughter Erica: New York Times, 'Erica Garner, Activist and Daughter of Eric Garner, Dies at 27,' 2017
- Bratton: Transcript: Mayor de Blasio Hosts Roundtable on Police-Community Relations, 2014
- $35 million: New York Post, 'Cops say training after Eric Garner's death is a 'waste of time,' 2015
- multi-day training program: ibid.
- waste of time: ibid.
- high-ranking police official: ibid.
- "Reckless": media reports and documents from New York City Police Department disciplinary case number 2018-19274
- "gave his victim a death sentence over loose cigarettes.": ibid.
- "This officer didn't let go even after Mr. Garner fell to the ground": ibid.
- He said Pantaleo applied pressure to Garner's neck for 15 seconds: ibid.
- "Eric Garner's pleas for air is ignored … buries this man's face in the ground": ibid.
- "lethal dose of deadly force": ibid.
- Fogel paused for effect for 15 seconds: ibid.
- "a ticking time bomb": ibid.
- "set these facts in motion by resisting arrest": ibid.

- London: ibid.
- "Had he accepted the summons, he would be here today": ibid.
- "Scapegoat" ibid.
- "seatbelt technique": ibid.
- He was serving time for gun and drug charges at the time: New York Times, *"I Can't Breathe' Case: 7 Takeaways From Disciplinary Hearing on Eric Garner's Death,'* 2019
- Orta: media reports and documents from New York City Police Department disciplinary case number 2018-19274
- "knew for a fact": ibid.
- "Twin": ibid.
- "to take to the store": ibid
- "take it up the block.": ibid.
- Garner's mother and his sister Ellisha left in tears: New York Post, *'Eric Garner's sister breaks down after seeing video at Daniel Pantaleo's NYPD trial,'* 2019
- "Around": media reports and documents from New York City Police Department disciplinary case number 2018-19274
- "trying to interlock his fingers": ibid.
- "He kept saying, 'I can't breathe ... Then I saw his eyes roll back, and that was it": ibid.
- Bannon: ibid.
- "the condition": ibid.
- from the end of March through mid-July: ibid.
- Eric Garner was arrested twice during this period: ibid.
- "Huddled": ibid.
- He testified that he did not observe any illegal cigarette sales: ibid
- text messages: ibid.
- Gasps: New York Post, *'Not a big deal' NYPD Lt. texted after Eric Garner's death,'* 2019
- "My reasoning...To try to bring him down to a level where you put him at ease": media reports and documents from New York City Police Department disciplinary case number 2018-19274
- "bad situation." ibid.

- "I don't know how to answer that ... I don't know if he was or wasn't": ibid.
- Officer Justin D'Amico testified he was about 100-200 feet away from Garner: ibid.
  - "328 feet": ibid.
- "More than a football field": ibid.
- D'Amico said that distance might be correct: ibid.
- "Irate": ibid.
- "verbal judo.": ibid.
- "You did that because you believed he was playing possum?": ibid.
- "Yes,": ibid.
- D'Amico rode with Garner in the ambulance that day: ibid.
- Back at the precinct, he continued to process the arrest of Garner: ibid.
- D'Amico entered "no": ibid.
- D'Amico confirmed that Garner did not possess enough cigarettes to warrant the felony charge: ibid.
- He never said on the stand that Pantaleo put Garner in a chokehold: ibid.
- "It was around his body ... Upper body": ibid.
- "seatbelt maneuver": ibid.
- Jung: ibid.
- "There's a million maneuvers we do in the street that we're not trained to do": ibid.
- IAB investigators interviewed 16 civilians and 21 uniformed witnesses, including Pantaleo: ibid.
- Deputy Inspector Charles Barton: ibid.
- In a memo, Barton requested a charge against the officer "for violation of Patrol Guide 203-11, 'Use of Force,' in that he placed Eric Garner in a chokehold.": ibid.
- In the report, she ruled that the cause of death was: "Compression of neck (choke hold), compression of chest and prone positioning during physical restraint by police.": ibid.

- London ripped up a copy of Persechino's report: media reports from New York Times, Reuters, New York Daily News and others.
- "worthless, completely worthless.": ibid.
- "set into motion a lethal sequence of events.": media reports and NYPD trial judge's opinion, New York City Police Department disciplinary case number 2018-19274
- autopsy photos: ibid.
- Persechino agreed with London: ibid.
- She said that forearms, being soft and broad, do not necessarily leave marks: ibid.
- She added that she had only seen fractured bones in a minority of choking and strangling cases: ibid.
- Michael Graham: ibid.
- "probably felt he couldn't breathe ... the fact is he could breathe": ibid.
- Graham believed the fact that Garner was talking during the incident backed this argument up: ibid.
- "it was heart disease exacerbated by his interaction with law enforcement": ibid.
- London announced that his client would not testify: ibid.
- transcript of Pantaleo's interview with internal affairs investigators was entered in the record: ibid.
- "It's disconcerting that the US attorney was here, but we have nothing to hide": ibid.
- After London said Pantaleo wouldn't testify, the US attorney left the courtroom: media reports from CNN.com, New York Daily News and New York Post.
- "That we are not supposed to use them": media reports and NYPD trial judge's opinion, New York City Police Department disciplinary case number 2018-19274
- "you take your two hands ... the windpipe preventing him from breathing": ibid.
- "No, I did not": ibid.
- "I was able to push him forward ... was in the crook of my elbow" ibid.

- "pressuring the neck": ibid.
- "There was no pressure to the neck ... preventing him from trying to get back up on all fours": ibid.
- The IAB investigators played the video for Pantaleo during the interview: ibid.
- "termination without his pension" ibid.
- "was enough to set in motion the chain of events that killed Eric Garner": ibid.
- "He couldn't breathe. God help us, he could not breathe": ibid.
- "his own compromised health conditions": ibid.
- "He was obese. He had hypertension, cardiovascular disease. That's why he died": ibid.
- Stuart London said that he thought Maldonado's recommendation might come before the July deadline for the DOJ to file federal charges: media reports from New York Daily News and New York Post
- Department of Justice announced it was declining to file federal civil rights charges against Pantaleo: New York Times, 'Eric Garner's Death Will Not Lead to Federal Charges for N.Y.P.D. Officer,' 2019
- "The DOJ has failed us": New York Times, "The D.O.J. Has Failed Us': Eric Garner's Family Assails Prosecutors,' 2019
- "The streets of New York City are not safe with them walking around. Five years ago, it was me. It was my family. Today or tomorrow, it could be your family": ibid.
- "This makes my heart smile": Gothamist, "Nothing Has Changed': Protesters Rally On 5th Anniversary Of Eric Garner's Death,' 2019
- "He needs to be scared everywhere that he go! We will find you Pantaleo!": ibid.
- Good Morning America: ABC News, 'New York City Mayor Bill de Blasio announces 2020 presidential bid,' 2019
- de Blasio pumped up his accomplishments as mayor: ibid.
- "Con Don" ibid.
- "Fire Pantaleo!": media reports from Associated Press, New York Times, New York Post and others.
- "He should be fired. He should be fired now": ibid.

• "To the protestors in the audience today: I heard you. I saw you. I thank you.": tweet from @BilldeBlasio, 2019

• "This is what democracy looks like and no one said it was pretty": ibid.

• "Garner family is going to get justice in the next 30 days." media reports from Associated Press, New York Times, New York Post and others.

• the judge who presided over Pantaleo's department trial delivered her decision: New York Times, *'Daniel Pantaleo, N.Y.P.D. Officer in Eric Garner's Death, Should Be Fired, Judge Says,'* 2019

• "It is important to underscore ... did not seek to gain compliance of the subject by setting up for, or by using, a prohibited chokehold": New York City Police Department Final Order of Dismissal, disciplinary case 2018-19274

• "exceptionally qualified and unbiased": ibid.

• "without substantiation.": ibid.

• "substantial pain": ibid.

• "Recklessness": ibid.

• "cohesive, fact-based and reasoned summary of medical findings that support a conclusion.": ibid.

• "was a significant factor in triggering the acute asthma attack which contributed to [Garner's] tragic death.": ibid.

• "apparent physical distress" until Pantaleo "put his forearm around his neck.": ibid.

• "implausible and self-serving.": ibid.

• "questionable reliability.": ibid.

• "Untruthful.": ibid.

• "Disingenuous": ibid.

• "unhelpful or unreliable.": ibid.

• In finding he acted recklessly, the judge noted the numerous times that the police department informed Pantaleo ... chokeholds were not to be used in his interview: ibid.

• "Unequivocal": ibid.

• "Absolute.": ibid.

• "Deadly,": ibid.

- **"reduce the possibility of in-custody deaths.":** ibid.
- **"department prohibitions":** Under the 2015 Patrol Guide, Members of the New York City Police Department were prohibited from using chokeholds. In the 2016 Patrol Guide, a note was added to the section of the Patrol Guide stating that chokeholds and other force prohibitions —may be reviewed on a case-by-case basis by the Use of Force Review Board to determine, whether, under the circumstance, the actions were reasonable and justified. The review may find that, under exigent or exceptional circumstances, the use of the prohibited action may have been justified within guidelines."
- **"under exigent or exceptional circumstances, the use of the prohibited action may have been justified and within guidelines."** ibid.
- **Maldonado ruled that the CCRB proved its case to satisfy the high threshold of establishing all of the elements of Assault in the Third Degree:** New York City Police Department Final Order of Dismissal, disciplinary case 2018-19274
- **She wrote that the prosecution failed to establish that Pantaleo acted with intent to strangle Garner and impede his breathing:** ibid.
- **"Target":** ibid.
- **"Lawful"** ibid.
- **"Undoubtedly, [Pantaleo's] forearm moved up ... the tribunal is not persuaded that [Pantaleo's] intent, even when his hands were clasped, was to impede Mr. Garner's breathing"** ibid.
- **"singular in its facts"** ibid.
- **"strikingly similar set of circumstances and medical issues":** ibid.
- **"forbidden chokehold":** ibid.
- **"neck and chest compression with chronic asthma as a contributing factor":** ibid.
- **Anthony Baez:** New York Times, *'Federal Jury Indicts Officer In Choking Of Bronx Man,'* 1998
- **Officer Livoti:** ibid.
- **Baez fell limp and died:** ibid.

• Two years after the incident, a Bronx judge acquitted him on negligent homicide charges: ibid.

• But in 1998, Livoti was found guilty in federal court of violating Baez's civil rights and sentenced to seven years in prison: New York Times, *'Former Officer Gets 7 1/2 Years In Man's Death,'* 1998

• "The Police Department let him remain on the streets, knowing that one day a real tragedy would occur,'": ibid.

• Ultimately, Livoti was dismissed from the police department for using a prohibited chokehold against Baez: ibid.

• "is only one appropriate penalty for the grave misconduct that yielded an equally grave result .. can no longer remain a New York City Police Officer.": New York City Police Department Final Order of Dismissal, disciplinary case 2018-19274

• O'Neill fired Pantaleo: media reports from New York Times, Associated Press, NBC News and others.

• He became the first officer fired over the use of an illegal chokehold since Livoti: Associated Press, *'5 years later, officer faces reckoning for chokehold death,'* 2019

• "Today, we have finally seen justice done": media reports from New York Daily News, New York Post, CBS News and others.

• "The place that we had turned for generations to, the place that was synonymous with making things right *failed us*...even to come to any decision for five long years": ibid.

• "fairly and impartially": ibid.

• "Brokenhearted": ibid.

• "There's no confidence for the leadership at City Hall and One Police Plaza...The leadership has abandoned ship and left our police officers on the streets, alone": CBS News, *'Pat Lynch, Police Benevolent Association Speak Out On Firing Of Officer Daniel Pantaleo,'* 2019

• "to cringe in fear of the anti-police extremists, rather than standing up for New Yorkers ... them and their families": ibid.

• "With this decision, Commissioner O'Neill has opened the door for politicians to dictate ... police officers' due process rights": ibid.

• "wake up tomorrow to discover that the cop-haters are still not satisfied, but it will be too late.": ibid.

- "The damage is already done": ibid.
- Pantaleo sued in state court to get his job back: Associated Press, *'Court upholds firing of NYPD officer in Eric Garner's death,'* 2019
- "shocking to one's sense of fairness": ibid.
- "substantial evidence": ibid.
- "recklessly caused injury to Eric Garner ... thereby disregarding the risk of injury": ibid.
- "in my DNA." New York Times, *'Daniel Pantaleo, Officer Who Held Eric Garner in Chokehold, Is Fired,'* 2019
- "I can tell you that, had I been in Officer Pantaleo's situation, I may have made similar mistakes": ibid.
- "Every time I watched the video, I say to myself, as probably all of you do, to Mr. Garner: 'Don't do it. Comply.'": ibid.
- "To Officer Pantaleo: 'Don't do it.' I said that about the decisions made by both Officer Pantaleo and Mr. Garner.": ibid.
- "very difficult decision": ibid.
- "I've been thinking about this since I was sworn in as police commissioner": ibid.
- "I've been a cop for a long time": ibid.
- "And if I was still a cop, I'd probably be mad at me — 'You're not looking out for us.' But I am.": ibid.
- "We recruit from the human race ... We're not perfect. But, the next time you're walking down the street and you feel safe, thank the N.Y.P.D." New York Times, *'How the N.Y.P.D. Commissioner Grappled With the Eric Garner Decision,'* 2019
- "I'm not stopping this fight...I'm out here for the long run.": New York Times, *'Daniel Pantaleo, Officer Who Held Eric Garner in Chokehold, Is Fired,'* 2019
- "They all need to lose their jobs": ibid.
- Sergeant Kizzy Adonis: media reports from New York Post and Staten Island Advance, 2019
- "Pantaleo, you may have lost your job, but I lost a son," she said. "You cannot replace that. You can get another job, maybe at Burger King.": New York Times, *'Daniel Pantaleo, Officer Who Held Eric Garner in Chokehold, Is Fired,'* 2019

NOTES: CHAPTER 13

- On May 25, 2020, Minneapolis police officer Derek Chauvin killed George Floyd: media reports from the Associated Press, New York Times, Washington Post and others.
- On May 28: New York Times, *'George Floyd Protests: A Timeline,'* 2021
- The next night in Brooklyn: ibid.
- Vincent D'Andraia: ibid.
- One night later, near the intersection of Flatbush and St. Mark's Avenue: ibid.
- Mullins: New York Post, *'NYPD sergeants union boss loses bid to squash trial over profane tweets,'* 2021
- "Unconscionable": New York Times, *'Police Union Discloses Arrest of de Blasio's Daughter in Privacy Breach,'* 2020
- more than 345 people had been arrested over the course of three nights: New York Times, *'George Floyd Protests: A Timeline,'* 2021
- The NYPD said that 33 officers had been injured and more than 40 cop cars damaged: ibid.
- Curfew: media reports from the New York Daily News, NY Post, New York Times and others.
- On June 4, 2020, a group of about 300 people gathered in the

Mott Haven section of the South Bronx: Human Rights Watch, 'New York Police Planned Assault on Bronx Protesters,' 2020

- **FTP:** ibid.
- **At least 100 officers were dispatched to the Bronx, including dozens of high-ranking "white shirt" officers:** ibid.
- **SRG:** Gothamist, 'How An NYPD Anti-Terror Squad Became A Tool For Cracking Down On Protests,' 2021
- **"advanced disorder control":** ibid.
- **"not be involved in handling protests and demonstrations"** ibid.
- **2015:** ibid.
- **Within a year of its creation, the SRG also doubled in size and its budget grew from $13 million to nearly $90 million:** ibid.
- **NYPD Legal Bureau:** NYPD on NYC.gov, Bureaus, Legal
- **"They're good to go":** Human Rights Watch, 'New York Police Planned Assault on Bronx Protesters,' 2020
- **In total, the NYPD arrested 263 people in Mott Haven that night, more than any single protest in New York during the George Floyd demonstrations:** ibid.

NOTES: CHAPTER 14

• Jesse Hamilton: New York Times, *'Breakaway Group in New York Senate Becomes an Island of Power,'* 2016

• In September 2018, Myrie defeated Hamilton in the primary: New York Times, *'Democratic Insurgents Topple 6 New York Senate Incumbents, 2018*

• He was one of a handful of new candidates during the election cycle to take out Democratic senators who had joined forces with the Republican side: ibid.

• "defeats accountability, increases public skepticism, and foments distrust.": transcript from New York State Assembly, *hearing on criminal justice reform,* May 2015

• "The effect of 50-a ... is to make the public employees who have often the greatest power over the lives of New York residents the least accountable to the public": ibid.

• "So long as 50-a remains on the books, other efforts to increase police accountability that have been proposed are less likely to be effective": ibid.

• "outright repeal": ibid.

• "serve as a positive step toward increasing transparency in law enforcement.": ibid.

• a report that showed the NYPD had 2,000 complaints of racial profiling and they failed to substantiate even a single complaint: OIG-NYPD report, *'EXAMINATION BY DOI'S OFFICE OF THE INSPECTOR GENERAL FOR THE NYPD IDENTIFIES DEFICIENCIES AND RECOMMENDS IMPROVEMENTS IN HOW NYPD HANDLES COMPLAINTS OF BIASED POLICING,'* 2019

• **Mullins:** New York Post, *'Don't let activists and lawyers weaponize police-discipline records,'* 2019

• **Codes Committee:** NYS Senate Hearing, *'PUBLIC HEARING: POLICING (S3695), REPEALS PROVISIONS RELATING TO PERSONNEL RECORDS OF POLICE OFFICERS, FIREFIGHTERS, AND CORRECTIONAL OFFICERS,'* October 2019

• "impossible to truly fight for justice for Eric": ibid.

• "It's been five years since my son's murder, and there's been a widespread cover-up": ibid.

• "be Ramarley's voice": ibid.

• "I had sleepless nights ... I don't want to have to bury another son.": ibid.

• "The Republican senator who wrote 50-a before he passed away said, 'We never intended it to be like this'": ibid.

• "there's a total misconception for what 50-a does and does not do": ibid.

• "not a hell of a lot": ibid.

• "There's no other profession in the world that has as much oversight ... keep the police away from them": ibid.

• "somehow diminishes the complaints ... weak.": ibid.

• "If you had two restaurants ... Doesn't make sense.": ibid.

• "I wonder how many people in this room remember ... I dare say not.": ibid.

• "Garner, Bell, and the third one I do not know": ibid.

• "That's the thing about pointing fingers ... I'm a little admonished by your testimony because it comes across as if you think that because you wear a badge you are better than us": ibid.

• "The Mayor has been vocal in his advocacy of 50-a reform ...

must balance transparency and safety": Politico, *'De Blasio does not support full repeal of police secrecy law,'* 2019

• *New York Post* reported that the mayor blocked the representatives from the city from testifying at the hearing: New York Post, *'De Blasio muzzled NYPD, CCRB from testifying on planned repeal of records law,'* 2019

• "fact-based publication...they will say anything they want all the time.": Mayor de Blasio interview with WNYC's The Brian Lehrer Show, October 2019

• "I personally support repeal": tweet from @RevFredDavie, October 2019

• tweeted a photo: tweet from @zellnor4ny

• "I would sign a bill today that reforms 50-a": Governor Andrew Cuomo delivers daily Coronavirus update, May 2020

• "I would sign it today ... I can't be clearer or more direct than that.": ibid.

• more than 100,000 emails and placed over 20,000 phone calls to lawmakers pushing for the repeal of 50-a: Refinery29, *'Why Advocates In New York Are Working To Repeal The 50-A Law,'* 2020

• State Senator Brad Hoylman: tweet from @bradhoylman, 2020

• "We have heard from some folks that our grievances ... us taking advantage of a political moment": NYS Senate speech on 50-a by Senator Zellnor Y. Myrie, October 2019

• "Some people have said that it isn't a real grievance. That this is not happening here in New York ... and you're only doing it now": ibid.

• "So you're right. This is the moment. We are tired," Myrie said. "There has been no consequence for the brutality against our people.": ibid.

• "has a history of excessive use of force.": ibid.

• "That is what this bill is about...This is pro people": ibid.

• The bill to repeal 50-a passed along party lines in the senate, 40-22 ...In the Assembly, it was approved by a margin of 101-43: New York Daily News, *'New York lawmakers vote to repeal 50-a, making police disciplinary records public,'* 2020

- "unavoidable and irreparable harm to reputation and livelihood.": ibid.
- "We, as professionals, are under assault": ibid.
- Governor Cuomo signed the bill: media reports from New York Daily News, New York Post, New York Times and others.
- Another piece of legislation made the state attorney general's special unit for prosecuting police killings permanent: ibid.
- "Eric Garner Anti-Chokehold Act": ibid.
- NYCLU: court documents from *NYCLU v. NYPD*, 2020
- "Massive": Transcript: Mayor de Blasio Holds Media Availability, June 2020
- "Longer-term": ibid.
- "do something historic": ibid.
- "all records for every active member available in one place": ibid.
- "formal actions": ibid.
- "Transparency is not something to fear ... just as it would be for any of us as citizens": ibid.
- police unions filed lawsuits: New York Daily News, *'Cops, fire, correction unions sue de Blasio administration over release of disciplinary records,'* 2020
- "data dump": ibid.
- "absolutely destroy the reputation and privacy — and imperil the safety" of many police officers: ibid.
- "Unsubstantiated": ibid.
- "unfairly stigmatized": ibid.
- "We are defending privacy, integrity and the unsullied reputations of thousands of hard-working public safety employees": Gothamist, *'Police And Fire Unions Sue To Block Disciplinary Records From The Public,'* 2020
- temporary stay: Gothamist, *'Federal Judge Blocks Release Of NYPD Misconduct Records, Orders NYCLU To Keep Records Secret,'* 2020
- *ProPublica* published a database: ProPublica, *'The NYPD Files,'* 2020

- "unlawful scheme": Gothamist, *'NYCLU Publishes Over 300K Police Misconduct Records After Court Order Lifted,'* 2020
- "Where is the concern...perfectly legitimate request for public information": ibid.
- The Second Circuit: ibid.
- The database initially contained more than 300,000 disciplinary cases for 89,000 current and former NYPD officers: NYCLU, NYPD MISCONDUCT COMPLAINT DATABASE, 2020
- The data showed that nearly 20,000 officers had five or more civilian complaints of misconduct: ibid.
- 8,699 of those complaints resulted in an officer facing punishment from the department. Twelve officers were terminated and dismissed after receiving one of these complaints: ibid.
- Further analysis: New York Daily News, *'White cops in the NYPD have been accused of misconduct far more often than officers of color: report,'* 2020
- "not made haphazardly" Judge Katherine Failla ruling in *Uniformed Fire Officers, et. al. v. de Blasio*, et al., 2020
- "to aid underserved elements of New York's population" ibid.
- She denied the unions' motion and ruled the de Blasio administration could publish the disciplinary records online: ibid.
- "could not provide a single example": ibid.
- "There are numerous states with more robust ... I don't see any safety issues in those states" ibid.
- BuzzFeed database: ibid.
- the Second Circuit made its decision to uphold Judge Failla's decision: Associated Press, *'Appeals Court OKs Release of NYC Police Discipline Records,'* 2021
- "without any evidence of a resulting increase of danger to police officers": ibid.
- "The NYPD cannot bargain away its disclosure obligations": ibid:
- 83,000 current and former officers dating back to 2000: NYPD Member of Service Histories, NYC.gov, 2021

- **NYPD published its own database:** NYPDONLINE Personnel, https://nypdonline.org
- **"baseball card":** Gothamist, *'New NYPD Database Offers "Narrow" Glimpse At Police Disciplinary Records,'* 2021
- **Portillo:** ibid.
- **The disciplinary records initially put online by the NYPD were limited to decisions reached after a department trial. Cases that ended in "negotiated plea agreements" were not included:** NYPDONLINE Personnel, https://nypdonline.org
- **"slap in the face."** NYCLU STATEMENT ON NYPD MISCONDUCT AND DISCIPLINE DATABASE, 2021
- **"the anti-cop lobby":** tweet from @nycpba, 2021
- **"The anti-cop lobby got exactly what they wanted ... But they're still not happy. Why? Because "transparency & accountability" were never the goal.":** ibid.
- **As of January 2022, the NYPD said online that its databases included "charges and specifications and corresponding penalties resulting from a plea of guilty, plea of nolo contendere, or a finding of guilty after trial" for the years 2010 through 2021:** NYPDONLINE Personnel, https://nypdonline.org
- **"will continue to work towards increasing transparency by expanding the information displayed on this site."** ibid.
- **Commission to Combat Police Corruption:** Commission to Combat Police Corruption, annual reports on NYC.gov, 1994-2019
- **fails to mention that Marrero faced charges and was found guilty after he held down a person while they were stomped on:** NYPDONLINE Personnel, https://nypdonline.org
- **Marrero was promoted to sergeant in 2020:** NYPDONLINE Personnel, https://nypdonline.org
- **Lisa Marsh:** New York City Police Department disciplinary case number 2012-7072
- **Jose Ayala:** New York Post, *'Protect' & offend,'* 2011
- **Three other officers were criminally charged for the cover-up of the crime:** ibid.
- **Marsh was spared criminal charges but was suspended by the**

department for 30 days, docked 30 vacation days, and given a year of dismissal probation: New York City Police Department disciplinary case number 2012-7072

- "This officer does not have any applicable entries": NYPDON-LINE Personnel, https://nypdonline.org
- Officer Angela Polancobrito: New York City Police Department disciplinary case number 2011-6287
- Bronx DA Robert Johnson: New York Times, *'Authorities Move to Charge 16 Officers After Widespread Ticket-Fixing,'* 2011
- Scores of other officers were disciplined by the department: BuzzFeed News Secret NYPD files disciplinary database, 2018
- Roberson Tunis: New York City Police Department disciplinary case number 2011-3917
- But under Tunis's profile in the NYPD's database it says: "This officer does not have any applicable entries.": NYPDONLINE Personnel, https://nypdonline.org
- Jarrett Dill: New York City Police Department disciplinary case number 2012-8756
- a penalty of probation and suspension for a 2016 incident where he struck a motorcyclist while driving drunk: NYPDONLINE Personnel, https://nypdonline.org
- Myrie and Assemblywoman Diana Richardson sued the city and the police department after the protests. But two years later, he still hadn't learned the identity of any of the cops that arrested him on May 29, 2020: *NEW YORK STATE ASSEMBLYWOMAN DIANA C. RICHARDSON and NEW YORK STATE SENATOR ZELLNOR Y. MYRIE v. City of New York, et. al,* Case 1:21-cv-03609, EDNY

NOTES: CHAPTER 15

• **"had a plan"**: Transcript: Mayor de Blasio Holds Media Availability, June 2020

   • **"executed flawlessly"**: ibid.

• **The son of immigrants**: New York Daily News, *'Meet one of the NYPD masterminds driving down NYC's already historically low crime rates,'* 2017

   • **Shea rose through the ranks at the department**: ibid.

• **"tearing down society"**: Transcript: Mayor de Blasio Holds Media Availability, June 2020

• **He claimed a gun and gasoline were recovered from individuals who intended to use them as weapons at the protest**: ibid.

• **The gun, for instance, was recovered a mile from the protest from an individual with gang ties. As for the gasoline, there was none**: New York Post, *'NYPD Commissioner Dermot Shea ignores his own 'misinformation' warnings,'* 2020

• **Mayor de Blasio went on WNYC's** *The Brian Lehrer Show* **and parroted Shea's earlier comments**: Gothamist, *'Here's The Full Transcript Of Mayor De Blasio On The Brian Lehrer Show,'* 2020

   • **"extreme discretion"**: *Attorney General James Questions NYPD*

Commissioner Shea in Ongoing Investigation into Interactions Between Police and the Public, Virtual Hearing, Day 3, June 2020

- **"Violent":** ibid.
- **"Isolated.":** ibid.
- **"were set upon and attacked and got out of [the] situation with no injuries.":** ibid.
- **He also said that driving the car into the group was not a violation of the department's Use of Force policy:** ibid.
- **"I was never familiar with it until about two weeks ...But it's not something that to my knowledge exists in our policies":** ibid.
- **"Encirclement ...utilized when there is a need to take a group of people into custody":** The Intercept, *'NYPD "GOON SQUAD" MANUAL TEACHES OFFICERS TO VIOLATE PROTESTERS' RIGHTS,'* 2020
- **"Legal observers, I'm not sure what you're referring to there.":** *Attorney General James Questions NYPD Commissioner Shea in Ongoing Investigation into Interactions Between Police and the Public*, Virtual Hearing, Day 3, June 2020
- **"Having a shirt or a hat that says Legal Observer, does not mean that person is an attorney ... that they're actually performing any legal function"** ibid.
- **"Demonstration Observer Program":** NYPD Patrol Guide *'Demonstration Observer Program'* Procedure No. 213-11
- **"Observers shall be permitted to remain in any area ... as determined by the incident commander":** ibid.
- **James's office:** press release: 'Attorney General James Files Lawsuit Against the NYPD for Excessive Use of Force,' January 2021
- **"It is impossible to deny that many New Yorkers have lost faith in law enforcement":** ibid.
- **"phenomenal job.":** DOI's interviews with New York Police Commissioner Dermot Shea, December 2020
- **"flying blind":** ibid.
- **"I do.":** ibid.
- **"First time I heard kettling was when I read it in the paper":**

DOI's interviews with New York Police Chief of Department Terence Monahan, December 2020

• **During the week of demonstrations, he made headlines when he took a knee and locked hands with protesters:** New York Post, *'NYPD Chief of Department kneels in solidarity with George Floyd protesters,'* 2020

• "Justified": ibid.

• **In December 2020, DOI issued a 111-page report:** NYC Department of Investigation, *'Investigation into NYPD Response to the George Floyd Protests,'* 2020

• "contributed to the heightened tension": ibid.

• "clearly defined strategy": ibid.

• **"fact that the target of the protests was policing itself...in any meaningful way.":** ibid.

• "encirclement (commonly called "kettling"), mass arrests, baton and pepper spray use...failure": ibid.

• "Inconsistent ... selective enforcement": ibid.

• **"limited intelligence was used to justify a disproportionate response":** ibid.

• "prior to the curfew": ibid.

• **"Even if protesters received and heard the message ... prior to the curfew and blocked their ability to move":** ibid.

• **20 recommendations that DOI made in its report was that the department stop sending the Strategic Response Group to protests:** ibid.

• **They recommended that the department create a new 'Protest Response Unit,' that does not report to the SRG. They said the SRG should stick to handling "counterterrorism, riots, and other serious threats.":** ibid.

• **"crowd control...has proven to be a critical asset during events like parades, protests ... demonstrations, or other significant incidents":** NYPD Special Operations, NYC.gov

• **"shortcomings...did not otherwise identify any flaws":** NYC Department of Investigation, *'Investigation into NYPD Response to the George Floyd Protests,'* 2020

- "When DOI asked NYPD officials whether, in retrospect, the Department could have done anything differently ... officials offered none": ibid.
- "I wish I had done better," the mayor said, adding "our police department has to do better." Transcript: Mayor de Blasio Holds Media Availability, December 2020
- "makes clear that we should have had a better strategy": ibid.
- "We really missed an opportunity ... to try to exhibit a more understanding": ibid.
- He told the AG that only ten officers had been disciplined: *Attorney General James Questions NYPD Commissioner Shea in Ongoing Investigation into Interactions Between Police and the Public,* Virtual Hearing, Day 3, June 2020
- That Summer, reports surfaced of just two suspensions of officers seen harming people at protests: media reports from New York Times, NBC News and Gothamist.
- Vincent D'Andraia: The City, *'City to Pay Protester Shoved by Cop $387K, Officer Contributes $3,000,'* 2022
- compilation of police brutality that showed 64 cops attacking and beating demonstrators: New York Times, *'N.Y.P.D. Says It Used Restraint During Protests. Here's What the Videos Show.,'* 2020
- De Blasio responded that any officer caught on camera committing a violent act would be disciplined. New York Times, *'Under Pressure on Policing, N.Y.C. Mayor Toughens Discipline,'* 2020
- just five faced discipline while the rest were cleared by the department of any wrongdoing: The City, *'Just Five Cops Face Serious Penalties in De Blasio's Promised Accounting of NYPD Protest Misconduct Caught on Video,'* 2021
- Krystin Hernandez: ibid.
- "Exonerated": ibid.
- "was largely the result of a lack of proper protocol ... and improperly completing paperwork.": CCRB 2020 PROTEST DATA SNAPSHOT – OCTOBER 2021
- CCRB said it was only able to substantiate misconduct in just

27% of the 321 cases that fell under its jurisdiction: CCRB 2020 PROTEST DATA SNAPSHOT – MAY 2022

- "Out of the 321 cases, the CCRB conducted full investigations for 223 cases and substantiated misconduct in 87 cases... 88 of whom have been recommended the highest level of discipline": CCRB monthly board meeting, May 2022.

- But of those 143 officers that the CCRB recommended discipline for, as of May 2022, just 18 officers — or about 12% — were actually punished by the department: CCRB 2020 PROTEST DATA SNAPSHOT – MAY 2022

- **Monahan:** New York Daily News, *'Top NYPD chief retires to work for mayor as COVID recovery adviser,'* 2021

- **Regarding Monahan's actions at the 2020 protests, the mayor said that he would still be interviewed by the CCRB for their investigations:** Transcript: Mayor de Blasio Holds Media Availability and Makes Announcement with NYPD Leadership, February 2021

- **"Passionate":** ibid.

- **"loves this city":** ibid.

- **"loves making sure people are safe.":** ibid.

- "I think the message this sends is that we're moving the recovery forward and the city needs to move forward": ibid.

- **RNC:** Guardian, *'I was at the 2004 GOP convention protest. It was the worst of US policing,'* 2014

- **$18 million:** NYCLU, VICTORY IN UNLAWFUL MASS ARREST DURING 2004 RNC THE LARGEST PROTEST SETTLEMENT IN HISTORY

- **Terence Monahan:** New York Times, *'2 Top Officers Criticized for Arrests at 2004 G.O.P. Convention,'* 2006

- **Moments later, Monahan, a deputy chief at the time, ordered them to stop:** ibid.

- **In a 2006 letter to NYPD Commissioner Ray Kelly:** ibid.

- "They were blocked by a wrought iron fence on their left...did not hear the chief's dispersal order and therefore prevented civilians from passing." ibid.

- In the Fall of 2020, advocates from the NYCLU and the Legal

Aid Society, as well as the state's attorney general, filed lawsuits: court documents from *IN RE: NEW YORK CITY POLICING DURING SUMMER 2020 DEMONSTRATIONS* (SDNY, 1:20-cv-08924)

• **$750,000 settlement:** New York Post, *'NYPD use of sound cannons during protests limited by new $750K settlement,'* 2021

• **"rocket docket":** Gothamist, *'Federal Judge Promises "Rocket Docket" For NYPD Protest Lawsuits,'* 2021

• **The city moved to have the lawsuits dismissed:** Gothamist, *'City Must Answer Lawsuits Over NYPD's Response To 2020 Protests, Judge Rules,'* 2021

• **50-page request:** court documents from *IN RE: NEW YORK CITY POLICING DURING SUMMER 2020 DEMONSTRATIONS* (SDNY, 1:20-cv-08924)

• **filings from December 2021:** court documents from *IN RE: NEW YORK CITY POLICING DURING SUMMER 2020 DEMONSTRATIONS* (SDNY, 1:20-cv-08924)

• **By early 2022, the judge had sanctioned Law Department lawyer Dara Weiss, the senior attorney on the litigation who had worked at the Law Department for 18 years, five times for failing to comply with the court's direction:** Hell Gate, *'NYPD's Stonewalling Attorney Called Out for Lying and Forging Emails,'* 2022

• **Sierra sisters:** court documents from SAMIRA SIERRA, AMALI SIERRA, et. al v. City of New York, et. all (SDNY, 1:20-cv-10291)

• **"Don't come to a riot when you have MS, how about that!"** interview with attorney Rob Rickner and court records from SAMIRA SIERRA, AMALI SIERRA, et. al v. City of New York, et. all (SDNY, 1:20-cv-10291)

• **"Pay close attention to every word ... This is the best video I've ever seen telling the public the absolute truth.":** New York Post, *'NYPD union boss sent members overtly racist video in email,'* 2019

• **"Cops will continue to wade into that fray and Blacks will continue to attack and ambush us forever.":** ibid.

• **Willie Shields:** Gothamist, *'NYPD Police Union Boss: Sorry For Sharing Racist Video, 'I Have Black Friends,'* 2019

- "One of the most astonishing aspects of police work in an urban environment is that almost literally no one has a job": ibid.
- "Section 8 scam artists and welfare queens... impregnate as many women as possible." ibid.
- "Did you listen to this thing?": New York Post, *'NYPD union boss sent members overtly racist video in email,'* 2019
- "There is no one to blame but me for the video that was distributed ... I sincerely apologize.": New York Post, *'NYPD union boss sent members overtly racist video in email,'* 2019
- The judge ruled that the city had to turn over what it had on Mullins to the protest plaintiffs: court documents from *IN RE: NEW YORK CITY POLICING DURING SUMMER 2020 DEMONSTRATIONS* (SDNY, 1:20-cv-08924)
- When Rickner complained to the judge that Weiss hadn't responded to his emails about this meeting, she accused him of making a false statement in court: court documents from *IN RE: NEW YORK CITY POLICING DURING SUMMER 2020 DEMONSTRATIONS* (SDNY, 1:20-cv-08924)
- "While attempting to send the email to you as an attachment, I came to realize that the email was never actually sent, which explains why no counsel never received it.": ibid.
- "Misrepresentations": ibid.
- "Under great pressure I made an unintentional mistake.": New York Times, *'N.Y.C. Lawyer Fired Over Handling of George Floyd Protesters' Lawsuits,'* 2022
- "reiterated that NYPD did not conduct an investigation into the circulation of a 2019 video": court documents from *IN RE: NEW YORK CITY POLICING DURING SUMMER 2020 DEMONSTRATIONS* (SDNY, 1:20-cv-08924)
- In total, the city settled 183 claims from 2020 protesters out of court, according to data obtained from the comptroller's office. These settlements ranged from $3,000 to $185,000. All together, these out-of-court settlements cost the city's taxpayers $5,209,620: files from 2021 FOIL of NYC Comptroller

NOTES: CHAPTER 16

• New York City ended 2020 with 468 murders — a 47% spike compared to 319 the year before 2019. The police also tallied 1,531 shooting incidents in 2020, up 97% from 2019 (776): NYC Mayor's Office of Criminal Justice, 'Factsheet: 2020 Shootings & Murders'

   • A Spectrum News NY1/Ipsos poll: NY1, *'Exclusive: COVID-19, crime at top of Democratic voters' minds in NY1/Ipsos poll,'* 2021

   • "great tool": court records in *Floyd v. New York City* lawsuit.

   • Adams also decried the notion of defunding the police that several of his fellow candidates supported: New York Times, *'What Does It Mean to Be a New York Democrat These Days?,'* 2021

   • claimed to shift $1 billion from the NYPD budget: media reports from Politico, New York Times, Associated Press, NBC News and others.

   • Adams also vowed to revitalize the NYPD's anti-crime unit: New York Times, *"Keep an Eye on This Guy': Inside Eric Adams's Complicated Police Career,'* 2021

   • A report commissioned by the state's attorney general Eliot Spitzer: 'The New York City Police Department's Stop & Frisk Practices: A Report to the People of the State of New York from the Office of the Attorney General,' 2000

   • In 2002, Commissioner Ray Kelly announced that the NYPD

was disbanding the Street Crimes Unit: New York Times, 'Police Commissioner Closing Controversial Street Crime Unit,' 2002

- Between 2000 and 2018, the anti-crime cops were responsible for about a third of the police killings by the department, despite accounting for just 6% of the force: The Intercept, 'PLAINCLOTHES NYPD COPS ARE INVOLVED IN A STAGGERING NUMBER OF KILLINGS,' 2018

- NYPD Commissioner Dermot Shea announced that the police department was disbanding its anti-crime units: New York Times, 'N.Y.P.D. Disbands Plainclothes Units Involved in Many Shootings,' 2020

- Shea said that the roughly 600 plainclothes officers from 77 precincts around the city would be reassigned: ibid.

- "seismic shift": ibid.

- He declared that it was time for the police department to "move away" from the "brute force" tactics of the past: ibid.

- "We should not throw out the baby with the bathwater...we'll get it right, and we'll make sure our city is safe.": The City, 'Eric Adams Wants To Bring Back The NYPD's Most Controversial Unit,' 2021

- 103rd precinct in Queens: New York Post, 'Mayor Eric Adams warns NYPD cops not to be 'abusive',' 2022

- "an opportunity to go in and just aggravate people.": Columbia University, New York Police Department Guardians Oral History Collection, 'Oral history interview with Eric L. Adams, 2015,'

- "We have the finest among us and sometimes unfortunately we have a small number of the worst among us": New York Post, 'Mayor Eric Adams warns NYPD cops not to be 'abusive',' 2022

- "I'm going to have your backs ... But if you are abusive to my community, I'm going to make sure you don't serve in my department and you don't hurt your fellow officers.": ibid.

- As his first police commissioner, Adams appointed Keechant Sewell: media reports from NY1, CBS News, New York Post and others.

- "nationwide search": ibid.

- "the right woman to lead New York's Finest at this critical moment in our city's history.": ibid.

- "As someone who wore a bulletproof vest for 22 years ... ": ibid.

- "And I also have been a clear and consistent voice for accountability ... it undermines the nobility of public protection...it undermines the nobility of public protection": ibid.
- In March 2022, Adams and Sewell introduced their new iteration of the unit, rebranding it the "Neighborhood Safety Teams.": New York Times, *'N.Y.P.D. Rolls Out New Version of Anti-Gun Unit With Violent Past,'* 2022
- "right officers": City & State, *'Eric Adams to launch "modified" version of NYPD plainclothes unit,'* 2022
- "You must have the right training, the right mindset, the right disposition and be ... that they are the best fit for the unit.": ibid.
- "could endanger the life or safety": FREEDOM OF INFORMATION LAW REQUEST: FOIL-2022-056-04464 Re: Neighborhood Safety Team Rosters, Appeal letter, March 2022
- "would allow for an individual or group to modify their conduct to evade or undermine the NYPD's capabilities.": ibid.
- Chris Gelardi: NYFocus.com, *'Exclusive: Here Are the New NYPD Gun Units' Trainees. Many Have Histories of Excessive Force Complaints,'* 2022
- "164 patrol officers and 43 higher-ranked officers were listed as having taken both courses, while the NYPD said that 163 patrol officers and 45 "supervisors" had been assigned to the teams as of the same date": ibid.
- "13 percent of the officers who have taken both courses have at least five complaints, and eight of the officers have at least 10": ibid.
- Mervin Bennett: NYPDONLINE Personnel, https://nypdonline.org
- "If you want to be a zero, I'll treat you like a zero": NY Daily News, *'Second NYPD whistleblower testifies he was called a 'rat' for protesting stop-and-frisk quotas,'* 2013
- "So we're going to start correcting and treating those who want to fight the cause and fight the power ... your name is important": ibid.
- "do your 8 hours and 35 minutes a day and go home, and just do

your job.": New York Times, *'Stop-and-Frisk Trial Turns to Claim of Arrest Quotas,'* 2013

• "You could be disgruntled, fine ... Welcome to the NYPD. That's part of the nature of the job.": ibid.

• Ramiro Ruiz: NYPDONLINE Personnel, https://nypdonline.org

• Ruiz was the arresting officer among a group of plainclothes cops who allegedly choked a man and tried to delete video from his phone when he began recording them during a traffic stop: NYFocus.com, *'Exclusive: Here Are the New NYPD Gun Units' Trainees. Many Have Histories of Excessive Force Complaints,'* 2022

• adverse credibility list: 50a.org, *'Ramiro Ruiz'*

• Lieutenant Ruiz also had a documented history of abuse and dishonesty on his record: NYPDONLINE Personnel, https://nypdonline.org

• Jean Alejandro: NYPD Disciplinary Case No. 2017-18011

• Other documented misconduct history among the trainees for the new anti-gun unit included illegal stops and frisks, unlawful arrests and illegal strip searches: NYPDONLINE Personnel, https://nypdonline.org

• For example, one of the officers arrested someone and signed a criminal complaint claiming that he observed the person blocking pedestrian traffic when that was not true: NYPDONLINE Personnel, https://nypdonline.org

• Another officer was found guilty of wrongfully warning another officer of the imminent execution of a search warrant at a location that they were known to frequent: NYPDONLINE Personnel, https://nypdonline.org

• Kings Theater: NYC Mayor's Office YouTube, *'Mayor Eric Adams Delivers Address on Future of New York City,'* 2022

• He carried with him a framed photo of his late mother, Dorothy Mae Adams-Streeter: ibid.

• "I feel sorry for people who live in a small town and don't live in New York": ibid.

• "FDR, like ELA (Eric Leroy Adams) understood that people

needed an honest and reckoning of the problems...That is what I intend to deliver...": *ibid.*

• According to statistics from the NYPD, overall crime across the city was up more than 36% percent and shootings were up about 16% compared to the year before: NYC.gov *'NYPD Announces Citywide Crime Statistics for March 2022,'* 2022

• The Neighborhood Safety Unit was mostly pulling over suspects in cars for minor infractions including tinted windows, drug possession and bogus license plates: New York Post, *'NYPD anti-gun teams mostly make car stops, bust traffic offenders: records,'* 2022

• 448 arrests: City & State, *'NYPD's Neighborhood Safety Teams are mostly making low-level arrests, data shows,'* 2022

• "And so when you hear people say, "We don't need our police." Let me tell you right here and right now, I will support my police and we will make our city a safe city...That is our obligation. That's the partnership.": NYC Mayor's Office YouTube, *'Mayor Eric Adams Delivers Address on Future of New York City,'* 2022

NOTES: CHAPTER 17

- McLoughlin's online profile on the NYPD personnel website omits this information: NYPDONLINE Personnel, https://nypdonline.org
- In June 2020, Gwen Carr filed a petition calling for a judicial inquiry into her son Eric Garner's killing: media reports and court documents from *Matter of Carr v De Blasio*, NY SUPREME COURT, 2020
- Rarely used: ibid.
- "city taxpayers have been denied access to fundamental information concerning Mr. Garner's death.": ibid.
- After more than a year of fighting in court, a New York Supreme Court judge ruled: ibid.
- But the judge also ruled that top officials including de Blasio would not be compelled to testify: ibid.
- "due to the circumstances I wasn't thinking clearly." media reports from New York Daily News, Staten Island Advance, CNN. com and others.
- "total mistake": ibid.
- "Error": ibid.
- "bring their mindset back to center": ibid.
- Joseph Reznick: ibid.

- **After Reznick's testimony:** media reports and court documents from *Matter of Carr v De Blasio*, NY SUPREME COURT, 2020
- **"in high profile matters":** ibid.
- **"are briefed throughout the process":** ibid.
- **"However, they indicated knowledge of and input into the disciplinary process, but were not at liberty to disclose information about an open investigation":** ibid.
- **"To me, there's nothing new that came out ... that their testimony would be appropriate under the circumstances":** New York Daily News, *'Judge won't require Mayor de Blasio and NYPD brass to testify at city's Eric Garner inquiry,'* 2021
- **"I have been fighting for years to get the NYPD to fire the officers who helped kill my son and helped cover it up."** Communities United for Police Reform, *'STATEMENT: GWEN CARR & PETITIONERS RESPOND TO FINAL HEARING OF JUDICIAL INQUIRY IN ERIC GARNER'S KILLING, CALLING FOR FIRING OF OFFICERS WHO ENGAGED IN MISCONDUCT,'* 2022
- **"We fought for this once-in-a-century judicial inquiry and it exposed some of the misconduct by city officials and the NYPD... which is very frustrating":** ibid.
- **Mullins:** New York City Police Department Disciplinary Case Nos. 2021-23192 and 2021-23193
- **Hawa Bah filed a complaint with the CCRB:** media reports and court documents from *Mateo v. N.Y. City Civilian Complaint Review Bd.* Supreme Court of New York, 2020
- **The detective countered:** ibid.
- **Mateo retired before the board could vote on the charge:** NYC.gov, *'NYPD Member of Service Histories,'* 2022
- **Bah put out a statement saying she was "outraged" that he "escaped accountability" but not surprised:** JusticeCommittee.org, *'At Close of CCRB Investigation, Mom of Mohamed Bah Blasts NYPD and Mayor for Shielding Officers,'* 2022
- **"At least my tireless fight for justice means Mateo is no longer a police officer and cannot kill another mother's child":** ibid.
- **In early 2021, the CCRB substantiated second-degree assault**

charges against Wayne Isaacs: media reports and court documents from *'For a Judgment Pursuant to Article 78 of the Civil Practice Law & Rules v. The N.Y.C. Civilian Complaint Review Bd. (In re Police Officer Isaacs)'*

- **Sewell denied Isaacs' request to block the case:** Gothamist, *'NYPD commissioner OK's misconduct case for officer who killed Delrawn Small in 2016,'* 2022

- **But in early 2022, a judge denied his attempt to block the CCRB's case:** ibid.

KINGSTON IMPERIAL

Kingston Imperial
4045 Sheridan Ave. #360
Miami Beach, FL 33140
Email: Info@kingstonimperial.com
www.kingstonimperial.com

Thank you for reading this book published by Kingston Imperial. Kingston Imperial books and authors play an important role in sparking conversations about today's most important social and political issues.

We hope you enjoyed this book and will stay in touch with Kingston Imperial. Here are some ways to stay up to date on our books and events.

Sign up at www.kingstonimperial.com to receive updates on Kingston Imperial authors and events.

Like us on Facebook: www.facebook.com/kingstonimperialbooks

Follow us on Instagram: www.instagram.com/kingstonimperialbooks

Follow us on Twitter: www.twitter.com/KingImpBooks

Publicist
Finn Partners
www.finnpartners.com

INDEX

THE SECRET FILES

BILL DE BLASIO, THE NYPD, AND THE BROKEN PROMISES OF POLICE REFORM

MICHAEL HAYES

THE SECRET FILES

BILL DE BLASIO, THE NYPD, AND THE BROKEN PROMISES OF POLICE REFORM

MICHAEL HAYES